HOBBES AND THE LAW

Hobbes's political thought provokes a perennial fascination. It has become particularly prominent in recent years, with the surge of scholarly interest evidenced by a number of monographs in political theory and philosophy. At the same time, there has been a turn in legal scholarship towards political theory in a way that engages recognisably Hobbesian themes, for example the relationship between security and liberty. However, there is surprisingly little engagement with Hobbes's views on legal theory in general and on certain legal topics, despite the fact that Hobbes devoted whole works to legal inquiry and gave law a prominent role in his works focused on politics. This volume seeks to remedy this gap by providing the first collection of specially commissioned essays devoted to Hobbes and the law.

DAVID DYZENHAUS is Professor of Law and Philosophy at the University of Toronto, and a Fellow of the Royal Society of Canada.

THOMAS POOLE is Reader in Law at the London School of Economics and Political Science.

HOBBES AND THE LAW

Edited by
DAVID DYZENHAUS
and
THOMAS POOLE

CAMBRIDGE
UNIVERSITY PRESS

CAMBRIDGE UNIVERSITY PRESS
Cambridge, New York, Melbourne, Madrid, Cape Town,
Singapore, São Paulo, Delhi, Mexico City

Cambridge University Press
The Edinburgh Building, Cambridge CB2 8RU, UK

Published in the United States of America by Cambridge University Press, New York

www.cambridge.org
Information on this title: www.cambridge.org/9781107022751

First published 2012

A catalogue record for this publication is available from the British Library

Library of Congress Cataloguing in Publication data
Hobbes and the law / Edited by David Dyzenhaus and Thomas Poole.
p. cm.
Includes index.
ISBN 978-1-107-02275-1 (hardback)
1. Hobbes, Thomas, 1588–1679. 2. Law – Philosophy. 3. Natural law.
I. Dyzenhaus, David. II. Poole, Thomas (Thomas M.), Dr.
K457.H62H63 2012
340′.1–dc23 2012013364

ISBN 978-1-107-02275-1 Hardback

CONTENTS

CONTRIBUTORS

DAVID DYZENHAUS is a Professor of Law and Philosophy at the University of Toronto. The second edition of his *Hard Cases in Wicked Legal Systems* was published in 2010.

EVAN FOX-DECENT is an Associate Professor at McGill University, Faculty of Law. His book, *Sovereignty's Promise: The State as Fiduciary* (2011), is published in the Oxford Constitutional Theory series.

ROSS HARRISON is the Provost of King's College, Cambridge. His more extensive writing on Hobbes can be found in his *Hobbes, Locke, and Confusion's Masterpiece* (Cambridge University Press, 2003).

DENNIS KLIMCHUK is an Associate Professor of Philosophy at the University of Western Ontario. His main interests are in private law theory and the history of political philosophy.

DANIEL LEE is an Assistant Professor of Political Science at the University of Toronto. His research focuses on the history of political and legal thought and his recent publications appear in *History of Political Thought*, *Journal of the History of Ideas* and *Review of Politics*.

MICHAEL LOBBAN is Professor of Legal History at Queen Mary, University of London. He is one of the authors of volumes 11–13 of *The Oxford History of the Laws of England* (2010).

MARTIN LOUGHLIN is Professor of Public Law at the London School of Economics & Political Science. His most recent book, *Foundations of Public Law*, was published in 2010.

THOMAS POOLE is Reader in Law at the London School of Economics & Political Science. He writes on public law, constitutional theory and constitutional politics.

ALICE RISTROPH is Professor and Eileen Denner Research Fellow (2010–2013) at Seton Hall University School of Law. She teaches and writes in the fields of constitutional law, criminal law and political theory.

LARS VINX is an assistant professor in the Department of Philosophy at Bilkent University in Ankara, Turkey. He is the author of *Hans Kelsen's Pure Theory of Law: Legality and Legitimacy* (2007).

1

Introduction

DAVID DYZENHAUS AND THOMAS POOLE

Hobbes's philosophy provokes perennial fascination, such is its force and originality. But Hobbes's political thought has become particularly prominent in recent years, with a surge of scholarly interest, evidenced by a number of monographs in political theory and philosophy. At the same time, there has been a turn in legal scholarship towards political theory in a way that engages recognizably Hobbesian themes, for example: the law and politics of security; the law and politics of fear; and the relationship between security and liberty. It might even be the case that the scholarly surge and the turn to Hobbesian themes are connected in that Hobbes's focus on security and order as foundational values of civilized society seems particularly apt in unsettled times.

However, there is surprisingly little engagement with Hobbes as a juristic or legal thinker, despite the fact that Hobbes devoted whole works to legal inquiry and gave law a prominent role in his works focused on politics. This volume seeks to begin to remedy this by providing what we believe is the first collection of specially commissioned chapters devoted to Hobbes and the law.

The collection is in one way more in line with the surge than the turn in that it does not canvass Hobbesian themes, but Hobbes's thought. However, its interdisciplinary scope means that those themes recur within the particular discussions of aspects of Hobbes's juristic thought. For the collection contains original essays from scholars in the fields of political philosophy, the history of political thought, legal theory (jurisprudence), legal history, public law, and criminal law and criminal justice. Our aim in publishing the collection is thus to add to the scholarly study of Hobbes and to enrich inquiry into Hobbesian themes.

Perhaps the most surprising feature of Hobbes's juristic thought, both to scholars who have not turned their attention to it and to those whose understanding of Hobbesian themes does not draw on it, is its complexity and depth. Hobbes took law seriously, as one of the constitutive elements of the stable order of the civil society that we establish in order to escape the state of nature. So he was deeply concerned with the relationship between politics and law. But he was as deeply concerned with the task of elaborating a legal theory that would explain the internal workings of law – the legal nature of sovereignty as a product of human artifice, authority, adjudication, and the role of both criminal law and contract in sustaining legal order. Moreover, this elaboration requires, in his view, attention to a long list of the laws of nature and to the way in which these laws interact with the enacted law of the sovereign in a civil society.

There is, as this collection well illustrates, no uncontroversial interpretation of Hobbes's juristic thought. But one can discern from the essays collected here three main interpretive possibilities.

First, Hobbes's account of the relationship between the laws of nature and the enacted law of the sovereign is designed to establish an entirely secular basis for sovereignty, which enables the sovereign to rule effectively by law, though in a way that makes the sovereign not answerable to any standards that transcend his publicly expressed judgements about the collective welfare of his subjects. Thus Martin Loughlin argues that Hobbes uses natural law as an instrument to overthrow the idea that the laws of nature are transcendent standards to which the sovereign is answerable, which transforms the laws of nature into a set of axioms of civil peace; they become the 'immanent laws of civil government' and so help to constitute a science of political right. Loughlin's treatment presents a snapshot of Hobbes within what we might think of as a genealogy of modern political thought about the state. It is an exercise, that is, in the history of political and legal thought. But driving to the same conclusion though by dint of a philosophical reconstruction of the logic of Hobbes's argument, Ross Harrison investigates Hobbes's puzzling statement that 'The law of nature and the civil law contain each other and are of equal extent'. Harrison argues that, properly understood, natural law and civil law are neither equal in the extent of their power, nor in the extent of their content. Rather, natural law merely shows that there has to be civil law, but does not thereby limit its content. Similarly, Michael Lobban sets a detailed analysis of Hobbes's theory of contracts within his general philosophy to argue that the main function of the laws of nature was to impel men to set up a sovereign who would be the source of all laws governing them and to provide the tools to set the sovereign on firm foundations.

Together these three essays support what might be said to be the orthodox view of Hobbes, as an early legal positivist thinker, but who diverges from the kind of positivism that united Bentham, Austin and Hart because of the role of natural law in his theory to provide a secular legitimation of de facto sovereign power. The second line of interpretation is presented by Thomas Poole who exploits the rich resources of Hobbes's discussion of law in *Behemoth* to display a tension in Hobbes's legal theory between the commitment to government by an entirely artificial sovereign who makes his judgements known only by enacting public laws that create a stable framework for social interaction, and a commitment to the necessity for the sovereign to be able to act against the law by relying on his prerogative authority to decide what is best for the safety of his subjects. On Poole's interpretation, this tension between the commitment to rule by law and the commitment to natural law – the safety of the people – does not make Hobbes's system unstable, but rather holds it together.

The third line of interpretation also does not seek to reduce Hobbes's account of law to the enacted law of the sovereign, with natural law supplying the reason to obey enacted law since, like Poole, it seeks to give natural law an independent role within civil society. However, unlike Poole, that role is located in the way that the sovereign's artificial role is constituted by the laws of nature in ways that give a moral shape to civil society thus softening considerably Hobbes's reputation for authoritarianism. Thus Alice Ristroph analyses Hobbes's theory of punishment to show that Hobbes thought that a state had to punish non-compliance with the law but was deeply concerned about the inhuman character of punishment. He was therefore anxious to moderate the inhumanity of punishment by subjecting it to the rule of law. Evan Fox-Decent argues that the sovereign and subject in Hobbes are in a trust-like or fiduciary relationship that explains how the sovereign's possession of public power yields authority and obligation independently of consent. Dennis Klimchuk explores Hobbes's discussions of equity to show that equity serves as a criterion of legality in the common law and as a principle of statutory interpretation. Lars Vinx argues, against neo-republican critiques of Hobbes, that Hobbes shared the republican aim of understanding law as a way of avoiding arbitrary treatment and domination, but had sound reasons to avoid constructing the more demanding account of non-domination favoured by neo-republicans. And David Dyzenhaus sets out an account of Hobbes's theory of legal authority in which the subordinate judiciary play a role, arising from their duty to the sovereign, in ensuring that the sovereign's laws do in fact serve the legal subjects' interest in equality and liberty, with the result that consent to the sovereign's rule is rendered intelligible to those subject to it.

There is much more in these essays than can be conveyed in this exercise of bringing them into direct dialogue with each other. And there is finally one essay that is not involved in this dialogue though it shares with all others the aim of displaying the depth of Hobbes's juristic thought. Daniel Lee shows how Hobbes, despite his disavowal of Roman civil law, was nevertheless dependent upon it, and used elements of Roman private law such as ownership, guardianship and suretyship to craft more precisely the different forms of authorization and representation central to his understanding of the state.

2

The political jurisprudence of Thomas Hobbes

MARTIN LOUGHLIN

Introduction

Thomas Hobbes was a jurist of the first rank, and his *Leviathan* stands as the greatest masterpiece of political jurisprudence written in the English language. Commonly regarded as a political philosopher,[1] 'political jurisprudence' more precisely specifies the nature of his scholarship. Hobbes was certainly a philosopher in some sense, yet he remained very critical of abstract theorizing and so-called philosophical thinking, believing that true wisdom, 'the knowledge [*scientia*] of truth in every subject', comes only from experience.[2] His speculations were continually fixed on practical matters.[3] He thought he was engaged in a thoroughly practical undertaking which he himself termed 'civil science' but which, given its juristic orientation, could also be called 'political jurisprudence'.

I have benefited from presentations at the seminar on Hobbes and Law at the LSE Legal and Political Theory Forum in May 2010 and at a Cardozo Law School Faculty Seminar in September 2011. In addition to the participants in those seminars, I thank Philip Cook, Neil Duxbury, Chris Foley and Grégoire Webber for their written comments.

1 See, e.g., Michael Oakeshott, 'Introduction to Leviathan' [1946] in Michael Oakeshott, *Hobbes on Civil Association* (Indianapolis: Liberty Fund, 2000), 1, 3: '*Leviathan* is the greatest, perhaps sole masterpiece of political philosophy written in the English language'.

2 See Thomas Hobbes, *On the Citizen*, edited by Richard Tuck and Michael Silverthorne (Cambridge University Press, 1998), 4–5 (hereafter: *De Cive*, DC). Noting in his introduction to *De Cive* that 'the war of the sword and the war of the pens is perpetual', Hobbes suggested that one reason was that 'both parties to a dispute defend their right with the opinions of Philosophers'. Much of what passes for philosophy, he complained, 'has contributed nothing to the knowledge of truth': its appeal 'has not lain in enlightening the mind but in lending the influence of attractive and emotive language to hasty and superficial opinions'.

3 Cf. G.W.F. Hegel, *Lectures on the History of Philosophy* [1805] (London: Bell, 1894), Pt I B 3, who notes of Hobbes's books that 'there is nothing speculative or really philosophic in them'. He continues: 'The views that he adopts are shallow and empirical [i.e. there is "nothing properly philosophical" in them] but the reasons he gives for them, and the propositions he makes respecting them, are original in character, inasmuch as they are derived from natural necessities and wants.'

This chapter addresses the ambition and significance of Hobbes's political jurisprudence. One immediate barrier concerns his status as a jurist. He is occasionally regarded as a founder of legal positivism, but this tends to be a cursory acknowledgement that overlooks his pivotal role.[4] The reason for this is that, finding his authoritarianism repugnant and his criticisms of the common law method objectionable, many regard Hobbes's contribution to jurisprudence as thoroughly discreditable.[5] Contemporary legal positivists also seem embarrassed at the way Hobbes, having defined law as the command of the sovereign, proceeded to give natural law such a prominent place in his account.[6] Such criticisms reveal more about the

[4] It might be noted, e.g., that contemporary Anglo-American legal positivism takes its cue from H.L.A. Hart, *The Concept of Law* (Oxford: Clarendon Press, 1961), a work which does not address Hobbes's account of law and which treats John Austin's more reductive account as definitive of the older tradition.

[5] This type of assessment dogged Hobbes from the outset. Herman Conring, one of the leading German jurists of the seventeenth century, argued that: 'Hobbes philosophises in the *Elementa* and *De Cive* in an outrageous manner when he grounds sovereignty as a whole in the most powerful authority and explains hatred or enmity between human beings as the basis of the government of the state. Which upright person would expound something so preposterous? The author appears to deserve the hatred of all.' Cited in Horst Dreitzel, 'The Reception of Hobbes in the Political Philosophy of the Early German Enlightenment' (2003) 29 *History of European Ideas* 255, at 258. More recently, it has often been noted that Hobbes's statements to the effect that 'every man to every man, for want of a common power to keep them in awe, is an Enemy' forms the basis of Carl Schmitt's claim that 'the specific political distinction to which political actions and motives can be reduced is that between friend and enemy'. See Thomas Hobbes, *Leviathan* [1651], edited by Richard Tuck (Cambridge University Press, 1991) (hereafter L), 102 and Carl Schmitt, *The Concept of the Political* [1932], translated by George Schwab (University of Chicago Press, 1996), 26. Strauss offers an explanation. He refers to Hobbes as 'that imprudent, impish, and iconoclastic extremist [who] was deservedly punished for his recklessness, especially by his countrymen. Still he exercised a very great influence on all subsequent political thought, Continental and even English, and especially on Locke – the judicious Locke, who judiciously refrained as much as he could from mentioning Hobbes's "justly decried name"'. See Leo Strauss, *Natural Right and History* (University of Chicago Press, 1953), 166.

[6] George H. Sabine, *A History of Political Theory* (London: Harrap, 3rd edn, 1963), 460–461: 'It would undoubtedly have been easier for Hobbes if he could have abandoned the law of nature altogether, as his more empirical successors, Hume and Bentham, did. He might then have started from human nature simply as a fact, claiming the warrant of observation for whatever qualities … he might have seen fit to attribute to it'. Some argue that, because of his account of this relationship, Hobbes was not in fact a legal positivist: see Mark C. Murphy, 'Was Hobbes a Legal Positivist?' (1995) 105 *Ethics* 846 (showing Hobbes's affinities with Aquinas); David Dyzenhaus, 'Hobbes and the Legitimacy of Law' (2001) 20 *Law & Philosophy* 461 (showing Hobbes's affinities with Fuller and labelling Hobbes an 'anti-positivist'). Coyle states that: 'In the face of the foregoing account of (Hobbes' perception of) the relationship between natural law and the positive laws of a civil society, it may

construction of modern schools of legal thought than about Hobbes's contribution to jurisprudence. We should move beyond the argument of whether he is a natural lawyer or a legal positivist. Following his own injunction that one should try to understand the overall point of a scholar's writing,[7] we might focus on how Hobbes drew a clear distinction between natural law and positive law for the purpose of crafting a rich, ambitious and comprehensive account of the modern idea of law.

Political jurisprudence

In later life, Hobbes claimed to be the founder of a new field of knowledge, that of civil science. This subject, which he defined in contrast to the natural sciences, was concerned with the relations of 'politic bodies', and especially of the rights and duties of sovereigns and subjects.[8] The subject of 'civil science', he boasted, is 'no older than my own book, *De Cive*'.[9] It was inspired by dramatic shifts in European thought since the sixteenth century which were to lead to the formation of the modern idea of the state. Governmental ordering was de-personalized: instead of focusing on the figure of the ruler and the conditions that legitimated his rule, attention came to rest on the commonwealth or state. This institution, rather than those who exercised its powers, set the agenda for Hobbes's inquiries: 'I speak not of the men', he explained, 'but (in the Abstract) of the Seat of Power'.[10] Rulership was displaced as the central object of political inquiry once it was recognized that the ruler's basic responsibility was to maintain the state.[11]

seem perplexing to persist in regarding such an account as positivist'. He does, however, recognize that there is a 'deeper sense in which Hobbes's thought should be regarded as the foundation of the modern positivist tradition': Sean Coyle, 'Thomas Hobbes and the Intellectual Origins of Legal Positivism' (2003) 16 *Canadian J. of Law & Jurisprudence* 243, 254–255.

7 It is not, he claimed, 'the bare words, but the scope of the writer that giveth the true light, by which any writing is to be interpreted; and they that insist on single texts, without considering the main design, can derive no thing from them clearly, but rather ... make everything more obscure than it is': L, ch.43, 414–415.

8 L, ch.9.

9 Thomas Hobbes, *The Author's Epistle Dedicatory to De Corpore* [1656]: see *The English Works of Thomas Hobbes of Malmesbury*, edited by Sir William Molesworth (London: J. Bohn, 1839), vol. I, ix.

10 L, 3.

11 L, 231: 'The office of the sovereign ... consisteth in the end, for which he was trusted with the sovereign power, namely the procuration of *the safety of the people* ... But by safety here, is not meant a bare preservation, but also all other contentments of life.'

In these emerging conditions of modernity, received ideas of natural law underwent important changes. The commonwealth was no longer seen as a natural or organic entity: the institution of the state was created as an act of imagination. Not by Nature, claimed Hobbes, but 'by Art is created that great Leviathan called a Commonwealth or State'.[12] The state was an artefact of 'self-government', an institution created by humans to serve human purposes. Although the 'laws' by which this institution was established and maintained might be categorized as 'laws of nature', they were derived entirely from human characteristics and from scientific investigations into the nature of the politico-legal world. The state was brought into existence through the exercise of political reasoning. This was a distinct, autonomous attempt to explain governmental ordering: if we cannot rest such claims on divine sanction or unchanging custom, how could obedience to authority be justified?

Hobbes was one of the most insightful scholars of the early-modern period to examine this question. The characteristics of his civil science were later specified by Rousseau in the opening sentence of *The Social Contract*. I want to know, said Rousseau, whether in the civil order (i) there can be some sure and legitimate principle of governmental ordering, (ii) taking men as they are and (iii) laws as they can be.[13] What Hobbes called civil science, Rousseau referred to as the science of political right (*droit politique*). Rousseau's statement made plain that this science was not limited to the task of proposing a logical, aesthetically pleasing normative scheme of government. It had also to recognize law's practical character, to draw on a plausible account of human psychology, and to provide a realistic portrayal of the nature of collective existence. Like Hobbes, Rousseau sought to explain how governmental authority could be established and maintained in the actually-existing world.

Both scholars recognized that civil science was not just a speculative undertaking. The world was, after all, littered with imaginative schemes that had foundered on the rocks of political realities. Even as thought experiments, they had often foundered because they were unable to reconcile two equally powerful but contrary human dispositions: the desire to be autonomous and the desire to be a participant in a common venture.[14] The difficulty was that since the disjuncture between freedom

[12] L, 9.

[13] Jean-Jacques Rousseau, *The Social Contract* [1762] in *The Social Contract and Other Later Political Writings*, edited by Victor Gourevitch (Cambridge University Press, 1997), 39, 41.

[14] See Martin Loughlin, *Foundations of Public Law* (Oxford University Press, 2010), ch.6.

and belonging could be neither eliminated nor reconciled, it could only be negotiated. It followed that a 'science', in any strict sense of the term, could never be established.[15] So-called civil science did not simply entail the explication of principles of political right; it required the exercise of prudential judgment.[16] It therefore seems better to characterize this undertaking as an exercise in political jurisprudence.

If we accept that Hobbes was engaged in political jurisprudence, the apparent discrepancies that some legal scholars believe characterize his work are resolved. We can make sense of the apparently paradoxical claim that Hobbes belongs to the natural law tradition yet also founds the modern school of legal positivism. We can also appreciate that although Hobbes's account is authoritarian, it is not absolutist. We can, most significantly, appreciate the sheer ambition of Hobbes's undertaking.

Hobbes on law

The contention that Hobbes was a progenitor of legal positivism is certainly justified.[17] The overriding objective of his work was to establish the authority of the state, conceived as a human artefact. Central to that objective was the claim that the office of the sovereign possessed the absolute power of law-making. Hobbes defined law as 'the Reason of this our Artificial Man the Commonwealth'.[18] Sovereign was the name given to the person (office) that represented the commonwealth, and it was 'his Command that makes Law'.[19] It was the authority of the sovereign, rather than the wisdom of scholars and philosophers, that made law: *Auctoritas, non veritas facit legem.*[20]

Law was the command of the sovereign. This concept of positive law (*lex*) should not be confused with right (*jus*). Hobbes argued that many

[15] This is a point that Rousseau himself recognized: see Jean-Jacques Rousseau, *Emile, or On Education*, translated by A. Bloom (New York: Basic Books, 1979), 458: 'the science of political right is yet to be born, and it is to be presumed that it will never be born'.

[16] Quentin Skinner points us in the right direction when suggesting that Hobbes came to recognize that the proper conduct of civil science rested as much on the art of persuasion as that of reasoning: Quentin Skinner, 'Hobbes's Changing Conception of Civil Science' in Skinner, *Visions of Politics: Vol. 3 Hobbes and Civil Science* (Cambridge University Press, 2002), 85. See also Skinner, *Reason and Rhetoric in the Philosophy of Hobbes* (Cambridge University Press, 1996), Conclusion.

[17] See, e.g., M.M. Goldsmith, 'Hobbes on Law' in Tom Sorell (ed.), *The Cambridge Companion to Hobbes* (Cambridge University Press, 1996), ch.12.

[18] L, 187. [19] L, 187.

[20] Thomas Hobbes, *A Dialogue between a Philosopher and a Student of the Common Laws of England* [1681], edited by Joseph Cropsey (University of Chicago Press, 1971), 55.

people were confused about the distinction between right and law: right 'consisteth in liberty to do, or to forbeare' whereas law 'determineth, and bindeth'. Law and right therefore 'differ as much as Obligation and Liberty; which in one and the same matter are inconsistent'.[21] As the supreme law-maker, the sovereign was the sole source of right and wrong, of justice and injustice. Justice, for Hobbes, was a purely legal concept: justice consisted in acting in accordance with those commands. Since positive law provided 'the measure of Good and Evil actions', there could be no such thing as an unjust law.[22]

Once law was acknowledged as the command of the sovereign, it was evident to Hobbes that the sovereign could not be bound by that law. It was not possible 'for any person to be bound to himself, because he that can bind can release'.[23] The manner in which the pact between individuals for the purpose of creating the sovereign was constructed also supported this position. Hobbes argued that since the sovereign was not a party to this pact, he could not commit any breach of legal obligation to the parties to it. Further, the so-called 'rights' of 'the people' could not act as a counterweight to the will of the sovereign. Since 'the people', as distinct from 'the multitude', came into existence as a result of the pact to create the sovereign, the office of the sovereign represented the will of the people.[24] For Hobbes, the sovereign was a 'Mortal God' and the source of law.[25] Established by art – by political pact – the office of the sovereign was in no way dependent on any higher authority.

Hobbes here deliberately broke with the ancient world of virtue and vice, good and evil. Moral arguments of right and wrong were transformed into political claims of peace and war.[26] The edifice of the state was designed to subordinate all other sources of morality, justice or law. Its authority could not be qualified by property, international law, common law or religion. First, the sovereign not only possessed sole dominion over property; he determined what constituted property.[27] Second, Hobbes argued that the norms of the 'international community' of nations could not be binding on states.[28] Third, he challenged Coke's argument that law

[21] L, 91. DC, 156: 'There is then a great difference between *law* and *right*; for a law is a *bond*, a *right* is a *liberty*, and they differ as contraries.'

[22] L, 223. [23] L, 184.

[24] DC, 75–76, 137. [25] L, 120.

[26] See Reinhart Koselleck, *Critique and Crisis: Enlightenment and the Pathogenesis of Modern Society* (Cambridge, MA: MIT Press, 1988), 25.

[27] L, 125.

[28] L, 244. See further Noel Malcolm, *Aspects of Hobbes* (Oxford University Press, 2002), ch.13.

constituted a special type of 'artificial reason': it was not the 'wisdom of subordinate judges but the reason of this our artificial man the commonwealth and his command that makes law'.[29] His final argument – about religion – was the most comprehensive. Hobbes's analysis of ecclesiastical questions takes up almost half of *Leviathan*. In an Erastian argument, he demonstrated that the church's claim to earthly power was based on error; the church was not an independent institution, but part of the commonwealth and entirely subject to the rule of its sovereign.[30]

It seems beyond doubt that Hobbes constructed, in Bobbio's formulation, 'the ideological framework for legal positivism'.[31] Modern legal positivism – the conviction that positive law forms an autonomous system of law that includes its own criteria of right and wrong, just and unjust – has its origins in his work.

Given his position on the authority of positive law, why then did Hobbes take so seriously the claims of natural law? Why in particular does he seem to rest his entire construction of positive law on a foundation of the laws of nature?[32]

The simple answer is that Hobbes could not ignore the claims of natural law without radically circumscribing the overall ambition of his civil science. Once we recognize his task as an exercise of political jurisprudence – of addressing the issue of legitimacy and not simply accepting the authority of positive law as a postulate of thought – it is evident that he could not avoid addressing claims of natural law. Much of his political

[29] L, 187: 'For it is possible long study may increase and confirm erroneous sentences: and where men build on false grounds, the more they build, the greater is the ruin: and of those that study and observe with equal time and diligence, the reasons and resolutions are, and must remain, discordant: and therefore it is not that *Juris prudentia*, or wisdom of subordinate judges; but the reason of this our artificial man the commonwealth, and his command, that maketh law.' See also Hobbes, *A Dialogue between a Philosopher and a Student of the Common Laws of England*, 54–77.

[30] L, Pt III. See Jeffrey R. Collins, *The Allegiance of Thomas Hobbes* (Oxford University Press, 2005), 10: 'He [Hobbes] understood the English Revolution not, primarily, as a constitutional struggle over monarchy, nor as an outburst of republicanism, nor as a theological struggle over Calvinism. Hobbes understood the Revolution as a war over the nature of the church as an independent corporate body, and the status of the clergy as an estate of the realm. In this sense, Hobbes interpreted the English Revolution as an ecclesial crisis, and as the culmination of the long Reformation struggle to redefine the political struggle of Christendom by submitting the universal church to the power of emerging modern states.' See further Thomas Hobbes, *Behemoth or the Long Parliament* [c.1668], edited by Stephen Holmes (University of Chicago Press, 1990).

[31] Norberto Bobbio, *Thomas Hobbes and the Natural Law Tradition*, translated by Daniela Gobetti (University of Chicago Press, 1993), 116.

[32] See DC, chs 2–4; L, chs 14 and 15.

writing was undertaken during a period of conflict and civil war, the period he calls, in the fourth part of *Leviathan*, 'the kingdom of darkness'. During these turbulent times, pernicious beliefs flourished: 'sovereignty may be divided; civil and spiritual power are distinct; the sovereign is subject to the law; private men can judge if laws are just or unjust; private conscience justifies resistance, not to mention tyrannicide'.[33] His civil science could not be adequately formulated without taking seriously the revolutionary claims being made in the name of natural law. Hobbes made natural law a central focus of his work,[34] but he did so in order to expose its errors and to rework its precepts for the purpose of rebuilding the authority of sovereign will.

In order to explain this, I first examine his treatment of natural right, then natural law, and finally draw on the relation between natural law and positive law to address more directly Hobbes's political jurisprudence.

Natural right

The concepts of natural right and natural law perform major roles in Hobbes's scheme. But right and law must be kept distinct, he argued, since one concerns liberty and the other obligation. This general distinction applied to natural right and natural law. We start with his treatment of natural right.

Hobbes belongs to a school of thinkers who placed the concept of natural rights at the core of their arguments.[35] Natural rights theories – especially those that a century later were enshrined in the words 'that all men are created equal and endowed by their Creator with certain inalienable rights'[36] – have had a great impact on the drafting of modern constitutional documents. In later schemes, natural rights as the inherent possession of every human being were declared either inalienable – liberties that no government could suppress – or regulated only with the consent of the

[33] Stephen Holmes, 'Introduction' to *Behemoth*, xxv–xxvi.

[34] DC, 156: '*Natural law* is the law which God has revealed to all men through his *eternal word* which is innate in them, namely by *natural reason*. And this is the law which I have been attempting to expound throughout this little book.' See further, L, 110: 'The Laws of Nature are Immutable and Eternal ... And the science of them, is the true and onely Moral Philosophy.'

[35] Richard Tuck, *Natural Rights Theories: Their Origin and Development* (Cambridge University Press, 1979), ch.6.

[36] American Declaration of Independence 1776; see also French Declaration of the Rights of Man and the Citizen 1789, Art. 1: 'Men are born and remain free and equal in rights.'

individual for the purpose of maximizing liberties.[37] But the role of natural rights in Hobbes's scheme is different.

Hobbes developed his argument about the nature of society and government through the frame of natural rights. Leo Strauss claims that Hobbes did more than any other theorist to bring about the shift in modern political theory from duty to rights, for which reason he is the true founder of modern liberalism.[38] That may be so, although 'modern liberalism' is an ambiguous notion. Tuck notes that 'most strong rights theories have in fact been explicitly authoritarian rather than liberal',[39] a point neatly illustrated in the radical twist Hobbes gave to the concept of natural right.

Hobbes argued that the fundamental right of the individual in the state of nature was self-preservation: 'the first foundation of natural *Right* is that *each man protect his life and limbs as much as he can*'.[40] It is a right built into our nature: 'we cannot be blamed for looking out for ourselves', he contended, for 'we cannot will to do otherwise'. The desire for self-preservation thus 'happens by a real necessity of nature as powerful as that by which a stone falls downward'.[41]

Hobbes replaced the Aristotelian claim that man was a social animal with the argument that humans were self-centred, competitive and driven by their passions and fears. Their fundamental right by nature is freedom to preserve the conditions of their existence. Hobbes's analogy to gravitational force suggests that he was seeking to put this basic natural right on a scientific foundation. The fundamental natural right of self-preservation is 'not a philosopher's thought imputed to mankind', but 'a rational claim immanent in human nature'.[42]

This basic right to preserve one's existence was directly connected to his concept of sovereignty.[43] In a state of nature, 'every man was permitted to do anything to anybody, and to possess, use and enjoy whatever he wanted and could get'.[44] Consequently, 'the effect of this *right* is almost the same as if there were no *right* at all'.[45] The drive for self-preservation and the right of liberty of each individual leads directly to 'a war of every man against every man'.[46] It followed that for the purpose of maintaining

37 French Declaration, Art. 2: 'The aim of all political association is the preservation of the natural and imprescriptible rights of man.'

38 Leo Strauss, *Natural Right and History* (University of Chicago Press, 1953), esp. 166–202.

39 Tuck, *Natural Rights*, 3.

40 DC, 1.7. 41 DC, 1.7.

42 Perez Zagorin, *Hobbes and the Law of Nature* (Princeton University Press, 2009), 28.

43 L, ch.30. 44 DC, 28. 45 DC, 29. 46 DC, 29.

this basic natural right, humans must pool their natural rights and vest them in the office of the sovereign. Hobbes argued that this was a necessary corollary of the existence of the fundamental natural right of self-preservation.

Hobbes was the first to draw a clear distinction between natural right and natural law, arguing that the former was not dependent on the latter. Natural rights inhere in humans for the purposes of ensuring their survival. Formulating natural rights in this way revealed the paradox that in order to realize natural rights, humans must agree to relinquish them and vest an absolute right of rule-making in the office of the sovereign.[47]

Natural law

Modern modes of thinking have eroded the medieval idea of natural law as disclosing an ordered world replete with meaning. Given Hobbes's scientific approach to matters of law and state, the retention of natural law in his scheme requires explanation. He was very critical of those who invoked the concept of natural law without defining it and he poured scorn on those who argued 'that a particular act is against natural law because it runs counter to the united opinion of all the wisest or most civilized nations'.[48] Such claims were naïve: 'men condemn in others what they approve in themselves, publicly praise what they secretly reject, and form their opinions from a habit of listening to what they are told, not from their own observation'.[49]

Hobbes retained the medieval formulation of natural law as 'the dictate of right reason'. But he placed the precepts of reason on a more scientific footing. Noting that geometry was 'the only science that it hath pleased God hitherto to bestow on mankind',[50] Hobbes saw reason as a type of

[47] Hobbes does qualify this point with the statement that 'not all rights are alienable', arguing that 'a man cannot lay down the right of resisting them that assault him by force, to take away his life': L, 93. It is sometimes argued that this right of self-defence undermines Hobbes's theory of absolute sovereignty: see, e.g., Jean Hampton, *Hobbes and the Social Contract Tradition* (Cambridge University Press, 1986), 197–207. But in a systematic account, Susanne Sreedhar shows that Hobbes's account of resistance rights are personal and peculiar, do not conflict with his prohibition on rebellion and are entirely compatible with his account of absolute sovereignty. In reality, Hobbes takes the potentially powerful conceptual tools of resistance and renders them politically innocuous. Sreedhar concludes that Hobbes's 'delimited set of cases of justified resistance ... serves to underscore all of the ways in which subjects are *not* at liberty to disobey the sovereign'. Susanne Sreedhar, *Hobbes on Resistance: Defying the Leviathan* (Cambridge University Press, 2010), 171.

[48] DC, 32. [49] DC, 33. [50] L, 28.

instrumental calculation. This helped him to reformulate the concept of natural law as a set of logical and purposive axioms.

For Hobbes, the laws of nature were axioms 'found out by Reason, by which a man is forbidden to do that which is destructive of life, or takes away the means of preserving the same'.[51] Natural laws yielded a catalogue of duties to maintain the fundamental right to self-preservation. Natural law did not prescribe the type of good conduct laid down in Scripture; since these laws were 'immutable and eternal', they predated any divine texts.[52] Natural law did not promote behaviour that was good in itself; it existed for the purpose of regulating action necessary for the maintenance of self-preservation. The main problem with these laws of nature, Hobbes suggested, was that they obliged *in foro interno*, in conscience only.[53] Strictly, they were 'dictates of Reason', not really laws at all for 'they are but Conclusions, or Theorems concerning what conduceth to the conservation and defence of themselves'. Law, by contrast, 'properly is the word of him that by right hath command over others'.[54]

Chapters 2 and 3 of *De Cive* and Chapters 14 and 15 of *Leviathan* list the primary laws of nature in some detail. But their essential purpose was expressed in the first law: 'to seek peace'.[55] Since the state of nature was one of perpetual war generated from the exercise of natural rights, this first law, seeking to ensure self-preservation by promoting peace, must lead to the giving up of the state of nature. It followed that 'the right of men to all things must not be held on to; certain rights must be transferred or abandoned'.[56] The overriding purpose of natural law was to promote peace 'for a means of the conservation of men in multitudes'.[57]

Hobbes retained the concept of natural law within his overall scheme mainly as a 'device … to provide an acceptable foundation of the absolute power of the sovereign, and thus to ensure the undisputed supremacy of positive law'.[58] His objective was to use natural law, a concept used by many of his contemporaries to justify revolution and resistance to oppression, to demonstrate that laws of nature require the very opposite: unconditional obedience to the sovereign. This is highlighted in his second law of nature: 'stand by your agreements, or keep faith'.[59] Yet this obligation is impossible to realize in the state of nature, where force or fraud prevail: 'Covenants, without the Sword, are but Words, and of no strength

[51] L, 91. [52] L, 110. [53] L, 110.
[54] L, 111. [55] DC, 34. [56] DC, 34. [57] L, 109.
[58] Bobbio, *Thomas Hobbes and the Natural Law Tradition*, 123.
[59] DC, 43.

to secure a man at all.'[60] These first two basic laws – maintenance of peace and fidelity to agreements – could be realized only by subjecting individuals to the rule of the sovereign.

Hobbes's longer list of the general laws of nature included gratitude, sociability, mercy, respect, impartiality, proportionality, equality of standing and fair adjudication of disputes.[61] His general point was that humans might adhere to these laws of nature, but they did so only as a matter of conscience and personal morality. For these laws to become obligatory they had to be converted into positive laws by command of the sovereign: 'Thus the practice of *natural law* is necessary for the preservation of peace, and *security* is necessary for the practice of *natural law*.'[62]

Hobbes's argument about natural right and natural law can be summarized. Left to the free exercise of inherent natural rights, individuals would end up destroying themselves. The sovereign's law was necessary because natural rights must be given up for the purpose of self-preservation. He recognized the existence of certain laws of nature, such as mutual respect and fair treatment, which propel humans to sociability. But he argued that these natural laws could not be realized outside the state. They became 'true' laws – that is, obligatory – only once recognized by civil law. For Hobbes, natural laws formed part of a regime of public reason, which meant the reason of the sovereign.[63] The difference between Hobbes and natural lawyers thus becomes clear. Natural lawyers say that positive law binds only if it complies with the precepts of natural law. Hobbes, by contrast, said that natural law binds only when expressed in the form of positive law.

Natural law and civil law

Although a legal positivist, Hobbes assigned to the precepts of natural law an important role. Some argue that in accepting a natural or rational mode of ordering, he was a suppressed natural lawyer, but this is to misconstrue the radical character of his argument. There are two main issues: first, his

[60] L, 117.

[61] See esp. DC, 47–54. For discussion see Gregory S. Kavka, *Hobbesian Moral and Political Theory* (Princeton University Press, 1986), 343; S.A. Lloyd, *Morality in the Philosophy of Thomas Hobbes: Cases in the Law of Nature* (Cambridge University Press, 2009), 52–55. For consideration of equality see Joel Kidder, 'Acknowledgement of Equals: Hobbes's Ninth Law of Nature' (1983) 33 *Philosophical Quarterly* 133.

[62] DC, 70.

[63] L, 306: 'we are not every one, to make our own private Reason, or Conscience, but the Publique Reason, that is the reason of Gods Supreme Lieutenant'.

claim that natural law and civil law are parts of a common concept; and, second, the question of the authority of the sovereign.

Hobbes contended that, once the state had been established, the 'law of nature and the civil law contain each other and are of equal extent'.[64] Laws of nature, 'being qualities that dispose men to peace and to obedience', undoubtedly form component parts of an orderly regime.[65] But natural laws were dependent on sovereign power for their obligatory force. 'Civil and natural law are not different kinds', he concluded, 'but different parts of Law; whereof one part being written is called Civil, the other unwritten, Natural'.[66]

Hobbes believed that if a dispute arose on which the civil law was silent – perhaps because the legislature had not foreseen the issue – the judge should refer to the precepts of natural law for a solution. He acknowledged that a good judge was impartial, patient and dispassionate and also had 'a right understanding of that principal law of nature called Equity', which depended 'not on the reading of other men's writings but on the goodness of a man's own natural reason and meditation'.[67] But this hardly constitutes evidence that Hobbes was at heart a natural lawyer. He recognized that the function of civil law was to promote peace and sociability through an impartially administered regime of rules.[68] When interpreting law, a judge had to have regard to this basic purpose and in this situation the so-called laws of nature provide guidance. They are therefore best understood as prudential precepts.[69] To say that an officer of the state relies on such precepts in interpreting laws is not to acknowledge natural law as an independent set of moral norms; it is to recognize

64 L, 185.

65 For an interpretation of Hobbes's account of natural law as founded in reciprocity and generating the obligations of governments to promote the peace and welfare of their citizens see Lloyd, *Morality in the Philosophy of Thomas Hobbes*, esp. ch.1.

66 L, 185. 67 L, 195. 68 DC, 14.10.

69 *Behemoth*, 44: 'To obey the laws is justice and equity, which is the law of nature ... Likewise to obey the laws is the prudence of the subject; for without such obedience the commonwealth (which is every subject's safety and protection) cannot subsist.' See further Philip Pettit, *Made with Words: Hobbes on Language, Mind, and Politics* (Princeton University Press, 2008), 165: 'Here I depart from the moralistic view of Hobbesian natural law that is associated with a number of people, most prominently Howard Warrender (1957). My view is much closer to the prudential view of natural law ascribed to Hobbes by John W.N. Watkins (1973). Debate continues on this issue, but the Watkins stance is now more or less accepted as the "orthodox" one.' The references are to Howard Warrender, *The Political Philosophy of Hobbes* (Oxford University Press, 1957) and J.W.N. Watkins, *Hobbes's System of Ideas* (London: Hutchinson, 1973).

that the judge must be attuned to the nature of the association, to political reason, to 'reasons of state'.[70]

The second issue, the relationship between civil and natural law, concerned the status of the sovereign. Although the sovereign was not bound by positive law, Hobbes did not confer the office with arbitrary power. As he explained in *Leviathan*, the office existed to procure '*the safety of the people*; to which he is obliged by the law of nature'.[71] For some, this again offers evidence that Hobbes based his account on natural law, but this too rests on a misunderstanding.

Hobbes's objective was to establish a governmental regime that possessed absolute validity. The only effective way of doing this was, as Bobbio has noted, to 'place it on the pedestal of natural laws, i.e., on a law which was … rationally deductible from another law of nature evident in itself'.[72] But on the critical question of whether a subject could appeal to a higher law which restricted the sovereign's power, Hobbes was unequivocal: the sovereign must 'render an account to God, the author of that law, and to none but him'.[73] Further, the sovereign 'may ordain the doing of many things … which is a breach of trust, and of the law of nature; but this is not enough to authorise any subject, either to make war upon, or so much as to accuse of injustice, or any way to speak evil of their sovereign'.[74]

Hobbes's argument that the authority of the sovereign rested on natural law precepts did not lead him to recognize the validity of a higher legal norm. His primary objective was to explain that there could be no valid law except that of civil law, and that the basic function of civil law was to meet the conditions of his civil science.

Hobbes's political jurisprudence

Hobbes's civil science was formed as a result of the secularization, rationalization and (partial) positivization of the medieval idea of natural law. It

[70] Hobbes did not engage in a detailed examination of what is often called 'reason of state' thinking. The most obvious reason was that his primary objective was to develop a science of politics rather than to offer guidance on the arts of governing. But in all probability he felt it presumptuous to instruct sovereigns on how best to exercise their power. Nonetheless, Malcolm's view that 'a number of themes and lines of argument' in Hobbes's works 'echo the teachings of *ragion di stato* theory' and that 'it seems reasonable to align Hobbes's political theory with that of *ragion di stato*' seems sound: Noel Malcolm, *Reason of State, Propaganda, and the Thirty Years' War: An Unknown Translation by Thomas Hobbes* (Oxford University Press, 2007), 114, 118.

[71] L, 231.

[72] Bobbio, *Thomas Hobbes and the Natural Law Tradition*, 143–144.

[73] L, 231. [74] L, 172.

was founded on the view that collective ordering was not divinely ordained but the result of a world we have made. In this constructed world, humans were conceived as free, equal and rational beings able to devise their own arrangements of collective ordering and to establish regimes of government resting on some notion of consent.

A key objective of Hobbes's civil science was to undermine any lingering authority of the medieval idea of natural law. Natural law – the metaphysical notion that all natural occurrences were subject to universal reason apprehended by our faculty of reason – had to be overthrown. Hobbes felt that this could most effectively be achieved using the instruments of natural law. Herein lies the critical importance of his civil science. He detheologized the concept of natural law, rejecting the idea of civil rule as an expression of natural order, and conceived the question of obedience to authority as a rational undertaking. He thereby transformed the concept of natural law, treating it instrumentally as a set of axioms that promoted civil peace. Rather than assuming that humans were governed by (God-given) reason, he understood them to be creatures possessed of reason but driven by potentially destructive passions.

The transformation of natural law was of critical importance in refashioning the instruments of modern political rule. Hobbes showed that to realize liberty and equality – the foundational precepts of public law – humans must first be subjected to government. The laws of nature he listed and the conditions for their realization – the promotion of civil peace and enforcement of the laws of sociability – became the immanent laws of civil government. Laws of nature were converted into precepts of political right.

This concept of political right must be distinguished from the concepts of natural right and natural law. As Hobbes says, it is not by nature but by artifice – i.e. by political imagination – that the state is created. And it is from this institution of the state that all rights and duties are derived. The concept of political right might perform a function similar to that of the medieval concept of natural law: that of generating 'laws' that establish and maintain the authority of rule. But Hobbes's claim about the originality of his civil science is that it broke with traditions of natural law.

Hobbes emphasized the importance of this break with his claims about the omnipotent nature of sovereign power: since positive law provided 'the measure of Good and Evil actions', there could be no such thing as an unjust law.[75] But he did accept that there could be such a thing as a

[75] L, 223.

'good' law, one that 'is *Needful*, for the *Good of the People*, and withall *Perspicuous*'.[76] A law that benefited the ruler but not the people could not be a good law.[77] 'It is a weak Sovereign, that has weak Subjects', he wrote, 'and a weak People, whose Sovereign wanteth Power to rule them at his will'.[78] Sovereign authority was a form of public power exercised for the good of the people, and a well-governed state was one in which, without endangering the public good, civil liberty was maximized. This, he explained, required acknowledgement of 'the art of making fit laws'.[79] This was the core of his civil science.

His objective was to create 'one firm and lasting edifice'.[80] Without the help of 'a very able Architect' what was likely to result was 'crazy building' which the people would regard as unstable and which 'must assuredly fall upon the heads of their posterity'.[81] To ensure this did not occur, the sovereign had to be skilled in the arts of government.[82] As Hobbes expressed it, the relationship between sovereign and subject was not regulated by positive law, but by the prudential art of governing. Though Hobbes himself – for good political reasons – called these 'laws of nature', they are actually precepts of political right.

This is the beauty of Hobbes's civil science: he invoked the concept of natural right to generate the constitutive rules of the modern state, arguing that natural law yielded the regulative rules of the modern state. For Hobbes, the autonomy of the public sphere was founded on liberty, equality and consent. Convinced of the necessity of authoritarian government, Hobbes accepted that 'the power of the mighty hath no foundation but in the opinion and belief of the people'.[83] And he recognized that, to maintain that authority, the sovereign had to act with restraint as well as engaging in the vital task of shaping the people to make them 'fit for society'.[84]

[76] L, 239. [77] L, 240. [78] L, 240.
[79] L, 221. [80] L, 221. [81] L, 221.
[82] Thomas Hobbes, *The Elements of Law Natural and Politic (Human Nature and De Corpore Politico)* [1640], introduction by J.C.A. Gaskin (Oxford University Press, 1994), Pt II, ch.28.1: 'And as the art and duty of sovereigns consist in the same acts, so also doth their profit. For the end of art is profit; and governing to the profit of the subjects is governing to the profit of the sovereign … And these three: 1. the law over them that have sovereign power; 2. their duty; 3. their profit: are one and the same thing contained in this sentence, *Salus populi suprema lex*; by which must be understood, not the mere preservation of their lives, but generally their benefit and good. So that this is the general law for sovereigns: that they procure, to the uttermost of their endeavour, the good of the people.'
[83] *Behemoth*, 16.
[84] DC, 21. See also L, 233: 'the Common-peoples minds … are like clean paper, fit to receive whatsoever by Publique Authority shall be imprinted in them'.

Hobbes's political jurisprudence – a combination of rhetoric as well as reason, of counsel as well as command[85] – marks a vital stage in the transition to modern public law. His argument for authoritarianism was an essential step in destroying the medieval worldview. Only by asserting the sovereign's absolute power to make law could the principle of representation transform hierarchical notions of medieval rulership into the immanent logic of the modern state. The concept of sovereignty thereafter evolved from its initial fixation on some transcendent figure that founded the regime into a representation of the entire political entity.[86] In the process, modern public law came to acquire its identity not from the figure of the sovereign but from the concept of sovereignty, not from the formal law-giver but from the prudential logic binding together the political entity of the state. In that transition, Hobbes's political jurisprudence performed a crucial role in replacing the moral reason of natural law with a form of political reason that led to the formation of the modern state as an institution promoting civil peace, security and prosperity.

[85] See Tom Sorell, 'Hobbes's Persuasive Civil Science' (1990) 40 *Philosophical Quarterly* 342, highlighting the importance of counsel as well as command in Hobbes's scheme.

[86] See Benedict de Spinoza, *Tractatus Theologico-Politicus* [1670], translated by R.H.M. Elwes (London: Routledge, 1951), 200–213.

3

The equal extent of natural and civil law

ROSS HARRISON

Chapter 26 of Hobbes's *Leviathan* is entitled 'Of Civil Laws'. My title is taken from the eighth paragraph of that chapter, which Hobbes starts by saying, 'The law of nature and the civil law contain each other and are of equal extent.' My puzzle is what this means, or how, at least on my fairly standard interpretation of Hobbes's general thought about natural and civil law, it could be so.

As this is, at least initially, a question of interpretation, I start with an extended quotation from this paragraph to set the general context and remind ourselves of several familiar Hobbesian themes that we should be able to bring to bear in resolution of the problem. Almost in its entirety, paragraph 8 of Chapter 26 reads as follows:

> The law of nature and the civil law contain each other, and are of equal extent. For the laws of nature, which consist in equity, justice, gratitude, and other moral virtues on these depending, in the condition of mere nature (as I said before in the end of the 15th chapter) are not properly laws, but qualities that dispose men to peace and to obedience. When a commonwealth is once settled, then are they actually laws, and not before, as being then the commands of the commonwealth, and therefore also civil laws; for it is the sovereign power that obliges men to obey them. For in the differences of private men, to declare what is equity, what is justice, and what is moral virtue, and to make them binding, there is need of the ordinances of sovereign power, and punishments to be ordained for such as shall break them; which ordinances are therefore part of civil law. The law of nature therefore is a part of the civil law in all commonwealths of the world. Reciprocally also, the civil law is part of the dictates of nature. For justice (that is to say, performance of covenant and giving

With thanks to Alasdair Cochrane for his helpful comments. References to *Leviathan* are in the form [x.y, p.z]. This gives the chapter [x], paragraph [y], and page number [z] of the 1651 'Head' edition; 'Head' page numbers enable reference to Tuck's Cambridge University Press and Curley's Hackett editions.

> to every man his own) is a dictate of the law of nature. But every subject in a commonwealth hath covenanted to obey the civil law ... and therefore, obedience to the civil law is part also of the law of nature. Civil and natural law are not different kinds, but different parts of law, whereof one part (being written) is called civil, the other (unwritten), natural. But the right of nature, that is, the natural liberty of man, may by the civil law be abridged and restrained. [26.8, p.138]

This is enough, or more than enough, to set the problems. Anyone worried about the deletion represented by the ellipsis should be reassured that I haven't suppressed any additional problem; it is simply a restatement, familiar from previous chapters, of the particular ways in which, at least according to Hobbes, subjects have subjected themselves by covenant.

As with other parts in Hobbes's work, it's easier to understand the separate parts than understand how the whole fits together. Hobbes is a deeply ambiguous writer. If this were not so, interpretative disputes such as the position of God or the essence of the law of nature would not persist in the way they have; the persistence of sharply incompatible interpretations can only be explained by each of the parties having a footing somewhere in the text. Therefore every way that I put the different familiar strands in the above long quotation together is liable to be similarly contested.

There is, however, a fairly common interpretative line on natural law in which, for Hobbes, natural law is not really law at all, but is rather what he calls 'theorems' [15.41, p.80]. It is, that is, a set of truths deducible by reason much in the way that geometric propositions are deduced in Euclid; the statements of supposed natural law state no law but are instead contributions to moral science.

That they are not properly laws can easily be explained. In the previous chapter (Chapter 25) Hobbes distinguishes between 'counsel' and 'command' and he uses the distinction in the current chapter to make the crucial claim that 'it is manifest that law in general is not counsel but command' [26.2, p.137]. So the law of nature is therefore strictly speaking counsel. It is good advice. It is what can be worked out by reason (or at least by a person of superior reason like Hobbes). It tells us what there is good reason for us to do. In Chapters 14 and 15 Hobbes deduces what he himself calls the 'laws of nature'. Examples are keeping covenant, striving to accommodate ourselves to others, and not being proud. They are for Hobbes the rational means to what he considers the supreme rational goal, which is seeking and maintaining peace. Therefore, although he calls them 'laws', they are not strictly speaking or really laws. To become real laws we have to shift from counsel to command.

Both counsel and command are examples of practical reason; they are both about why I should act. Someone tells me to do something and I do it. But if my reason for action is based on the content of what is said, it is in Hobbes's terms counsel. The person is giving me good advice and I follow it because it is good advice. Rationality, as worked out by the good adviser Hobbes, tells me (anyone) that I should acknowledge everyone else as my natural equal (Hobbes's ninth law [15.21, p.77]). This is a 'theorem' he can deduce. However, so far, this is all advice. If I think that is likely to be right, either because it seems rational to me or else because I think it must be right because worked out by the great moral geometer Hobbes, then I follow it.

The difference with command is that I do it because of its source rather than its content. Hobbes defines command as 'where a man saith *do this*, or *do not do this*, without expecting other reason than the will of him that says it' [25.2, p.131]. So again someone speaks to me and I do what is said. But now I do it because of who that person is, not because I think that what they say is likely to be correct. I have no other reason than, as just quoted, 'the will of him that says it'. Another way of putting this important and convincing distinction is as the difference between scientific authority, where someone is an authority because what they say is likely to be true, and political authority, where someone is an authority because the fact they say something gives in itself sufficient reason for obedience. The political authority's will alone gives sufficient reason independently of the adequacy or correctness of what is said.

The distinction could be contested and fitting the different parts together can cause problems. But it seems to me incontestable that it is a correct interpretation of Hobbes. So with this material available from the earlier chapters, how may it be brought to bear on the interpretation of our current chapter and our long starting quotation? What in Hobbes is the relation between natural and civil law? Well, this additional material does seem to explain the first part of our long quotation satisfactorily. As was laid out in the earlier Chapter 15, justice, equity and so on are parts of the law of nature. From this it follows, as he puts it here at the start of the long quotation, that they 'are not properly laws, but qualities that dispose men to peace'. This echoes precisely what he had said in Chapter 15 where he concluded that 'these dictates of reason men use to call by the name of laws, but improperly; for they are but conclusions or theorems concerning what conduceth to the conservation and defence of themselves' [15.41, p.80]. So far, so good.

Our long quotation repeats the points that the laws of nature are not properly laws and that the reason for this is that law needs command. We get command with the state (or what Hobbes more usually calls the commonwealth). Our long quotation proceeds to make precisely this point. It says that 'when a commonwealth is once settled, then they are actually laws, and not before'. Hobbes even here clearly gives the reason for this, saying that they are 'then the commands of the commonwealth, and therefore also civil laws'. So far the account of civil law fits exactly with the statement of Hobbes's thought in the previous chapters that I sketched and summarized. We furthermore get here a sense of why someone has good reason to respect the will, or command, of the commonwealth. It is based on the commonwealth's threatening power; it follows from its ability to make people conform. Behind the reason of the law lies the threat of punishment. Hobbes says in our long initial quotation, 'it is the sovereign power that obliges men to obey them'. I understand 'obligation' here as not merely moral obligation but, rather, a much more literal sense of someone being forced to act. The key is power. Because the commonwealth, the great Leviathan, is a mortal god, it has the same power to terrify as the original leviathan (a great sea monster described in the Book of Job in the Bible; a quotation from this part of Job is Hobbes's epigraph to *Leviathan*).

It might be thought that this is to read too much into the chance juxtaposition in our long quotation of 'power' and 'obliges'. If so, a sentence later the threat of punishment becomes completely explicit. Here Hobbes says, 'to make them binding, there is need of the ordinances of sovereign power, and punishments to be ordained for such as shall break them'. Obligation is a ligature; it is a tie; it is a binding. We need to explain why subjects are obligated; that is, why they are bound in obedience to political authority. For Hobbes the answer is power. Once we have a 'sovereign power', we have something of sufficient terror to enforce obedience. The sovereign power ordains punishments for breaking ordinances and the sovereign power uses its punishing power to see that these ordinances are obeyed.

All now seems to be exactly in step. With the commonwealth we get real law, civil law. And it is real law because it is based on real command. It is based on real command because the commonwealth's instructions are based on real, terrifying, power. The great power of the state makes 'ordinances' (or laws) and threatens punishment for non-compliance. Hence it obliges its subjects to keep them. They do so not because of the content, or inherent goodness, of these ordinances. They do so not because they are thought up by a moral geometer like Hobbes. They do not follow them because they are assumed to be rational. They are not accepted because they are good advice. No, it is none of these. Instead, they are accepted because they are command and not counsel, and it is this that makes them laws. We obey these commands because they have been proposed by the terrifying Leviathan, the mortal god with the power to compel obedience. Source, not content, gives the reason for obedience and all that is needed, both to know what the law is and also why it should be obeyed, is that it is the will of the sovereign.

So that should be the end of the matter: we now know both what natural law is and what civil law is. Natural law is counsel and civil law command. Yet is this enough to explain the claim at the start of the long quotation, which gives the title to this chapter, that civil and natural law are of equal extent? At first sight, perhaps, yes. If only civil law is real law, then natural and civil law must be equal in extent. That is, insofar as natural law is law, then it has to be equal in extent to civil law because civil law is all the law there is. However, and this is my problem, Hobbes says other things that make this simple delivery of equality by reduction and identity more problematic.

Natural law has for Hobbes a fully described, detailed, content, whether or not we think that it is really law. It is justice, equity, and so on. It is the nineteen 'laws' laid out in Chapters 14 and 15. It is what follows from the golden rule ('Do not that to another, which thou wouldest not have done to thyself' [15.35, p.79]), which according to Hobbes is an 'easy sum, intelligible even to the meanest capacity' from which the other 'laws' can be deduced. He repeats the golden rule as a device for eliciting the content of the whole natural law in the current chapter, where he gives it as 'do not that to another which thou thinkest unreasonable to be done by another to thyself' [26.13, p.140]. So, for Hobbes, natural law has extensive, determinate, content, which he accords considerable care in delineating.

We may allow that this carefully delineated content only becomes the content of real law when it is willed by the sovereign power. So the simplest way of taking our starting quotation, that 'the law of nature and the civil law contain each other, and are of equal extent' is that this natural law content is made also into civil law content by being willed by the sovereign. Yet this can't be right. If it is so willed, it does indeed become law. However there is nothing necessary about it being so willed. Some of the natural law content may not be made into civil law by the sovereign; conversely, some of the civil law that is so willed may not have the natural law content. So how could they be equal in extent?

The initial quotation that gives the title to this chapter is not just that natural and civil law 'are of equal extent' but also that they 'contain each other'. But how on the above account is such containment possible? If the sovereign can depart from the natural law content in its will, it doesn't seem to be contained by the natural law. Conversely, the natural law content as laid out in Chapters 14 and 15 seems to be independent of the content of the civil law. It was fully described before Hobbes starts his description of commonwealth, sovereigns, and so civil law. Therefore how can this independently described content be contained by the civil law?

It is true that for Hobbes civil law does affect or constrain natural law, although more than this is required, I think, to show that it 'contains' it. Near the end of our long initial quotation, Hobbes says that 'the right of nature, that is, the natural liberty of man, may by the civil law be abridged and restrained'. Although this claim might at first sight seem surprising, it actually also fits in well with the earlier stated general theory. In it, people start with a natural right to anything that they think necessary for their self-protection. So, in the state of nature, 'every man has a right to everything, even to one another's body' [14.4, p.64]. To enter the commonwealth, everyone has to agree, each with each, to relinquish this right and instead to be bound by the will of the sovereign. If natural rights are, as it says here, 'abridged and restrained' by civil rights (so my natural right to your body or book is constrained by your civil personal and property rights created by the sovereign distinguishing who has a right to what), then in some sense for Hobbes civil law does 'contain' natural law. It does, that is, limit and in that sense contain its scope. But this does not show that it contains it in the sense that the whole content of natural law is included (or contained) in civil law. Yet it is the latter that would have to be the case if natural and civil law were 'equal in extent'.

Coming at this point from the other direction, Hobbes also claims in our initial long quotation that 'the civil law is part of the dictates of nature'. So, being a 'part', it could, perhaps, be said to be 'contained' in it. The reason why Hobbes says it is a part is because 'justice (that is to say, performance of covenant and giving to every man his own) … is a dictate of the law of nature' [26.8, p.138]. We might expect him to go from here as follows: natural law determines justice (which Hobbes often defines as keeping one's covenants). Civil law, to be just, must hence contain natural law; or, more specifically, civil law must include keeping of covenants. But this is not in fact what Hobbes does. He is aiming to establish the converse proposition, namely that natural law contains civil law. So what he does is remind readers of his earlier account of how covenant is essentially involved in the creation of the commonwealth. (And, as I said, the part I omitted in the long quotation merely repeats the ways in which he has already said that this happens; he refers to what he earlier called a commonwealth by institution and to a commonwealth by acquisition.) So the argument is that natural law contains civil law because something essential for the construction and creation of civil law (the keeping of covenants) is already part of natural law; hence, as he puts it here, 'obedience to the civil law is part also of the law of nature'.

However, as before, even if we count this as containment, it is again containment only in the sense of limitation rather than inclusion. For Hobbes, civil law to some extent limits or constrains the content of natural law. As we have just seen, natural law also for him constrains civil law. It constrains it in that, for Hobbes, it renders it both possible and desirable. This is because he holds that it is a fundamental part of natural law that we should seek peace and the most important thing that he wishes to show is that the leviathan state is an essential means for seeking peace. Hence to fulfil natural law we need civil law, the kind of law provided by states.

In Hobbes, therefore, whether we start with natural or civil law, we find the other variety. Examining natural law means that it has a civil part whereas examining civil law shows how it constrains natural law. Examining natural law will give us, as a part, that we have to obey civil law. Examining civil law will give us, as a part, the limitations of natural law. However, in each case we will only find a part and because these parts are of different scope and dimensions, this will not give us anything like natural and civil law being 'equal in extent'. The most we get is something like a partial overlap. Indeed even this is charitable: although civil law trenches on natural law's content, natural law merely shows there has to be civil law but does not thereby limit its content.

Let us return to natural law being included in civil law. Earlier, I was looking at this in terms of content and I concluded that there was nothing necessary about this: if the sovereign willed, the content of civil law might contain natural law but whether this happens or not depends on the will of a particular sovereign. However, in the last bit of the quotation with which I started, Hobbes adds something much more traditional about the difference between natural and civil law. He says: 'Civil and natural law are not different kinds, but different parts of law, whereof one part (being written) is called civil, the other (unwritten), natural.' Now we seem to be in a different game in which we have two parts of (real) law. One of these, willed by the sovereign and declared in writing, is civil law. The other, eternally there in natural reason, needs no writing and is natural law. It is a familiar picture, but how is it compatible with what Hobbes says (including the rest of the paragraph under examination)?

If we hold to the line that real law is willed, civil, law, then the question returns to whether this could have as a part something that is unwritten (and perhaps therefore also natural law). Suppose we identify the natural law part of the civil law as the unwritten part, which anyone of the meanest capacity could deduce from the golden rule. Then at first sight it might seem that it could not be a part of civil law, since civil law depends on the declared will of the sovereign and something unwritten (and unspoken) could not be part of declared will.

However this merely makes the question one of whether the civil law could have unwritten parts. Hobbes in fact has already answered this, earlier in this chapter and before the long quoted passage. He considers whether, as we would now put it, custom can be a source of law. He declares that 'when long use obtaineth the authority of law, it is not the length of time that maketh the authority but the will of the sovereign' [26.7, p.138]. Again, as always, if it is law it depends on sovereign will; custom, however ancient and however well respected, will not on its own make something law. However Hobbes here immediately continues (after 'will of the sovereign'): 'signified by his silence (for silence is sometimes consent); and it is no longer law than the sovereign shall be silent therein'. So custom, or unwritten law, is a perfectly possible part of civil law for Hobbes. What is required is the consent (or will) of the sovereign; but this consent may be tacit, silent. What is allowed to continue to be respected has, as long as it is allowed, the full status of civil law; that it depends on the sovereign will follows from the fact that it can be stopped from being law at any time by the mere will of the sovereign.

What Hobbes says here for unwritten custom can be applied in the same way for unwritten natural law. Again it can be contained, even though unwritten, in the civil law that depends on the will of the sovereign. But it is only law because the sovereign gives tacit consent to its inclusion, and this consent may be explicitly withdrawn at any time. So, as before, although the content of natural law may be included in the content of the civil law, there is nothing necessary about this. It may or may not be so, and whether it is, or how far it is, may alter through time at the mere whim of the sovereign. Some inclusion is possible. But nothing requires it, and nothing would entail it being equal in extent.

Whether (some) natural law is included depends upon the actual nature of the civil law of a particular jurisdiction and this depends upon interpretation. The sovereign (acting usually through agents) has the power of final interpretation. These agents, the lawyers acting on behalf of the sovereign, both do and should for Hobbes use reason (i.e. the principles of justice and equity) to guide their interpretation. This is how he thinks that they should decide whether a custom should be legally approved and whether to follow the precedent of previous decisions. They should, that is, use natural law in their interpretation, and hence production, of civil law. Hobbes ends the paragraph immediately before our long starting quotation by saying that 'the judgement of what is reasonable, and of what is to be abolished, belongeth to him that maketh the law, which is the sovereign assembly or monarch' [26.7, p.138]. The sovereign (acting often through the judges as agents) controls interpretation. Hobbes thinks that this interpretation should follow equity, justice, natural law as he earlier described it. But, like that earlier description, this is but counsel, theorems. In the end the judges can do what they want, assuming only that this is consented to by the sovereign.

We here reach another ambiguity, or tension, in Hobbes's thought that gives rise to conflicting interpretations. For on the one hand, as seen, he thinks that the unwritten content of natural law could be known to the simplest intelligence, and can certainly be proved as theorems by a rational master like Hobbes. But on the other hand, because it is unwritten its content can be disputed. It needs determination; this determination can only come through interpretation; and this interpretation can only be provided by the sovereign and the sovereign's agents. So, whatever the ontological facts about the independent truth of the natural law, for epistemological purposes we have to take it as it is allowed and described by the civil law. The law for us is what the sovereign says. In our starting long quotation there was a hint of this when Hobbes says that 'in the differences of private men, to declare what is equity, what is justice, and what is moral virtue, and to make them binding, there is need of the ordinances of sovereign power'. When I looked at this remark before, I concentrated on the need for sovereign power and the threat of punishment to make the law 'binding'. But the sovereign ordinances are also needed because of the 'differences of private men'. As individuals considered in isolation from state power (as 'private' men), they may well think about the material of natural law (which for Hobbes, as here, is equity, justice, moral virtue). But they have different views and the declaration of sovereign power is required to make the ordinances determinate as well as to make them compelling.

Hobbes's use of the story of the Gordian knot, to which he refers later in this chapter, is revealing. 'All laws, written and unwritten', he says, 'have need of interpretation' [26.21, p.143]. He specifically concentrates on natural law, saying 'it is now become of all laws the most obscure, and has consequently the greatest need of ablest interpreters'. He here, that is, leans towards the difficulty of knowledge option rather than its possibility of being made clear to the meanest intelligence. He says that for the sovereign (here called 'the legislator') 'there cannot be any knot in the law insoluble, either by finding out the ends to undo it by, or else by making what ends he will (as *Alexander* did with his sword in the Gordian knot) by the legislative power, which no other interpreter can do'. We have a tangle of natural law, of supposed truth. We have different opinions, and the tangle is in part caused by this difference of private opinion. How can we get determination, a single authoritative account of law? We might be looking for our rational interpreter, our great moral geometer like Hobbes, to reduce it to theorems and exude his or her scientific authority. But this is just one more interpretation; it is advice to the judges and sovereign; it is counsel.

In the end, only one interpreter is king. The sovereign does something 'which no other interpreter can do'. He (or his judges) could untie the threads, retracing the same course as Hobbes or academic lawyers, working out what is the right answer according to the principles of justice, equity, reason and natural law. The sovereign could do this, or at least attempt it. But the sovereign doesn't have to. The sovereign has a completely separate resource. Wanting to find the ends and untie the knot, he does not have, like the purveyors of counsel, to use reason. He can instead, like Alexander, use the sword. He can use his legislative power to cut the knot and produce what ends he will. Law as the command of the sovereign is what is produced by sovereign power. Sovereign power as well as being compelling can also be determinate. All tangles, differences, conflicting advice can be set aside and the answer reached by sheer power. As the Bible shows, you do not reason with leviathan; instead, you respect its stupendous power. The awesome power of the mortal god, the state, is a power to make decisions as well as enforce them. If we do have natural law, then it is the natural law that the sovereign enforces. It is what the sovereign decides is natural law, cutting whatever knots he will.

One way to give natural law more content than has been allowed so far is to bring in God. With the immortal god we get even more punishing power than the mortal god of the state and even more rationality than the greatest mortal writer of moral theorems. In Hobbesian terms, we get as much power as we could possibly require to terrify people into the keeping of the law and to cut every imaginable knot that might impede determinacy of content. Just as the mortal sovereign by will makes civil law, the immortal sovereign by will makes natural law. On this account, natural law becomes divine positive law. There is nothing incompatible with Hobbes in such an account; we have another legislator, and therefore another example of civil law, even if we call this one 'natural'.

Hobbes describes 'divine positive law' in the course of this long chapter on civil law. The crucial point is again epistemological. As Hobbes puts it here, 'how can it be known?'. Revelation is an answer. But, he asks, 'how can a man without supernatural revelation be assured of the revelation received by the declarer?' [26.40, p.148] 'Natural reason', he says, is not enough. So, again, it might be true that there is divine positive law. But, because we can't prove it to be true, it won't work as determinate law for us. It is the same for the punishing aspect. God obviously has sufficient power to punish. But whether this power poses an adequate (or sufficiently motivating) threat depends upon the accuracy of the last judgement story. God's divine punishment is supposed to follow the last judgement after our deaths. But again, at least for Hobbes, acceptance of this story depends on revelation and the correct account of life after death cannot be established by natural reason alone. As he says in an earlier chapter, 'there is no natural knowledge of man's estate after death' [15.8, p.74]. We cannot, that is, prove by reason alone what happens to us after we die. Hence, lacking revelation, we don't know whether we'll be there to suffer the threatened punishment. No person, no suffering; no suffering, no sanction; no sanction, no law. So, again, what may be in superb ontological shape as an account fails through epistemological reasons to have the impact that for Hobbes is a necessary condition of real law.

A further much fought over interpretative area is the proper extent of God's role in Hobbes's thought. With respect to the material quoted earlier, he notoriously concludes Chapter 15, just after saying natural law was 'improperly' called law and was 'but conclusions or theorems' by saying, 'But yet if we consider the same theorems as delivered by the word of God, that by right commandeth all things; then are they properly called laws' [15.41, p.80]. Notoriously also, Hobbes left out this sentence when he translated *Leviathan* into Latin to produce an international version. Here we may take our choice, but I think the best interpretation is to have natural law (as above) as not properly law but for those who believe in God it can become a sort of divine positive law.

What if a people adopt this divine law by covenant? They are then a chosen people, like the Old Testament Jews, and all the same considerations apply as were spelled out for more mundane civil law above. The divine law for them has, by their covenant, been made their civil law.

It applies to them but is not necessarily true for all people. It needs an interpreter (a king or high priest) and so all the same points about interpretation apply. We now have an approved revelation, or approved sacred text, be it the Bible or Koran. But if they therefore take this to contain the eternal, immutable, natural law, it is true for them only because of their covenant and positive adoption. Eternal and immutable they may think it, but it is law not because it is divine but because it is civil. They adopted it because it is divine but it is law only because they adopted it and their adoption makes it civil. They are obliged, but only because they obliged themselves, 'there being', as Hobbes puts it, 'no obligation on any man which arises not from some act of his own' [21.10, p.111]. By their own act, they created a sovereign and it is law for them because it is what their created sovereign wills.

What if the natural law applies, as law, directly to the sovereign even if not to the sovereign's subjects? Hobbes is quite clear, both in this chapter and extensively elsewhere, that the civil law does not apply to the sovereign. As he puts it here, 'the sovereign of a commonwealth, be it an assembly or one man, is not subject to the civil laws' [26.6, p.137]. But, if the sovereign is not subject to his own civil law, is he not still subject to natural law, applying as it does to all persons at all times? And, if so, then would not the civil law be 'contained' in natural law to the extent that the natural law, controlling the sovereign, controls the civil law that the sovereign wills? This is a traditional story, as might be found for example in the writings of King James I and VI, and Hobbes need not, as such, resist it. The important thing (just as in James) is that this gives the subject no lever to criticize the legislator on the basis of justice or legality. Whether or not the sovereign is subject to natural (or divine) law, his following of it can only be judged by himself (or God); it is not a matter that can be determined by any of his subjects.

The sovereign is absolute and the civil law is determined solely by the sovereign's will; if the sovereign feels constrained in any way, or has any particular beliefs about the appropriate shape of the law, that is a matter only for the sovereign. (Or is a matter between the sovereign and God.) Even if a particular sovereign happens to think in this way, or even if it is true from a divine or rational perspective that natural law binds the sovereign and so the sovereign's civil law, this does not in any sense make natural law part of civil law. Once again, the relation is not necessary. Once again, it depends upon the facts of what is actually willed by the particular sovereign. And, once again, from the epistemological perspective of the subject the apparatus is irrelevant; all that makes something law is the sovereign's will and what influences or determines that will is not relevant to whether it is or is not law.

But should not the sovereign be just (where 'justice' is understood in a Hobbesian manner as the content of natural law)? Well, yes, and Hobbes also, presumably, thinks yes. But the point is that this justice is given by a set of 'theorems'. They set out what to do if law is to have its right purpose of preserving 'the conservation and defence' of the sovereign's people. This is the way to get peace, and *salus populi* is a right or appropriate aim of the sovereign. But this is all morality or, indeed, prudence. The good, sensible, sovereign does these things; the sensible sovereign bases legislation on the principles of natural law. One body of thought should influence the other. But this is not because it is one part of law constraining, or determining, another part of law, let alone because the natural and civil law are in some way equal. It is because as well as what law is, we can also think of how law ought to be. The will of the sovereign makes it what it is. But we can still think what a sensible, or good, sovereign should do.

We can think how the law could be better, or how it might better fulfil its point. According to what Hobbes calls natural law, which he expounds before he considers the commonwealth, the aim of natural law is to preserve peace and the course of his argument is that this can only be done with a commonwealth. So, as seen above, starting with natural law, we are led to the natural need for civil law. If this is the point of having (civil) law in the first place, it also gives the overriding point to this law once we have it. Hobbes thinks that a subject's obedience to the sovereign lasts as long as the sovereign can give protection to the subject (for such protection, or peace, is the point of sovereigns). The sensible sovereign, therefore, seeks protection and peace for his subjects, *salus populi*. We can, rationally, say on two grounds that this what the sovereign should do. First, only thus will the point of the enterprise be realized. Second, and more prudentially, a sovereign that fails to do this is liable to lose the obedience of his people and so cease to be a sovereign.

In the last paragraph of *Leviathan*, Hobbes says that he wrote his discourse, 'occasioned by the disorders of the present time, without partiality, without application, and without other design than to set before men's eyes the mutual relation between protection and obedience, of which the condition of human nature and of the laws divine (both natural and positive) require an inviolable observation' [*Review and Conclusion* 17, p.395]. Once we study natural (and/or divine) law, we see that there should be states to give protection, that this depends upon obedience, and that they are in mutual relation. People's obedience to the civil law and subjecting their private wills to the public will of the sovereign is given point by the protection of the sovereign. No protection, no obedience, no law.

In Hobbes, as in other philosophers, there's the bit where you say it and the bit where you take it back. It starts by seeming very radical. Natural law disappears (as law); the state is absolute without any form of control; religious practice has to be as the sovereign wills, and so on. Yet once we look at the reasons for having this absolute state, where the law is only the uncontrolled sovereign's will, we find reasons (in the same philosopher, Hobbes) why in fact the civil law should conform in parts to natural law, fully recognizable in traditional terms in its content. We see why the sensible sovereign should be constrained by these same principles of justice and equity. We even see (although I haven't dealt with this here) that although the sovereign can in principle do anything with religion, the sensible sovereign respects existing practice. So first it goes, but then it comes back. First no more natural law (of a form we all recognize, keeping covenants and so on). Then back it comes again (of the same, recognizable, form of keeping covenants and so on).

Is the whole Hobbesian show therefore a mere finesse with terms and descriptions in which the important content remains unaltered? No. It is important both that the content comes back but also that it comes back differently. We do, indeed, get much traditional natural law. So the same content returns, and we can use this traditional natural law content to make remarks about positive law, such as why we have it in the first place, what it would be to be equitable, that people should not judge when they have an interest, that the innocent should not be punished, and so on.

However, the important point is that it comes back differently. Not only its content matters but also its shape and effect. The voice is the voice of Jacob but the hands are the hands of Esau. It is similar in substance but it differs importantly in its purchase. Among reasons for action are that some things are law, obliging us. Hobbes gives an account of this obligation by explaining what it is for something to be law. His answer is that it is the commands of the sovereign that oblige us. They constitute what obliges us as law and nothing ensures the consistency of these commands with natural law. We can also think of how law should be. We can think of what this actual law should be like if it is best to fulfil the purpose of law, or, more generally, the principles of justice and equity. In doing so, we use much of the content of what has traditionally been called natural law. The natural law content can still be applied, but it is no longer being applied as law. We can still use it to give reasons to guide conduct but these reasons are moral or prudential rather than legal.

As well as knowing what we should do, we need to know why we should do it. This Hobbes provides, and he provides it in part by raiding or repeating natural law. But he also makes clear that although this still provides reasons for action it does so in a different way. Doing something because it is the right thing to do is doing it for a different reason than doing it because it is the law; and this is still true even if, as in Hobbes, among the right things to do are that we should do something simply because it is the law.

This can be expanded to meet a criticism made by Alasdair Cochrane when I first presented this chapter. It might be argued that I am too robust in my interpretation of 'equal extent' when I understand it to mean having the same content. Perhaps, instead, it could be suggested, we should understand Hobbes as meaning something like having the same point or power. So when he says that natural and civil law have the same extent, he could be (rather loosely) interpreted as meaning that they have the same power. The idea, that is, is not that they have an equal ('same extent') content, but rather that they have equal ('same extent') power.

If they both lay down obligations that give reasons for action, this might seem to be the case. Where Hobbes lays out the natural law, he gives us good reasons for doing certain things, such as not judging in our own cause, giving safe transit to 'all men that mediate peace' [15.29, p.78], and so on. Then when he lays out civil law he gives us more good reasons, this time to do what our sovereign commands. And therefore it might be thought that they both give good reasons and so are of equal power. Furthermore, it would seem that they both provide prudential reasons, holding things to be good because they are good for us: things will go better for us if we keep our covenants, give safe passage to ambassadors, do what the sovereign says, and so on. So, supposedly, they equally provide prudential reasons; we are lucky if they head in the same direction and unlucky if they conflict.

However, this is not right. We do not have equal prudential reasons, albeit from different sources. The different source of natural law means that, on the contrary, it does not directly give any particular individual any prudential reasons at all. Partly this is reflected in natural law being counsel rather than command. But, so far, this just reflects that they are different kinds of reason; so far, they could both be thought of as different sorts of prudential reason and that we are just lucky if we are commanded to do what is an advisable thing to do anyway. However and importantly, the difference is much deeper than this. In a straightforward sense, the advice in natural law does not give us reasons at all.

This is because natural laws only give any individual a reason if it can be assumed that others will act in the same way. Natural law in Hobbes tells us how to act if we are to gain peace (which it is assumed that we all want) and it also gives us that we need the state to deliver it. Natural law gives us that we should keep our covenants. But for Hobbes 'covenants without the sword are but words and are of no strength to secure a man at all' [17.2, p.85]. We need the sword for security; that is, we need the state or civil power. Only then do I rationally, prudentially, keep my part of a bargain. I do so because I can reasonably expect that the other party to the bargain will do so as well, but I only reasonably expect it if the agreement is backed by the punishing power of the commonwealth. Therefore, in Hobbes, it is only when the natural law precept that covenants should be kept becomes also civil law that it gives me real prudential reasons for action. Until that happens (that is, while it remains merely natural law) it is but words and gives me no real reason at all.

The central point here is earlier explicitly picked up by Hobbes himself in his second chapter on the laws of nature. He says there that 'the laws of nature oblige *in foro interno*' [15.36, p.79]. He explains this by saying 'they bind to a desire they should take place: but in *foro externo*; that is, to the putting them in act, not always', pointing out how a person keeping their promises when others do not merely makes themselves a 'prey'. It is the same point: without extra security, natural law should not oblige our actions. They show what we would like to be the case. We would like them observed because it is good for us if they are. However, this means (as Hobbes in his next chapters goes on to demonstrate) that what we need is the commonwealth because without a state we won't get what we like. And until we have a state the merely *in foro interno* binding of natural law is not translated into the *in foro externo* obligation that guides action.

As we have seen, the content of natural law is counsel rather than command. But for whom is it counsel? It would seem that it is really counsel to the sovereign: it is counsel about what makes good law. The only counsel to the individual is to become (or remain) a citizen: in prudentially seeking peace, a state is needed to enforce the law. Hence, even as a matter of supposed equal power, natural and civil law do not act with the same power on the individual. The power of the natural law, given prudential good reasons, is of no strength at all until backed by the punishing state. Hence it is not just that civil law is the only real law but also, for similar reasons, only civil law gives real reasons for action.

Another way of putting this important and central point is by using an *is/ought* distinction more firmly delineated than it is in Hobbes himself.

Civil law says what our obligation is; at best natural law tells us what our obligation ought to be. Yet specifying the theorems of moral science, or how things ought to be, does not as yet give anyone a real obligation, or a real reason for action. Hence it is not true that, in Hobbes's account, natural and civil law are equal in the extent of their power. Nor, more obviously, is it true that they are equal in the extent of their content.

The *is* does not contain the *ought*, nor does the *ought* contain the *is*. Hence and otherwise, they are not of equal extent.

4

Thomas Hobbes and the common law

MICHAEL LOBBAN

Thomas Hobbes has generally been regarded as one of the founders of legal positivism, since he defined law in terms of sovereign commands, whose validity did not depend on their moral quality.[1] Recently, however, a number of scholars – and in particular legal ones – have re-examined Hobbes's discussion of the laws of nature in order to develop an argument that Hobbes might better be described as an 'anti-positivist' with a commitment to the rule of law.[2] According to this argument, in Hobbes's vision of a political system, 'the sovereign has to rule by law', and 'rule by law is necessarily rule in accordance with the laws of nature'.[3] The revisionist argument claims that the laws of nature itemized by Hobbes acted as constraints on the sovereign's ability to make arbitrary laws, and that the judges maintained the rule of this law through their interpretation both of the sovereign's statutes and of the unwritten law. Thomas Hobbes, the argument goes, was not a 'Hobbist'.

Such a reading would have surprised late seventeenth-century readers of Hobbes's work.[4] As a defender of the king's right to levy ship money, he had placed himself on the opposite side from those common lawyers

I should like to thank Christopher Brooks, Alan Cromartie and Mike Macnair for their help. All remaining errors are my own.

[1] John Austin was therefore an admirer: see, e.g., *Lectures on Jurisprudence*, edited by R. Campbell (London: John Murray, 5th edn, 1885), vol. I, n. 268.

[2] The most prominent proponent of this view is David Dyzenhaus: see especially his articles, 'Hobbes and the Legitimacy of Law' (2001) 20 *Law and Philosophy* 461; 'How Hobbes met the "Hobbes Challenge"' (2009) 72 *Modern Law Review* 488; and his contribution to this volume (Chapter 10). For another treatment of Hobbes which regards him as outside the positivist tradition, see Mark C. Murphy, 'Was Hobbes a Legal Positivist?' (1995) 105 *Ethics* 846.

[3] Dyzenhaus, 'How Hobbes met the "Hobbes Challenge"', 493.

[4] For responses to Hobbes, see Jon Parkin, *Taming the Leviathan: The Reception of the Political and Religious Ideas of Thomas Hobbes in England, 1640–1700* (Cambridge University Press, 2007).

who questioned the king's use of his prerogative powers. Moreover, Hobbes was not a lawyer, and frequently made plain his disdain for the common lawyers. Nonetheless, the questions posed by the revisionists – of how he imagined a legal system would operate, and of how his view related to the common law tradition – are important ones, and will be explored here. As shall be seen, Hobbes's vision both of the sources of law and of the manner in which judges were to adjudicate was radically different from that of Tudor and early Stuart common lawyers. For these lawyers, the common law was developed by the 'artificial reason' of learned judges, who interpreted a customary system which was both a manifestation of and an elaboration of natural law.[5] By contrast, Hobbes made the sovereign's commands the source of all law. In his theory, the law of nature was not a set of precepts which could be figured out by judges, or elaborated in custom. It was natural equity, which only became binding law to the subject when articulated by the sovereign in a statute or in the post hoc judgment of a court. Hobbes's anti-common law theory of adjudication failed to convince the common lawyers, for it failed to address their core concerns. While it might have been an adequate theory to explain how judges should deal with correcting wrongs, it said nothing about how legal rights were established and developed. Most importantly, Hobbes said very little about how property was acquired and transferred – the very questions which made up the bulk of the work of early modern common lawyers. As Sir Matthew Hale explained in his response to Hobbes, ad hoc adjudication was not the same as the rule of law. Instead, it required judges to develop and interpret a body of rules which could co-ordinate and guide social interaction.

At the same time, while Hobbes's version of the command theory proved uncongenial to many common lawyers,[6] his careful analysis of legal concepts was more influential on lawyers than has generally been realized. Unlike later positivists, who largely eschewed discussion of the normative

[5] On these issues, see M. Lobban, *A History of the Philosophy of Law in the Common Law World* (Dordrecht: Springer, 2007), chs 1–2 (vol. VIII of E. Pattaro (ed.), *A Treatise of Legal Philosophy and General Jurisprudence*). On Hobbes and the common law, see also Alan Cromartie's editorial introduction to *A Dialogue between a Philosopher and a Student, of the Common Laws of England*, in Thomas Hobbes, *Writings on Common Law and Hereditary Right*, edited by Alan Cromartie and Quentin Skinner (Oxford University Press, 2005), xxvi–xliv.

[6] It should be noted that John Selden and Sir Matthew Hale also developed command-centred theories of law, but ones which did not share Hobbes's rejection of custom and precedent: see Lobban, *History*, ch. 3.

bases of the legal system, Hobbes rooted the citizen's obligation to obey the commands of the sovereign in a social contract.[7] His theory rested on a legal device; and in figuring out the theory, Hobbes needed to engage in a very careful analysis of legal concepts. As shall be seen, Hobbes's analytical formulations were very influential on at least one important common lawyer, Sir Jeffrey Gilbert, who found Hobbesian analytical reasoning helpful in explaining and ordering a set of concepts relating to rights in property and contract, while at the same time rejecting Hobbes's view that such rights needed the sovereign to come into being.

Hobbes and the laws of nature

If Thomas Hobbes's use of the law of nature often seems puzzling,[8] it is at least clear that he was seeking to use the concept in a way which was very different from his predecessors. Hobbes himself proclaimed his originality and claimed to have founded the science of civil or political philosophy.[9] He rejected the premises of the Thomist view of law, which held that it was possible to understand the 'essence' of any substance through reason, and that it was hence also possible to uncover an objective morality by reasoning on the end of man.[10] Insofar as Tudor and early Stuart common lawyers had drawn on the concept of natural law, it was this Thomist notion that there was a knowable law of nature which was drawn on.[11]

[7] See David Gauthier, 'Thomas Hobbes and the Contractarian Theory of Law' (1990) 16 *Canadian Journal of Philosophy* (Supplement) 5.

[8] See esp. David Gauthier, 'Hobbes: the Laws of Nature' (2001) 82 *Pacific Philosophical Quarterly* 258.

[9] Thomas Hobbes, *The Elements of Law Natural and Politic*, edited by F. Tönnies and M.M. Goldsmith (London: Frank Cass, 1969), xvi. The following abbreviations will be used in the text: EL for *Elements of Law*; DC for Hobbes, *Elementa Philosophica De Cive* (Amsterdam: H. & V.T. Boom, 1642), translated as *On the Citizen* by R. Tuck and M. Silverthorne (eds.) (Cambridge University Press, 1998); L for *Leviathan*, edited by R. Tuck (Cambridge University Press, 1991); B for *Behemoth, the History of the Causes of the Civil Wars of England* in *Tracts of Thomas Hobbes of Malmesbury* (London: W. Cooke, 1682); A for *An Answer to Arch-Bishop Bramhall's Book, called the Catching of Leviathan* in *Tracts of Thomas Hobbes of Malmesbury* (London: W. Cooke, 1682); and D for *A Dialogue between a Philosopher and a Student, of the Common Laws of England*.

[10] In Richard Tuck's view, Hobbes saw his task as putting political philosophy onto new, firm foundations, in order to overcome the challenge of sceptical philosophers, who had undermined this Thomist tradition of natural law: *Philosophy and Government, 1572–1651* (Cambridge University Press, 1993), ch. 7.

[11] See, e.g., Christopher St. German, *Doctor and Student*, edited by T.F.T. Plucknett and J.L. Barton (London: Selden Society, vol. XCI, 1974), which was influenced by the works of Aquinas and Jean Gerson. Robinson A. Grover has argued (in 'The Legal Origins of

Instead of building his theory on a concept of a right reason, which gave man insight into God's eternal law,[12] Hobbes commenced by exploring the nature of human reasoning, rooting all knowledge in subjective individual experience.[13] As is well known, for Hobbes, all knowledge came from the impact of matter in motion on the senses (EL I.2, L 13). Impressions on the senses were the sources of desires and fears (DC 3.31). Whatever a man desired, he called good; whatever was the object of his aversion, he called evil (L 39). Unlike beasts, man sought not only immediate enjoyment, but wanted 'to assure for ever, the way of his future desire' (L 90). It was his capacity for speech and reason which made this possible. The power of speech allowed him to register and name the causes and effects found by experience. The power of reason allowed 'a reckoning of the consequences of Appellations'. For Hobbes, '*truth* consisteth in the right ordering of names in our affirmations' (L 26–7). Reason was 'nothing but *Reckoning* (that is, Adding and Subtracting) of the Consequences of generall names agreed upon, for the *marking* and *signifying* of our thoughts'. To reason rightly was to maintain consistency in one's propositions, or non-contradiction. When men erred in reasoning, the result was 'an Absurdity, or senselesse Speech' (L 32–3).[14]

Words allowed men to reason, but they did not provide the tools for a common conception of right and wrong in the state of nature. Unlike words denoting simple objects, words which dealt with 'such things as affect us', such as virtue and vice or justice, were 'of *inconstant* signification'. They could 'never be true grounds of any ratiocination', for 'besides the signification of what we imagine of their nature', words dealing with such matters 'have a signification also of the nature, disposition, and interest of the speaker' (L 31). Even if men could have a general conception of the nature of virtue and vice, since they judged '*good* and *evil* by the different measures which their changing desires from time to time dictate'

Thomas Hobbes's Doctrine of Contract' (1980) 18 *Journal of the History of Philosophy* 177) that Hobbes's discussion of contract drew heavily on St. German. However, Hobbes's philosophical underpinnings and his view of the law of nature were quite different from St. German's. Hobbes's contemporary, the common lawyer John Selden, developed his own 'modern' theory of natural law.

[12] St. German, *Doctor and Student*, 15.

[13] Both the *Elements of Law* and *Leviathan* begin with chapters on Man, while *De Cive* (which did not) announced itself as the third part of a work on *Elements of Philosophy*, which was to deal first with 'Matter' and 'Man'.

[14] For an important recent discussion of Hobbes's 'proceduralist' reasoning, see Alan Cromartie, '*The Elements* and Hobbesian Moral Thinking' (2011) 32 *History of Political Thought* 21.

(DC 3.31), they would always be prone to disagree over what amounted to vice or virtue in any particular instance. In Hobbes's epistemology, reason was therefore not the tool to generate a common standard of morals in a state of nature: rather, it was the tool used by each man in planning his own actions. Man used 'reason to look for the means to the end which he proposes for himself; if he reasons rightly (that is, starting from the most evident principles he weaves a seamless discourse of necessary consequences), he will go the straightest way' (DC 14.16).

Hobbes argued that right reasoning led men to the laws of nature. But his conception of the nature of natural law differed significantly from that held by his contemporaries. The key foundation of Hobbes's system was the notion that man's most important end was self-preservation. The laws of nature were nothing but the 'dictate of right reason about what should be done or not done for the longest possible preservation of life and limb'. This being so, right reason always dictated '*peace and self-defence*' (DC 3.29; cf. L 87). The laws of nature were violated 'in false reasoning or in stupidity, when men fail to see what duties towards other men are necessary to their own preservation' (DC 2.1). They were consequently not strictly speaking *laws*, 'but Conclusions, or Theoremes concerning what conduceth to the conservation and defence of themselves' (L 111). Right reason taught men to seek a way out of the state of nature. A man who wished to remain in the state of nature, which was a state of war, reasoned wrongly, since he 'contradicteth himself. For every man by natural necessity desireth his own good, to which this estate is contrary, wherein we suppose contention between men by nature equal, and able to destroy one another' (EL 14.12).

Scholars have long debated whether Hobbes in fact regarded these laws of nature not merely as theorems of reason, but as proper laws, derived from God's command.[15] For in the very passages where Hobbes himself described them as theorems, he added phrases to suggest that they might be called laws, which were commanded by God.[16] Other passages

[15] Scholars who emphasize the centrality of God's command to Hobbes's moral theory include Howard Warrender, *The Political Philosophy of Hobbes: His Theory of Obligation* (Oxford University Press, 1957) and A.P. Martinich, *The Two Gods of Leviathan: Thomas Hobbes on Religion and Politics* (Cambridge University Press, 1992).

[16] In DC 3.33, Hobbes spoke of these laws as 'legislated' (*latae*) in 'Scripture'. He followed this with a chapter showing how the laws of nature could be found in Scripture. In L 111, he noted these theorems might be laws 'as delivered in the Word of God': the reference to Scripture was thus altered, and no chapter on the law of nature in Scripture followed. On this, see Jon Parkin, *Science, Religion and Politics in Restoration England: Richard Cumberland's De Legibus Naturae* (Woodbridge: Boydell, 1999), 69. Cf. EL I.17.12 and A 3.

in Hobbes's works also suggest the existence of a divine law which was discoverable by reason and was of a higher order than human law (e.g. L 202, 245, 248, 290, 403). However, there is reason to doubt whether Hobbes intended these passages to do more than pacify those of his critics who regarded his works as too atheistical.[17] Firstly, it is not insignificant that the key passage in *Leviathan* suggesting that the 'theorems' might be regarded as the commands of God was omitted from the 1668 Latin edition. Secondly, passages where he seems to restate a Thomist view of how man came to know God's commands are hardly compatible with his wider epistemology. Thirdly, Hobbes's persistent arguments about the centrality of the sovereign in determining the meaning of Scripture are not easily compatible with a view that men could by their own natural reason know God's commands.

Even if the laws of nature were seen as divine commands, they did not command actions, so much as dispositions. Hobbes argued that the laws of nature always bound a man's conscience, even though they did not always bind his actions (L 110, DC 3.29): 'The force … of the law of nature is not *in foro externo*, till there be security for men to obey it; but it is always *in foro interno*, wherein the action of obedience being unsafe, the will and readiness to perform is taken for the performance' (EL I.17.10). Hobbes's point was that it was imperative always to have the disposition to act in the equitable ways which tended to one's self-preservation.[18] But one should only *act* in this way where it was safe to do so, for otherwise men 'would certainly not be acting rationally' (DC 3.26–7). To act equitably in an inequitable world would be self-contradictory, since it would lead to one's destruction rather than to one's desired self-preservation. Insofar as the law of nature could be conceived as a command, it was a conditional one: 'That a man be willing, *when others are so too*, as farre-forth, as

[17] Cromartie, '*Elements*', 41–2 sees these passages as afterthoughts to tie up loose ends, which made the point that the laws of nature only count as laws to the extent that they are considered as being God's commands. Contrast Kinch Hoekstra, 'Hobbes on Law, Nature, and Reason' (2003) 41 *Journal of the History of Philosophy* 111, 111–12.

[18] Hobbes's natural law (even in its theological formulations) focused squarely on the individual who sought his self-preservation, and was not altruistic. Hobbes made the point (in L 202) that 'Facts Contrary to any Morall vertue, can never cease to be Sinne'. But in *De Cive*, he showed that sin could not be conduct which was blameworthy in others (since there was no common standard of blame), but that it was 'everything *done, said* and *willed*' against that right reason which taught individuals how best to reach their ends. When a man reasoned wrongly, he acted contrary to his own purpose: 'when he does that, he will indeed be said to have *erred* in reasoning, and to have *sinned* in acting and willing; for *sin* follows *error*, as *will* follows *understanding*', DC 14.17, 16.14.

for Peace, and defence of himself he shall think it necessary, to lay down [his] right to all things; and be contented with so much liberty against other men, as he would allow other men against himselfe' (L 92, emphasis added).[19] Man was only obliged to act on this law of nature if others did so; he was equally only obliged to act on the other laws of nature, insofar as he had security that other people would do so as well.

Even though Hobbes felt that each man's understanding of good and evil was a subjective matter, he did not argue that men could not discover what general rules of conduct were taught by reason. Anyone who cared to 'think himself into the other person's place' would immediately find that 'the passions which were prompting him to act will now discourage him from action, as if transferred to the other pan of the scales'. There was an easy rule: *Quod tibi fieri non vis, alteri ne feceris* (*'Do not do to another what you would not have done to you'*: DC 3.26). If this rule was so easy, why was the state of nature a state of war? Hobbes's answer was that people were not by nature calm and dispassionate. Their reason was often blinded by their passions. Although men were equal by nature, many were not merely selfish, but vainglorious, seeking to acquire more than others had, and to force others to acknowledge their value. In setting out this view of human nature, Hobbes explicitly rejected the Aristotelian idea that man was a political animal, born fit for society. It was 'vain-glory', which made some men acquisitive and selfish, which led to the state of war: for 'the will to do harm derives from vainglory and over-valuation of his strength' (DC 1.4).[20]

In the state of nature, the passions, which sought immediate gratification, tended to govern reason, which looked to future goods. While the use of reason allowed men to see that the virtues necessary for future peace should be followed, their present passions made them disagree on the nature of the virtues, seeing them only in subjective, selfish terms which led them to the state of war (DC 3.32–3). Although there were some 'modest' individuals who were inclined to practice the equality of nature, allowing others that which they allowed themselves, they were very few in number and were far outnumbered by those ruled by passion (EL I.14.3, DC 1.4, L 190–2). In such a state, it was folly for them to follow the laws of nature, since 'the law abiding would fall prey to the lawbreakers' (DC,

[19] See the discussion in Jean Hampton, *Thomas Hobbes and the Social Contract Tradition* (Cambridge University Press, 1986), 90.

[20] On this, see Philip Pettit, *Made with Words: Hobbes on Language, Mind, and Politics* (Princeton University Press, 2008), ch. 7.

3.26–7). The law of nature did not bind *in foro externo* where there was no mechanism to ensure that others would not simply follow their own passions, judging the rightness and wrongness of their actions from their own perspective.

Most crucially, men ruled by passion in the state of nature would always disagree on whether there had been a *breach* of the laws of nature. Since every man was judge in his own cause, he would decide according to his own subjective view (EL 1.17.6, L 108). It was hence necessary to have a third party, an arbitrator who could judge between them. This did not mean that the third party, unclouded by passions, could determine precisely what right reason and the laws of nature dictated. Even in the mathematical sciences, where one might arrive at truth via reason, the most able, attentive and practised men might still fall into error and come to false conclusions. In moral questions, 'For want of a right Reason constituted by Nature', men had to 'set up for right Reason, the Reason of some Arbitrator, or Judge' (L 32–3, cf. EL II.10.8). It was for this reason that they needed a sovereign.[21]

Hobbes's view of the law of nature was thus radically different from the Thomist tradition, which saw it as the participation of human reason in divine law. Although natural law played a minor role in common law reasoning, it was still seen as the foundation on which the common law had developed into a complex system which needed the specialized knowledge of the lawyers to understand it. By contrast, for Hobbes, it consisted of the conclusions of individual men's reason regarding the best means of their self-preservation. Its prime function was to impel men to set up a sovereign who would be the source of all laws governing them. As shall now be seen, it also provided the tools for Hobbes to set his sovereign on firm foundations.

The social contract

Hobbes was not a lawyer.[22] Nevertheless, his theory of the state and of political obligation was built on the foundation of that most legal of concepts, the contract. This has often seemed paradoxical to scholars. Hobbes

[21] One might therefore doubt Dyzenhaus's argument that Hobbes felt that 'in civil society subjects as well as judges have independent access to the content of the laws of nature' ('How Hobbes met the "Hobbes Challenge"', 495).

[22] Nevertheless, he did deal with legal affairs as tutor to William Cavendish: see Grover, 'Legal Origins', 178–9, Noel Malcolm, 'Thomas Hobbes', *Oxford Dictionary of National Biography*.

famously argued that contracts in the state of nature lacked validity, since there was no sovereign to enforce them. So how could a sovereign power whose existence was necessary for binding contracts to come into being be created by a contract which had no validity absent a sovereign?[23] In resolving the dilemma, Hobbes sought to develop the juristic concepts he used with great care. His analysis not only provided him with the tools to place his sovereign on sound foundations: as shall be seen in the final section, his analytical reasoning also put forward a theory of contract which proved influential on at least one important common lawyer thinking about private law.

Hobbes defined three different kinds of contract, which he labelled differently. The first kind consisted of reciprocal transfers of rights, wholly executed on both sides (DC 2.9, L 94). Hobbes used the general term 'contract' when referring to these. He used the term 'covenant' or 'pact' to refer to two kinds of executory agreements,[24] where one party trusted the other to perform his part in future. The first kind was that which was executory on one side only, where one party performed, trusting the other to perform in future. The other kind was executory on both sides, where both trusted each other to perform in future. Although Hobbes's use of the words 'covenant' and 'pact' had echoes of the terminology made use of by both civilians and common lawyers,[25] his analysis of contracting was not drawn from any existing legal text.[26] Indeed, his discussion was

[23] The nature of Hobbes's social contract has been very usefully discussed in M.T. Dalgarno, 'Analysing Hobbes's Contract' (1975–6) 76 *Proceedings of the Aristotelian Society* 209 and in Larry May, 'Hobbes's Contract Theory' (1980) 18 *Journal of the History of Philosophy* 95. Both are reproduced in Claire Finkelstein (ed.), *Hobbes on Law* (Aldershot: Ashgate, 2005).

[24] He used 'covenant' in EL (I.15.9), 'pactum' in DC (2.9) and 'Pact, or Covenant' in L (94).

[25] On Hobbes's use of Romanist language, see Daniel Lee's contribution to this volume (Chapter 11). On the common law side, Hobbes may have read William West's *Symbolaeographia* (London: Richard Tothill, 1590), which stated (book 1, sect. 5) that a 'couenant therefore in Latine *Pactum Pactio, Conuentum vel conuentio*, is a mutuall consent and agreement of two or more persons in one, concerning their mutuall promises of giving or doing … For as they which are gathered and come out of diuers places into one, are said *Conuenire* (that is to say) to come together: so they which out of diuers motions of the mind doo consent into one, that is do concur and condescend into one self sentence and meaning are saide *conuenire*, to covenant, whether the same be doone by worde, thing, writing or consent'. In contrast to Hobbes, West defined a 'contract' as 'a couenant grounded upon a lawful cause or consideration'. I am grateful to Mike Macnair for drawing this passage to my attention.

[26] Pufendorf pointed out that Hobbes's distinction (between contracts and pacts) was between the types of execution of contracts, rather than any distinction in the contracts

pioneering, for there was very little theoretical discussion of the nature of contract law in England in the era in which he was writing.

At the centre of his conception of contract stood his theory of the will. For Hobbes, the will was the last appetite or deliberation made on a matter in which an agent had free choice. By exercising his will, the agent put an end to his liberty in respect of the matter in question (EL I.12.2, L 44).[27] While every man had the right to every thing in the state of nature – since right or liberty existed in the absence of an obligation – he could transfer his right by an act of will, which curtailed this liberty. If he did so, whether by contract or by gift, he was obliged not to hinder those to whom the right was transferred. For having transferred the right, he was 'without right' – *sine jure* – and hence committed an injury (*iniuria*) if he sought to recover it by claiming it as his own. To do so would 'contradict what one maintained at the Beginning', which was a philosophical absurdity (L 93, cf. DC 3.3). To will and deny the transfer of a right at the same time violated the logical principle of non-contradiction. Analysing the nature of contracting in this way established the conclusion that the first kind of contracts – purely executed ones – were valid in the state of nature.

What of executory contracts? Again, all depended on the exercise of the will. For Hobbes, any transfer of right had to be made in words referring to present (or past) acts of will. Words relating to the future – such as, 'I will give you this tomorrow' – did not transfer any rights, for they left the speaker still free to change his mind with a new deliberation. But if the speaker used words importing the present transfer of a right, the will was exercised and the transfer made, even if the thing itself was not to be handed over until the next day (DC 2.6, L 94–5; cf. EL I.15.6). Using this analysis, Hobbes explained that a 'pact' where one party had performed was obligatory (in the state of nature) on the party yet to perform, since the party performing understood the other party's words as importing an immediate transfer of the right, with delivery of the object of the right to be made in future: '*Promises* therefore which are made in return for *good* received … are signs of will, that is … signs of the last act of deliberation by which the liberty not to perform is lost; consequently they are obligatory; for obligation begins where liberty ends' (DC 2.10). The party who exercised his will in relation to the future performance but failed to

themselves. He proceeded to a detailed discussion of Roman law terms, which Hobbes did not use: Samuel Pufendorf, *The Law of Nature and Nations*, translated by B. Kennett (Oxford: L. Lichfield *et al.*, 2nd edn, 1710), 378 (V.2.1).

27 On this issue, see Quentin Skinner, *Hobbes and Republican Liberty* (Cambridge University Press, 2008).

perform it contradicted himself, by willing the thing to be done and not to be done at the same time. He committed a wrong, on the principle that a wrong 'is a kind of *absurdity* in behaviour, just as an *absurdity* is a kind of *wrong* in disputation' (DC 3.3).

Transfers of rights also required the will of the recipient: 'no one can *make an agreement* with someone who gives no sign of acceptance' (DC 2.12; cf. L 97). But this did not mean that a contractual obligation was generated in the state of nature by the mere agreement. For, when he turned to discuss contracts executory on both sides, Hobbes argued that they were only valid where a civil power existed to enforce them. In the state of nature, wherever 'a just cause of fear arises' on either side that the other would fail to perform, the contract was void (L 96, DC 2.11). Hobbes was quite clear that it was the fear that the contract would not be performed which rendered the contract void, and not the fear which drove men into contracts. A man who, in exchange for being spared his life, promised to pay a highway robber 1,000 gold pieces the next day, and to do nothing which might result in his arrest, was bound by a valid contract. Having received the benefit of being spared his life, his promise had to be taken as the final exercise of his will, even if his promise was to transfer his right in the future (DC 2.16 ('traditurum ... postero die'), L 97–8).[28] The notion that the fear impelling a person into a contract did not vitiate it was crucial for Hobbes, since if such contracts were void, then the social contract by which one submitted to government itself would be void, since it was motivated 'by fear of mutual slaughter'.

Hobbes's claim that a fear of non-performance vitiated a contract seems at first glance to mix up the distinct issues of validity and enforceability. But Hobbes was not unaware of the distinction. In *Elements of Law*, he wrote that promises to transfer rights in future 'upon consideration of mutual benefit, are covenants and signs of the will ... whereby the liberty of performing, or not performing, is taken away, and consequently are obligatory'. This was to suggest that purely executory contracts could be 'valid', since they were the product of exercises of the will, which could not be undone without self-contradiction. But he immediately added that where performance of such promises could not be compelled, they were 'of none effect', since the person who performed first 'would betray himself thereby to the covetousness, or other passion

[28] Hobbes added in parentheses that the obligation to pay the highwayman applied 'where no other Law ... forbiddeth the performance' (L 98), showing that the sovereign could overturn natural obligations.

of him with whom he contracteth' (EL I.15.9–10). If he was aware of the distinction, why did Hobbes in his later works describe the initial promise as invalid rather than as merely ineffective? Two explanations might be offered. According to the first (which finds more support in the earlier two works), in the state of nature, where it was left to each man to judge of the likelihood of the other party performing, no sensible promisor would make any final determination of his will until he had received the benefit. Only when the security of the state intervened would the party promising be seen to have made an irrevocable exercise of the will when entering into the agreement. According to the second (which finds more support in *Leviathan*, where Hobbes spent less time discussing how the will was exercised when contracting), failure to perform would not violate the principle of non-contradiction, given that he who performed first betrayed 'himself to his enemy; contrary to the Right (he can never abandon) of defending his life, and means of living' (L 96). Since acting in any way which endangered one's life was the ultimate self-contradiction, the duty to preserve one's life would override any other obligation.

The notion that there were some forms of contracting which were valid in the state of nature gave Hobbes the ingredients to devise a social contract whose validity did not depend on the existence of the sovereign it created. Hobbes's formulation changed over time. His first attempt at modelling the social contract, in *Elements of Law*, was flawed. Describing the origins of democracies – presented here as the first form of government – Hobbes argued that every man covenanted with every other man to obey whatever the majority commanded, in consideration of the benefit he obtained from peace and defence (EL II.2.2). The contractual formulation here suggested a series of executory promises, where each person promised to obey in future, in exchange for every other person's promise to obey in future. Such promises were invalid in the state of nature, requiring the presence of a sovereign to give them validity. This formulation therefore begged the question of how a sovereign could be created by contracts whose validity depended on his existence.[29] In *De Cive*, he

[29] Earlier, at EL I.19.7, Hobbes had spoken of unions being made when 'every man by covenant oblige himself to some one and the same man'. By the covenant, each man made a final determination of his will, resigning 'his strength and means to him, whom he covenanteth to obey'. The wording appears to suggest that Hobbes had in mind that each person entered into a covenant with the ruler (rather than every person agreeing with every other person to resign their strength to the ruler). However, he does not here specify any reciprocal obligation on the ruler. This might have fitted a common law concept

altered the formulation. Here he argued that, for the sake of peace, each man had to submit his will to that of one man or assembly, whose will was to be taken to be the will of all; and that this submission came about when each man entered into a pact with each of the others not to resist that man or assembly submitted to (DC 5.7). This generated a double obligation, only one of which was contractual:

> if a citizen fails to show obedience to the sovereign power, he is a *wrong-doer* ... both against his fellow citizens on the ground that each man has agreed with every other man to show obedience, and against the *sovereign* because wrongdoers are taking back without his consent the right which they had given to him. (DC 7.14)

In this formulation, the sovereign's powers did not derive from the contract between all the people, but from the 'transfer' made by each man to the sovereign of 'the *Right to his strength and resources*' (DC 5.8). And as Hobbes had shown, even in the state of nature, asking for the return of a transferred right was a wrong, a kind of absurdity in behaviour. There were still, however, some problems with this formulation. Firstly, the 'grant' given to the sovereign was in fact a promise not to resist – 'since no one can literally transfer his force to another' (DC 5.11) – which looked more like a one-sided executory promise than a gift or grant. Secondly, the mutual contracts between the citizens were also executory promises of future obedience, which (in Hobbes's definition) needed an existing sovereign to be valid.

The formulation was further refined in *Leviathan*, where he set out a new theory of the sovereign as representing the people. He now defined the contract as the 'covenant' of each man with every other to authorize the actions of that man or assembly chosen by the majority to represent them all (L 121). Rather than being a set of executory promises not to resist, this was a set of mutual promises by each person to confer authority on the sovereign, in a contract executed at one moment. In *Leviathan*, Hobbes presented two versions of how sovereignty was instituted: one, where each man authorized a specific person or assembly, on condition that everyone else also did so (L 120); and another where each man 'covenanted' that he would authorize that person or assembly chosen by the majority (L 121). The first of these was clearly 'executed'. Hobbes's language on the

of the covenant (as a one-sided obligation, formally entered into); but in his later works, Hobbes was at pains to stress that the sovereign was not party to the contract (e.g. DC 7.12, 14, L 122) and consequently could never be in breach of his obligations. Hobbes's notion of contracting seems to have required the notion of reciprocity.

second seems to suggest that the mutual promises were executory.[30] But if so, the contract would not, in Hobbes's terms, be valid. To be valid, the transaction must be seen as executed. It could be seen as executed, as the promisor 'sufficiently declared his will' to stand by the majority decision by entering the congregation (L 123). In so declaring his will, he made a present transfer of authority to a party who was yet to be chosen. He was doing what any man did who offered a prize. For when a man offered a prize, Hobbes explained, 'the Right is transferred in the Propounding of the Prize ... though it be not determined to whom, but by the Event of the contention'.[31]

As in *De Cive*, Hobbes identified two obligations which were owed: a contractual one to the other citizens, and a non-contractual one to the person bearing the sovereignty not to 'take from him that which is his own' (L 122). These two obligations had to be independently valid in the state of nature for the theory to be coherent. The social contract could not depend on a sovereign yet to be created for its validity; nor could the sovereign's rights depend on an invalid social contract. Hobbes himself saw that the sovereign's *law* could not uphold the social contract. As he explained, a civil law which forbad rebellion was 'not (as a Civill Law) any obligation, but by vertue onely of the Law of Nature, that forbiddeth the violation of Faith; which naturall obligation if men know not, they cannot know the Right of any Law the Sovereign maketh'.[32] The sovereign could not guarantee that everyone else would keep their contracts by passing a law forbidding rebellion. He could not himself 'validate' a set of executory contracts constituting him, by removing their fear of non-performance through laws forbidding rebellion. The obligation to obey the sovereign

[30] Hobbes's language is that each man 'do Agree and *Covenant*' (i.e. Hobbes's term for executory contracts) that he 'shall *Authorise*'.

[31] L 95. In this passage, Hobbes introduced (for the first time) the theological distinction between *meritum congrui* (which imported an appropriate but non-obligatory reward) and *meritum condigni* (which imported 'satisfaction', or the payment of a just debt). *Pace* Martinich, Hobbes had no particular theological concerns in mind when using these terms: they were used to illustrate his point that the winner of the prize did not merit that the giver should part with his right (*meritum condigni*), in the way that a party who had executed his part of an agreement 'merited' that the other perform his part; but he did merit (*meritum congrui*) 'that when he has parted with it, it should be mine, rather than anothers'. Although Hobbes did not spell this out later, it might be inferred that the sovereign chosen by the assembly merited by *meritum congrui*, like the prize winner. This point has also been made in Dalgarno, 'Analysing Hobbes's Contract'.

[32] L 232. Cf. David Gauthier's arguments (on this passage) showing that the duty to obey the sovereign rested on a prior obligation: 'Hobbes: the Laws of Nature' (2001) 82 *Pacific Philosophical Quarterly* 258, esp. 282.

came from a natural obligation, not from the sovereign's command or his power to enforce.[33] This natural obligation rested on the principle of non-contradiction found out by reason. Having transferred authority to the sovereign, each individual was bound not to withdraw his authority and rebel not only because it would entail the 'philosophical' contradiction of unwilling what one willed, but also because it would tend to the destruction of one's own life (L 102–3). To return to the state of war was 'contrary to the designe they had in the Institution' (L 123). Only by seeing the transactions in terms of transactions 'valid' in the state of nature could Hobbes set the sovereign on solid foundations, and avoid the problem of bootstrapping.

The law of nature and the sovereign

It is well known that for Hobbes, the laws of nature only became binding as laws when the sovereign defined and commanded them. Since men in their natural state decided all questions by their own judgment, the sovereign had 'to come up with rules or measures that will be common to all, and to publish them openly', to determine what was 'mine and yours' (DC 6.9) and determine 'what is Equity, what is Justice, and what is morall Vertue' (L 185). It was not the reason of any private man (or the 'artificial reason' of the common lawyers) which made the law, but the 'Reason of this our Artificiall Man the Common-wealth, and his Command' (L 187, cf. D 10). But Hobbes also stated that the sovereign had certain *duties*, derived from the law of nature, the most important of which was to procure the safety of the people.[34] Moreover, he said that the 'law of nature and the civil law contained each other and were of equal extent'. This raises the question whether Hobbes's sovereign and his judges should be seen as interpreters of the law of nature, who were bound to act according to its dictates, as the revisionists have argued.

As has been seen, Hobbes spoke of the law of nature in two senses. The first sense was theological, making the law of nature God's command. Although he often spoke of the sovereign being accountable to God ('under the pain of eternal death': EL II.9.1), he made it clear that

[33] DC 14.2, where Hobbes points out that 'An *agreement* obligates of itself; a *law* keeps one to one's obligations in virtue of the universal *agreement* to render obedience'. The obligation to obey the sovereign came from agreement, not from command.

[34] In EL II.9.1 used the word 'duty' (as well as noting that it was 'the law over them that have sovereign power'); DC 13.2 spoke of duties (*de officiis*); *L* used the word 'office', an Anglicization of the Latin word for duty, 'officium'.

such accountability was to 'none but him' (L 231), so he could not be held accountable to other humans for the breach of divine law. The second sense was philosophical: following natural law was to follow the dictates of reason and the principle of non-contradiction. This more 'functionalist' view of the law of nature stood at the heart of Hobbes's discussion of the duties of the sovereign. A sovereign who used his powers 'otherwise than for the people's safety', would be acting against the principles of peace, and thus in contradiction to his very purpose (DC 13.2). A sovereign unable to maintain peace would lose the obedience of the people, and sovereignty would dissolve.

The natural law of reasoning rightly dictated *how* the sovereign should rule. He had to rule by *laws* applied equally (L 231), since it was the very purpose of sovereignty to set out rules, to end the state of war in which everyone had the right to everything and was judge in his own cause. The sovereign established peace by determining the boundaries between men's rights through laws and settling disputes about rights between the people in the manner of a neutral arbitrator. He could not act by arbitrary individual commands, since if he were to do so, he would not be acting as an equal arbiter making an objective 'third party' determination of rights. Many of Hobbes's statements in which he showed that the sovereign had to rule by law followed from his definition of sovereignty. It was of the essence of sovereignty to make laws by commands, which placed impediments on the free unrestrained exercise of liberty. It was equally 'necessary to the essence of a law' that citizens should know what the law said: '[f]or a law is a command of a legislator, and a command is a declaration of will; there is no law therefore if the will of the legislator has not been declared; and this is done by *promulgation*' (DC 14.11, 14.13; L 186–7). The corollary of this was that it was law 'only to those, that have means to take notice of it' (L 186): by definition, no man could be bound by a law he could not know in advance.

Other 'rule of law' consequences followed. By his definition, there could be no *ex post facto* law (L 204). By definition, 'punishment' was an evil inflicted for the transgression of a law, after 'precedent publique condemnation', aimed at inducing men to obey the law (L 215). Any other kind of evil inflicted was by definition an act of hostility, not a punishment. Punishing the innocent violated natural law, since it violated the principle of the equal distribution of justice (L 219). Hobbes also set out an elaborate theory of justice, whereby disputes were to be settled by judges who had to apply the sovereign's law to matters of fact elicited 'from none but witnesses' (L 195). The sovereign had to work through judges who were not corrupt: for to allow judges to be corrupt would contradict the sovereign's purpose in distinguishing 'mine' from 'yours', and tend directly to undermine the commonwealth.[35] Hobbes's theory of sovereignty thus required him to work through law, which required equal treatment (as, for instance, in the imposition of taxation). But it said nothing about the content of that law, for determining right and wrong was precisely a matter for the sovereign.

When it came to its content, no law could be *unjust*. Firstly, since the sovereign's commands defined justice, they could not be unjust. Secondly, because the sovereign broke no agreement when he made a law, he could commit no *injuria*, which in Hobbes's definition could only come from the breach of an agreement. Thirdly, every subject was 'by this Institution Author of all the Actions and Judgments of the Soveraigne Instituted', and one could not imagine a person to be so contradictory as to be unjust to himself. Hobbes did speak of the sovereign committing 'iniquity' (L 124, D 30) and said that sovereigns could 'sin against natural laws' (DC 7.14). However these passages should not be read as importing that the concept of equity provided 'a standard for judging the sovereign which is not dependent for its content on the sovereign's interpretation'.[36] The sovereign might be accountable before God for his iniquity, but he remained *legibus solutus*. Actions which were just in civil society could be 'unjust before God Almighty, as breaches of the laws of nature', but they were not remediable in this life (EL II.2.3, II.9.1).[37] The 'iniquity' lay in the bad moral disposition of the person enacting the law; but the law remained valid and binding.[38] The iniquitous would be punished in any afterlife for

[35] DC 13.17. This passage may answer the example in Dyzenhaus, 'Hobbes and the Legitimacy of Law', 478.

[36] Dyzenhaus, 'Hobbes and the Legitimacy of Law', 470.

[37] As has been seen, Hobbes argued that the very foundation of civil law was the natural law obligation to keep one's promises, so that obedience to the civil law was part of the law of nature. In his formulation of this argument in *De Cive*, Hobbes stated 'no civil law can be contrary to natural law (except a law which has been framed as a blasphemy against God)'. He was prepared to concede in this work that the civil law could not permit what was forbidden by divine law (DC 14.3), and even in *Leviathan* (where this parenthetical phrase was omitted) said that those commanded by the sovereign to breach divine laws should disobey such commands, lest they imperilled their 'eternal life' (L 403, cf. L 245). But Hobbes drew the sting of this with his long explanations that it was for the state, rather than private individuals, to determine what was the meaning of divine law.

[38] This is clear from Hobbes's discussion in DC 7.14 of decisions made by councils which were contrary to natural law. Any such decision, which expressed the artificial political will of the commonwealth, was a valid law, which all members of the commonwealth had consented to; but only those members of the commonwealth who voted for such a law offended against the laws of nature, through the expression of their 'natural will'.

their bad internal dispositions. But in the meantime, the sovereign could do whatever he thought fit.[39]

Hobbes repeatedly made the argument that natural law needed definition by the sovereign to become binding. The point was made abundantly clear in a passage in *De Cive*, where Hobbes explained that the rules to honour one's parents, not to kill, not to engage in illicit sexual intercourse, not to steal, and not to give false testimony had no purchase in the state of nature, where there was no law to define what counted as honour or property, and when it was licit to kill. Each of the above injunctions – crucially, taken from the Decalogue – only applied in a context of civil law: one was bound to give parents the honour '*prescribed by the laws*', one could not '*kill a man whom the laws forbid you to kill*', and so on (DC 14.9). Yet Hobbes also explained that while the sovereign was the source of all law, he did not need to promulgate all of its content. Much of the law of any state was the unwritten natural law, which was 'agreeable to the reason of all men', and which was encapsulated in the golden rule (L 188; cf. EL II.10.10). This seemed to suggest an uncomplicated notion of the law of nature: as if men, aware of the presence of an enforcing sovereign, would feel confident to act according to the rules of equity which applied *in foro interno*. The command of the sovereign appeared to be that 'one must follow the *law of natural equity*, which bids us to give equal to equals' (DC 14.14). In his *Dialogue between a Philosopher and a Student of the Common Laws*, Hobbes consequently argued that 'Murder, Robbery, Theft, and other practices of Felons' were 'Crimes in their own nature without the help of Statute' (D 79). Hobbes even argued that the legislator should not pass too many laws. Since men usually deliberated on how to act rather 'by natural reason than by knowledge of laws', if there were too many laws, 'men must necessarily fall foul of them … as they fall into traps' (DC 13.15; cf. L 239).

[39] Hobbes suggested at L 192 that the sovereign could not tacitly consent to judicial decisions violating 'Lawes immutable, such as the Lawes of nature' and thereby make them into a civil law, although he could so authorize 'mutable' decisions. His point was not that sovereigns were limited by mutable laws, but that irrational legal judgments could not be taken to be the sovereign's will. Hobbes illustrated his point by referring to the common law rule (given in Sir Edward Coke, *The First Part of the Institutes of the Laws of England*, edited by F. Hargrave and C. Butler (London: E. & R. Brooke, 15th edn, 1794), 373a–b that 'If a man that is innocent be accused of felony, and for fear flieth for the same, although he judicially acquitteth himself of the felony; yet if it be found that he fled for the felony, he shall notwithstanding his innocency forfeit all his goods and chattels'. Hobbes's objection was not to the punishment of men who fled (for he stated that the sovereign might make this an offence), but to imposition by the judges of a punishment on a man found guilty of no offence; and to their raising this into a fixed rule of law. For Hobbes, this judge-made rule was built on nothing but bad reasoning.

These apparently contradictory positions become compatible if we note that Hobbes's vision of the legal process was largely the backward-looking one of resolving disputes, rather than the 'forward-looking' one of setting rules for action. Judges had to make authoritative determinations of the law of nature when there were disagreements about whether it had been breached. Natural law was 'of all Laws the most obscure' and 'the most in need of able interpreters' whenever people were 'blinded by self love, or some other passion' (L 190–1), as occurred when they judged in their own cases. In one's own case, one would be ruled by one's subjective passions, finding fault in others but never with oneself. In this world of competing passions, 'it follows that the commonwealth must determine what is *to be blamed with reason*' (DC 14.17).

In making their determinations, the judges were to consider only whether the demand 'be consonant to natural reason, and equity', for the sovereign was presumed always to intend equity (L 188, 191). This did not mean that equity was a body of 'higher law', which bound judges and which could control the sovereign. After all, in Hobbes's theory, law was always to be identified by its source, and not by its content, and that source was always the sovereign.[40] Consequently, judges could not use equity to set aside 'iniquitous' statutes.[41] Nor could they claim that they had a special skill in understanding what equity required. In Hobbes's view, equity was simply the right reasoning of a well-cultivated mind looking at the case before it, capable of determining who between two parties had a better claim.

Hobbes's vision of equity was a clear challenge to the common lawyers' view that the rule of law required a specialist set of learned men, who were able to interpret the legal values of the community.[42] He assailed

[40] Some have sought to argue that Hobbes's sovereign was under some 'rule of recognition' constraints, that there were rules which the sovereign had to follow in order for his commands to be recognized as having authority: see Warrender, *Political Philosophy*, 258–63, D. Dyzenhaus, 'The Genealogy of Positivism' (2004) 24 *Oxford Journal of Legal Studies* 39, 59–60. However, in the discussion of the promulgation of statute laws at DC 14.13 and L 189, Hobbes took a rather 'plain fact' view of things: those who had not heard the sovereign's commands from his mouth accepted their promulgation through other intermediaries, who they had reason to believe (from consistent unchallenged practice) had been given authority to make them. Similarly, it had to be inferred that the judge had been given authority by the sovereign to make his pronouncement.

[41] Although Hobbes accorded judges significant leeway to make equitable interpretations of statutes (hardly a controversial view in the seventeenth century) he noted that no 'incommodity' could warrant a sentence against the law (L 194–5, cf. D 64–6, 68).

[42] Contrast David Dyzenhaus, 'The Very Idea of a Judge' (2010) 60 *University of Toronto Law Journal* 61, 70: 'Because, as Hobbes says, all laws require interpretation, it is essential

the very foundations of the common lawyers' system. Firstly, in contrast to the common lawyers, who rested their system on immemorial customs, Hobbes dismissed the very idea that custom could be a source of law. Those unwritten laws which obtained only in particular areas as 'local customs' were nothing more than the remnants of ancient statutes passed by previous local sovereigns which had been adopted by the present sovereign. Any unwritten law which applied throughout a kingdom was 'no other but a Law of Nature, equally obliging all man-kind' (L 186). In this way, Hobbes explained what the common lawyers referred to as 'particular customs' – local rules of law, such as gavelkind in Kent – while wholly undermining the concept of a 'customary' common law. In contrast to the common lawyers, who used reason as a test for the validity of a local custom, but presumed all common law to be reasonable, Hobbes used reason to test the whole body: 'if the Custom be unreasonable, you must with all other Lawyers confess that it is no Law, but ought to be abolished; and if the Custom be reasonable, it is not the Custom, but the Equity that makes it Law' (D 63). The very common law was nothing 'but Natural Reason, and Natural Equity' (D 25).

Secondly, Hobbes dismissed the idea that judicial precedents could create law: 'no Record of a Judgment is a Law, save only to the party Pleading' (D 56). Since any man might err in a judgment of equity, no subsequent judge could be bound to follow an earlier judge's decision, 'if he find it more consonant to equity to give a contrary sentence' (L 192, cf. D 55). For if judges simply applied each other's precedents, 'all the Justice in the World would ... depend upon the Sentence of a few Learned, or Unlearned, ignorant Men, and have nothing at all to do with the Study of Reason' if judges applied each other's precedents (D 83). Instead, in every new case, each judge had to act as a neutral arbitrator, in the place of the sovereign, studying what was equity from his own natural reason.[43]

in any legal order that there be a body of public officials who have the authority to interpret the law.' However, it may be suggested that Hobbes's notion of 'interpretation' was far from that of the common lawyers: see L 191.

[43] L 192. Grotius and Pufendorf had also discussed the use of arbitrators to settle controversies in the state of nature and in society. Grotius, citing Seneca, drew a distinction between judging according to law, and arbitration according to equity: H. Grotius, *The Rights of War and Peace* (London: W. Innys *et al.*, 1738), 710 (III.20.47). Pufendorf commented 'as he that judges between Fellow-subjects, judges according to the *municipal* Laws of the Place; so he who judges between those who acknowledge no common *municipal* Laws, ought to judge according to the Law of Nature': *The Law of Nature*, 435–6 (V.13.5). Hobbes did not make the distinction.

Thirdly, Hobbes attacked the 'artificial reason' of the common lawyers. In his view, the judges who claimed specialist knowledge and skills were often guilty of bad reasoning. The idea that the law could be seen as a matter of judicial interpretive practice was anathema to Hobbes, who derided the attempts of Sir Edward Coke to 'insinuate his own opinions among the People for the Law of the Land' (D 63; cf. D 19). If Coke's 'Definitions must be the Rule of Law', Hobbes's Philosopher asked, 'what is there that he may not make Felony, or not Felony, at his Pleasure?' (D 88). In the *Dialogue*, Hobbes set out to show how far from reason many of the definitions of the common lawyers' were. One of his main aims in composing the treatise was to show that there was no basis for the common lawyers' views on heresy, and to prove both by reasoning on the nature of heresy and by tracing the statute law of England on the subject that Bartholomew Legate, who was convicted of heresy and burned to death in 1612 – and whose case was cited by Coke as a precedent in his section on heresy – had been punished without legal authority. This showed how serious the consequences might be when the bad reasoning of professional lawyers made law.[44]

In contrast to Coke, who felt that the common law was the special preserve of judges like himself, and who was suspicious of encroachments on the part of the Court of Chancery or the king, Hobbes sought to downgrade the common law judges. In the view of his Philosopher, the Chancery was a higher court, which existed to remedy the errors of the lower common law judges (D 61). Hobbes also claimed (incorrectly) that the king retained the power to hear cases personally, having only 'committed' and not 'transferred' his power to the judges (D 27, 51–2, 55).[45] Since judges 'may err, and … the King is not Bound to any other Law but that of Equity, it belongs to him alone to give Remedy to them that by the Ignorance, or Corruption of a Judge shall suffer dammage' (D 31). In Hobbes's view, it was unnecessary to have men trained in law in charge of the system, since the decision-maker could take the facts from the witnesses and the law from the statutes or the pleadings. A good judge did not need to have made a profession of the laws: he only needed to have a right understanding of equity and natural reason (L 195). The point was reiterated in the *Dialogue*, where Hobbes argued for the appointment of

[44] On these issues see Cromartie's introduction to D, xlv–lviii.

[45] Contrast the view of Edward Coke, *The Fourth Part of the Institutes of the Laws of England* (London: E. & R. Brooke, 1797), 73 and Matthew Hale, *The Prerogatives of the King*, edited by D.E.C. Yale (London: Selden Society, 1986), 182–3.

clerics to hear cases, 'especially the Bishops, the best able to Judge of matters of Reason' (D 86, cf. 66).

Only occasionally do we have glimpses that Hobbes recognized that there might be a body of law apart from natural equity. Not everything was left to the decision of non-professional adjudicators. Even juries, who Hobbes stressed had the power to determine matters of right as well as of fact, were instructed by judges (the *juris consulti*) on the law (L 195).[46] Might these judges develop a body of law of their own? Hobbes laid the foundations for such an argument when he spoke of the *responsa prudentum* 'of the *judges*', which attained the status of 'written law' having 'attained customary authority with the consent of the sovereign' (DC 14.15; cf. L 196, EL II.10.10). But he did not develop this suggestion that judicial opinions might become a form of law to guide the ultimate decision-maker, obtaining their authority as rules from the sovereign. The one area where he did on more than one occasion treat judicial custom as generating rules which were to be followed was when discussing punishments. In *De Cive*, he argued that the amount of punishment inflicted on the first person to commit any offence was an entirely discretionary matter undetermined by reason; but added that once the first offender was punished, the appropriate punishment for other offenders was defined, 'for natural equity tells us that equal offenders should be equally punished' (DC 13.16; cf. L 202, EL II.10.10). This seemed to suggest that the custom of the judges might generate binding law when it came to the 'indifferent' matter of punishments.[47] In fact, by the time Hobbes composed his *Dialogue*, he had become more sceptical about allowing judges to settle punishments by precedent.[48] Keen to discredit the punishment of burning heretics, he now stated that to know what the 'custom' was which the sovereign approved, one should look not to a train of ancient precedents, but to the most recent ones (D 116).

For the most part, Hobbes did not feel there was great difficulty in knowing what the *law* was, which would require great technical learning. The skill which decision-makers most needed was that of being able to

[46] In D 110–11, Hobbes argued that the jury was not necessary for this process: other judges (such as the Chancellor) could equally determine and apply the law pleaded to them to matters of fact which had been 'judged' by witnesses. See also D 30–1, 123.

[47] Cf. D 117: 'Custome, so far forth as it hath the force of a Law, hath more of the nature of a Statute, than of the Law of Reason, especially where the question is not of Lands, and Goods, but of Punishments, which are to be defined only by authority.'

[48] By the time he wrote this work, he had also changed his mind about the nature of punishment, now arguing that reason dictated that punishment must fit the crime: D 102.

reason well, to understand what equity required in the individual case. He conceded that '[t]he work of a Judge … is very difficult, and requires a man that hath a faculty of well distinguishing of Dissimilitudes of such Cases as Common Judgments think to be the same' (D 83). Hobbes's worry was that, instead of reasoning carefully, to ensure that the best outcome was found in every individual case, judges would blandly follow the sweeping statements about what the common law required from men like Coke. In his view, if they examined much of common law closely, as he claimed to be doing in the *Dialogue*, they would find it had no foundation in statute or reason, but only in the formulations of private opinion.

Hobbes's system was thus radically sceptical of all the tools of the common lawyer. Against their view of artificial reason, Hobbes's view of law was a largely uncomplicated one. The sovereign was expected to make a limited number of rules on matters on which men could not know by their own reason what they should not do; and should enforce the rules of conduct which nature should tell each person. These rules would be generally, but imprecisely, known to each individual: and it took a retrospective determination by the sovereign in cases (on the unwritten law) to make an exact determination of right in each case. Where Coke felt that hard cases needed the 'artificial' reason of the judge for their resolution, for Hobbes it took the 'natural reason' of a disinterested party with the skill to understand the complexities of each case, and make an authoritative pronouncement on every case.

Hobbes's vision of law was almost entirely structured around a notion of adjudicating wrongs. He did not discuss how the law would set rules to determine rights to property and how they were transferred. Only at the end of the *Dialogue* did he turn to discuss property issues, and even here, his main concern was to explain the origins of political society. Hobbes's discussion of '*Meum* and *Tuum*' opened with a comment suggesting that property derived from positive law, whose 'justice' could not be disputed, for the classically Hobbesian reason that 'everyone must observe the Law which he hath assented to' (D 134). He immediately followed this comment with a discussion of the origin of 'dominion' among men, in which he argued that sovereignty arose originally from the lordship of fathers, whose absolute power over their families derived from the law of nature. The paterfamilias acquired property either by the right of first possession – which Hobbes had elsewhere laid out as one of the laws of nature (L 108, EL I.17.4–5, DC 3.18) – or by conquest. These early 'Lords' were treated by Hobbes as so many small family 'sovereigns' who had the right by nature to take anything that they needed for their subsistence, and to 'invade those whom they have just cause to fear'. Within their own families, they could deal with that property wholly as they saw fit. Hobbes discussed families as if they were little states. He was in effect putting forward a conjectural history of great monarchies growing out of small families, which then mutated into other forms as a result of rebellions.

In Hobbes's brief discussion here, ordinary subjects did not acquire the right to property by first possession, but by grant. In the final pages of the *Dialogue*, the argument was developed that there were no 'allodial' property rights in any kingdom, but that all property was held in the form of a conditional grant. In England, all property rights derived from the grants of William, who had acquired them all by conquest (D 136, cf. B 195). The *Dialogue* proceeded to describe the feudal nature of English tenures, with the Lawyer listing various feudal incidents. Hobbes's point in these brief passages was to show that property rights could never exclude the radical overriding rights of the sovereign: but it failed to explain the nature of the rights and duties which grew out of the feudal system of grants. Where earlier in the *Dialogue*, he had been critical of Coke's elaboration of the common law relating to crime, in these passages, he took for granted an elaborate system of property rights, which his legal theory made no effort to explain. At base, Hobbes had a very simple view of property rights, as originating in the grants of the sovereign, and then being transmitted either by the gift or testament of the owner, or by primogeniture, in cases of intestacy, which was (Hobbes argued consistently) the rule of nature.

But this said nothing about how valid grants or wills could be made, or about how these rules were affected by the body of legislation passed over time by English rulers. Hobbes's description of adjudication might have provided the basis for a system of corrective justice, to deal with torts and crimes, but it said nothing about the rules regulating the distribution of resources. For common lawyers, the question of how property was acquired and transmitted was a central one, which Hobbes's theory did not address. The flaw in Hobbes's system was that it failed to generate a system of *rules*, but seemed to leave large swaths of law – the entire 'unwritten' law – to ad hoc adjudications.

Two common lawyers' reactions to Hobbes

Early modern common lawyers reacted to Hobbes's work in two different ways, which reveal much about what they found of use in his work, and what they did not. On the one hand, common lawyers were unconvinced by his attack on their professional learning. On the other, they could find much of interest in his analytical reasoning. The first kind of reaction is to be found most clearly articulated in the work of Sir Matthew Hale,[49] who in a manuscript of 'Reflections' on the *Dialogue* defended the professional learning so derided by Hobbes. In this work, Hale seemed to share Hobbes's scepticism about the certainty of moral knowledge. He pointed out that while all men had common notions of what was 'just and fit', there was little agreement among men when it came to applying these notions in particular cases. It was for this reason that men needed to be ruled by law:

> to avoid that great uncertainty in the application of reason by particular persons to particular Instances; and to ye end that Men might understand by what rule and measure to live & possess; and might not be under the unknowne arbitrary, uncertaine Judgm^t of the uncertaine reason of particular Persons, hath been ye prime reason, that the wiser Sort of the world have in all ages agreed upon Some certaine Laws and rules and methods of administration of Comon Justice. (Reflections, 503)

In Hale's view, society needed rules: 'what a confusion would there be in the world', he noted, 'if the particular lawes and rules of property were not settled and governed by some established lawes or rules'.[50] These rules were not made simply by legislators, but grew from the activity of judges deciding cases as they came before them. This was a difficult task, for judges were not simply righting wrongs retrospectively, but were making rules for the future. As Hale put it, 'Itt requires a very large prospect of all the most considerable emergencies that may happen, not only in that wch is intended to be remedyed, but in those other accidentall, Consequentiall or Collaterall thinges that may emerge uppon the Remedy propounded' (Reflections, 504).

For Hale, law (like language) was the product of 'institution' rather than abstract reason.[51] It developed over time both through the passing of new statutes and through the interpretation of the common law by the

[49] On Hale, see Alan Cromartie, *Sir Matthew Hale, 1609–1676: Law, Religion and Natural Philosophy* (Cambridge University Press, 1995) and Lobban, *History*, ch. 3. Hale's engagement with Hobbes is to be found in 'Reflections by the Lrd. Cheife Justice Hale on Mr. Hobbes his Dialogue of the Law', in W.S. Holdsworth, *A History of English Law*, vol. 5 (London: Methuen & Co., 1924), 500–13 (cited henceforth as 'Reflections').

[50] Sir Matthew Hale, 'Treatise of the Nature of Lawes in Generall and touching the law of nature', British Library, MS Hargrave 485, fo. 83v.

[51] Custom was tacit institution: Hale, 'Preface to Rolle's Abridgment', in F. Hargrave (ed.), *Collectanea Juridica, consisting of tracts relative to the law and constitution of England* (London: E. & R. Brooke, 1791), 275. Reflections, 505.

judges.[52] It grew into a 'vast and comprehensive' system which consisted of 'infinite particulars', whose maintenance required 'much time and much experience, as well as much wisdom and prudence successively to discover defects and inconveniences, and to apply apt supplements and remedies for them'.[53] The reason of many rules was not self-evident to those with 'natural' reason, but it could be discovered by study and shown by experience. Knowledge of law was an expert study, just as knowledge of mathematics was. Consequently, for Hale, it was more rational to 'preferre a Law by wch a Kingdome hath been happily governed four or five hundrd years, then to adventure the happiness and Peace of a Kingdome upon Some new Theory of my owne, tho' I am better acquainted wth the reasonableness of my own theory then wth that Law' (Reflections, 504). However, such a system could only be maintained if judges were both learned, and applied the settled law, rather than their natural reason:

> Itt is one of the thinges of greatest moment in the profession of the Comon Law to keepe as neare as may be to the Certainty of the Law, and the Consonance of it to it Selfe, that one age and one Tribunall may Speake the Same thinges and Carry on the Same thred of the Law in one Uniforme Rule as neare as is possible; for otherwise that wch all places and ages have Contended for in Lawes namely Certainty and to avoid Arbitrariness and that Extravagance that would fall out, if the reasons of Judges and advocates were not kept in their traces wold in halfe an age be lost. (Reflections, 506)

Hale's response is important, for it shows that common law contemporaries of Hobbes's felt the sting of his attack, but considered that he had not developed a sustainable critique of common law adjudication.

The second kind of reaction is to be found in the work of Sir Jeffrey Gilbert,[54] who wrote an unpublished manuscript on the foundations of property and contract law, as part of his preparatory works for a projected treatise on English law.[55] Gilbert's draft (which was heavily influenced by Hobbes) shows that common lawyers who did not share his view of sovereignty could nonetheless find much of use in his analytical method. In this work, Gilbert used the kind of demonstrative argument found in *De Cive*, setting out numbered propositions, many of which closely followed

[52] Sir Matthew Hale, *The History and Analysis of the Common Law of England* (London: J. Walthoe, 1713), 59–60.

[53] Hale, 'Preface to Rolle's Abridgment', 266–7.

[54] For Gilbert's career, see Michael Macnair, 'Sir Jeffrey Gilbert and his Treatises' (1994) 15 *Journal of Legal History* 252.

[55] The manuscript (henceforth cited as *LI MS*) is Lincoln's Inn, MS Hargrave 13.

ones found in Hobbes's work. Like Hobbes, he began with a discussion of man in his natural state, as a creature of appetites, but one with a power of ratiocination denied to animals, which allowed him to contemplate future goods. Like Hobbes, Gilbert described reason in mathematical terms,[56] and sought to show what rules of conduct could be derived from reason. Like Hobbes, he began with the premise (from which 'all other laws and rules of living take their originall') that 'every man endeavours to preserve his own being' (*LI MS* ff. 3–4).[57] Gilbert also came to the same conclusions as Hobbes on the 'precepts' derived by reason from this principle. The manuscript concluded with the argument that even those prone to be ruled by the passions of 'hope, fear, and anger & severall other pertubations of the mind' could learn the law of nature, by putting 'themselves into the place of their neighbour', whereby 'those passions that persuaded them to the fact being cast into the other scale will disuade them from it'. It ended with a formulation of the golden rule borrowed from Hobbes: 'Do as you would be done by or quod tibi fieri non vis, alteri ne feceris' (*LI MS* ff. 110–11; cf. DC 3.26).

However, in contrast to Hobbes, who argued that these 'precepts' were rational dispositions which became law only when enforced by the sovereign, and who built a theory to show how that sovereign state came into being, Gilbert aimed to show that a law derived from human nature could be valid and binding in itself. Rather than using Hobbes's premises to build an argument about the state,[58] he drew on his methodology to analyse the nature of property and contract, in order to explain to judges how to handle disputes on these matters. In particular, Gilbert sought to explain the principles on which 'arbiters' settling disputes on matters of property and contract would act. Where Hobbes – the non-lawyer – had

[56] '[R]eason is nothing but a true consideration and right account of the agreement and disagreement of several Ideas the adding the severall single Ideas into one sum totall or into universall names and propositions or the subtracting and dividing universall propositions or compound Ideas into their severall parts which we call conclusions or consequences' (ff. 16–17). Cf. L 32. Gilbert was said to have had mathematical interests: see Macnair, 'Gilbert'.

[57] Although Hobbes was hardly unique in using this principle as a starting point, the centrality of the principle in his theory was seen as very distinctive. Jon Parkin, *Science, Religion and Politics in Restoration England: Richard Cumberland's De Legibus Naturae* (Woodbridge: Boydell, 1999), 99–100.

[58] In contrast to Hobbes, Gilbert sought to demonstrate the existence of God, and sided with the late seventeenth-century anti-Epicureans who were critical of Hobbes's view that there was no obligatory law of nature outside civil society. I shall discuss this and other aspects of Gilbert's work in a forthcoming article.

simply urged the arbitrator to use 'equity', Gilbert's aim was to show that judges had a rather fuller toolbox.

Hobbes's influence on Gilbert's reasoning can be seen particularly in his discussion of contract. Although the advent of 'will theory' in contract law has generally been associated with the influence of civilian theorists in the natural law tradition, Gilbert's treatment of contract was clearly influenced by Hobbes's writings on the will and on contracting.[59] His definition of a contract in the Lincoln's Inn manuscript has strong echoes of Hobbes's treatment: 'A contract is an act of the will made known by lawfull significant signs y[t] transfers my right to an other together with an act of his will concurring with mine to accept it.'[60] Moreover, several of his propositions on the nature of contracts follow Hobbes's treatment closely.[61] Discussing why contracts should be kept, Gilbert also used arguments which echo Hobbes's reasoning on executed contracts. Alongside an argument that contracting was necessary for man's self-preservation, he added a clear allusion to Hobbes:

> the breach of this law [that contracts are to be kept] we call injury and eminently injustice. Some men have wittingly compared this crime to absurdity in disputation for say they he who by argument is driven to deny the assertion that he first maintained is said to be brought to an absurdity ... for by contracting for some future action the party wills it done and by not doing it he wills it not done which is to will a thing done and not done at the same time which is a contradiction so that injury is a kind of absurdity in conversation or an absurdity is a kind of injury in disputation but there is a vast difference in their consequences for absurdity puts the opposor to silence and thereby ends the Debate but injury on the contrary raises the clamour of the opposor and becomes the beginning of war & contention.[62]

[59] This point has been made by David Ibbetson, who argues that Gilbert's manuscript treatise on contract was '[t]he best early example of the framing of contractual thinking on the Hobbesian model': *A Historical Introduction to the Law of Obligations* (Oxford University Press), 216.

[60] *LI MS* f. 43. Cf. DC 2.4–5. See also Gilbert's definition in his treatise on contract: 'Now Contract is the Act of 2 or more persons Concerning the one in parting with & the other in Receiving Some property right or benefitt' (British Library, MS Hargrave 265, f. 39).

[61] Thus, propositions 8–10 (*LI MS* f. 46) state that a man may transfer his right 'to commence at a day to come as well as presently', that 'the first contract makes void the latter because the first contract transfers all the right' and that 'a contract to do a thing impossible is void': cf. EL I.15.6, DC 2.6, L 94–8.

[62] *LI MS* ff. 44–5. Cf. f. 98: 'He that contracts in that he doth contract denies the action to be in vain for tis against reason for a knowing man do any thing in vain he therefore that contracts in such a manner so as he thinks he is not bound to keep his contract at once thinks his contract a thing done in vain which is an absurdity.'

Starting from his basic principle, Gilbert explained central features of contracts. Infants and madmen could not contract 'for they have no understanding no power of deliberation and consequently they cannot have any will that is the last act of deliberation and every contract is of its nature an act of the will' (*LI MS* f. 91, cf. L 187). Fraud or surprise vitiated a contract, 'for without a precedent act of the understanding there is no will or consent at all'.[63] If Gilbert did not agree with Hobbes's premises about the state, he learned a great deal from the author of *De Cive* about the nature of contracting.

As these reactions show, the common lawyers did not find Hobbes's radical rejection of specialist judicial reasoning convincing. Hale's defence of the common law as a body of rules developed over time by the judges was in effect a defence of the rule of *law*, against Hobbes's desire for a system of rule by natural equity. Gilbert's wider body of work demonstrated that he too shared Hale's view of the common law as a body which had developed over time through the decisions of expert judges. At the same time, his early theoretical writings show that common lawyers could find analytical approaches in Hobbes's work which could be turned to very un-Hobbesian ends: those of providing tools for the judges to develop the common law.

These early modern reactions to Hobbes may help shed further light on the recent debates about how far Hobbes was, and how far he was not, an 'anti-positivist' with a commitment to the rule of law. As has been seen, the common lawyers regarded Hobbes's vision as one which allotted no role to professional judges, and left no room for the development of the common law through a system of precedent. Insofar as Hobbes's theory of adjudication was focused on correcting past wrongs by an appeal to natural equity, and provided little explanation of how substantive rules regarding rights to property would develop, it appeared to them to fail to provide the rules of law which any settled society needed. As a result, the common lawyers did not think that Hobbes's vision of law offered a workable theory of adjudication; but (as Gilbert's manuscript shows) at least some of them felt that his analytical jurisprudence could be used to improve their approach to adjudication.

[63] *LI MS* f. 93: 'but if I mistake without any fraud in the buyer the thing is sold irrecoverably for the signs of transferring my right can be proved agt me but the want of knowledg of the nature of the thing sold or given in exchange cannot be proved for me, nay the presumption lies agt me that I had a knowledg of the thing bought since I take upon me to judg of the value of it.'

5

Hobbes on law and prerogative

THOMAS POOLE

We are familiar with the image of law as the study of social dysfunction and lawyers as pathologists of the human condition. But disorder is equally a natural habitat for the student of politics. It is 'characteristic of political philosophers', Michael Oakeshott claimed, 'that they take a sombre view of the human situation: they deal in darkness'.[1] This is certainly true of Thomas Hobbes, whose name is synonymous with a pathological treatment of politics. Hobbes is, for other reasons too, very much a philosopher for lawyers. The structure and texture of his thought is densely juridical, his theory presented 'in familiar terms – "reason", "right", "law", "authority", "obligation" – whose resonance is primarily legal'.[2] And he shares the lawyerly obsession with order, grounded in a sense of the

I would like to thank Philip Cook, Neil Duxbury, Martin Loughlin and Adrian Vermeule for their comments on various drafts of this chapter. I would also like to thank the participants at the Workshop on Droit Politique held at Université de Paris II Panthéon-Assas where a version of this chapter was presented, and in particular Denis Baranger and Olivier Beaud for their comments. In what follows, references to *Leviathan* are indicated by 'L' and are to Thomas Hobbes, *Leviathan*, edited by Richard Tuck (Cambridge University Press, 1996). References to *De Cive* ('DC') are to Thomas Hobbes, *On the Citizen*, edited by Richard Tuck and Michael Silverthorne (Cambridge University Press, 1998). References to *Behemoth* ('B') are to Thomas Hobbes, *Behemoth or the Long Parliament*, edited by Stephen Holmes (University of Chicago Press, 1990). References to *A Dialogue Between a Philosopher and a Student, of the Common Laws of England* ('D') are to Thomas Hobbes, *Writings on Common Law and Hereditary Rights*, edited by Alan Cromartie and Quentin Skinner (Oxford University Press, 2008). References to *The Elements of Law* ('EL') are to Thomas Hobbes, *Human Nature and De Corpore Politico*, edited by J.C.A. Gaskin (Oxford University Press, 2008).

[1] Michael Oakeshott, 'Introduction to *Leviathan*' in Michael Oakeshott, *Hobbes on Civil Association* (Indianapolis: Liberty Fund, 1975), 6.

[2] Alan Cromartie, '*The Elements* and Hobbesian Moral Thinking' (2011) 32 *History of Political Thought* 21, 21. See also Quentin Skinner, 'The Purely Artificial Person of the State' in Skinner, *Visions of Politics III: Hobbes and Civil Science* (Cambridge University Press, 2002), 177, 179: 'The inspiration for this approach – along with so much else in the conceptual apparatus of *Leviathan* – appears to be drawn from the *Digest* of Roman Law.'

fragility of civil life and a belief that only law conjoined with power can hold it together.[3]

This chapter explores the relationship between law and power in Hobbes. It asks the question: how is it that Hobbes's sovereign has plenitude of power, which must include not just legal authority but various extra-legal powers, and yet is expected to channel that power through ordinary law? I explore the question through the lens of the prerogative. At the heart of the constitutional disputes that tore the English polity apart in Hobbes's lifetime, the prerogative was the form in which discussions of excessive kingly power were framed. Keeping the prerogative in view helps us to identify what Hobbes finds distinctive about law and law's contribution to the stability of civil order. Against those who would turn the 'Mortall God' into a mere legal cipher, Hobbes maintains that ordinary law takes shape against the shadow of an untrammelled sovereign capacity that includes extraordinary and extra-legal powers.

'Champions of Anarchy': conflict in Hobbes

Hobbes's theory of political authority aims to provide an answer to the problems posed by conflict. Our natural condition, he argues, is one of inescapable and systemic disagreement, the source of which lies in our natural freedom. Each of us has a natural right to use our power to stay alive and a natural right to be 'judge himself of the necessity of the means, and of the greatness of the danger'.[4] It is not that we have no guide as to how best to exercise this right. Principles of natural law, which are general rules or theorems of reason conducive to our preservation, are available to us. But such laws even if self-evident are not self-applying.[5] Since 'men are by nature provided of notable multiplying glasses, (that is their Passions and Selfe-love,) through which, every little payment appeareth a great grievance',[6] the natural state is characterized by partial judgements supporting self-interested actions.

Conflict is endemic in Hobbes's world. But it arises not so much from man's antisocial character as from the 'self-destructive character of

[3] L, 90: 'Where there is no common Power, there is no Law: where no Law, no Injustice.'

[4] EL, 79; also L, 91.

[5] DC, 69: 'the natural laws do not guarantee their own observance as soon as they are known'.

[6] L, 129.

judgement'.[7] Conflict in the natural state is not contingent or factual, the kind that might not exist if people were less irascible or competitive. It is a result rather of a 'necessary jural conflict between people whose *rights* overlap or conflict in some sense with one another until they have been renounced'.[8] Such disagreement produces conflict which leads to disorder; disorder induces fear; fear in turn leads to more disagreement. While this condition lasts, 'there can be no Propriety, no Dominion, no Mine and Thine distinct: but onely that to be every mans, that he can get it; and for so long, as he can keep it'.[9] It is the ineluctably conflict-ridden condition of the natural state, and the exceptionally dour consequences attendant to it, that motivates people to form the commonwealth, even though this means signing away one of the core rights of natural personhood, the right to judge for myself what is best for me. Within the commonwealth, the plurality of voices is reduced to the single, authoritative voice of the sovereign, turning the disordered Babel of the natural state into a 'commonwealth of ordered words',[10] and the multiplicity of overlapping individual judgements about rights is replaced by a single, authoritative jurisdiction.

The commonwealth, then, vastly reduces the complexities that otherwise beset the interpretation of any body of law, whether written or unwritten. It resolves, if you like, a fundamental coordination problem that can only be solved by the introduction of an all-powerful sovereign.[11] That solution involves elements of both law and power, the sword and scales of sovereign capacity. The sovereign can impose a solution on the 'necessary jural conflict' that grows out of natural rights not just because he is supreme judge or ultimate source of legal authority but also because he has the power to impose his interpretation of the laws if necessary through the threat or use of overwhelming force. As Hobbes writes in *Leviathan*, for the sovereign alone there 'can not be any knot in the Law, insoluble; either by finding out the ends, to undoe it by; or else by making what ends he will, (as *Alexander* did with his sword in the Gordian knot,) by the legislative power; which no other Interpreter can doe'.[12]

[7] Richard Tuck, *Philosophy and Government 1572–1651* (Cambridge University Press, 1993), 307.

[8] Noel Malcolm, 'Hobbes and Spinoza' in J.H. Burns and Mark Goldie (eds.), *The Cambridge History of Political Thought, 1450–1700* (Cambridge University Press, 1991), 535.

[9] L, 90.

[10] Philip Pettit, *Made With Words: Hobbes on Language, Mind, and Politics* (Princeton University Press, 2008), chapter 8.

[11] Pasquale Pasquino, 'Hobbes, Religion, and Rational Choice: Hobbes's Two Leviathans and the Fool' (2001) 82 *Pacific Philosophical Quarterly* 406.

[12] L, 191.

'Man's tongue is a trumpet to war and sedition'

A finer-grained understanding of Hobbes's theory of law can be gained by turning to his late book on the English Civil War, *Behemoth*. Writing 'as from the Devil's Mountain',[13] Hobbes supplies in this work an anatomy of disorder, a crucial feature of which is the claim that the proliferation of private judgements at the expense of the public judgement of the sovereign leads to civil strife.

Behemoth is a litany of blame, holding group after group responsible for the collapse of social order. It begins with a parade of 'seducers'[14] who corrupted the kingdom. At the top of the list come religious groups: Presbyterians, Papists and various non-conformist sects. It also includes the educated who were led astray by classical authors, those 'champions of Anarchy',[15] into espousing 'democratical principles'. The universities that educated them are chastized for producing deliberately obfuscatory works on religion and politics on behalf of their paymaster the Pope.[16] Parliament is also criticized,[17] as are the independent-minded mercantile cities.[18] In each case, blame stems from the same source: encouraging the false belief that each individual should see himself as judge of matters of religion and politics eroded habits of obedience and led to the ruin of the commonwealth. In the constitutional-legal sphere, this attitude translated into a hardline opposition to the exercise by the king, on grounds of national security, of prerogative powers to raise revenue. Each 'thought himself to be so much master of whatsoever he possessed, that it could not be taken from him upon any pretence of common safety without his own consent'.[19]

It is not that the king's side escapes blame altogether. But here the reason for criticism is almost the opposite – not too much assertive independent-mindedness but rather too little. The king's party fell into strategic and conceptual error when, through their 'love with mixarchy', they threw away the chance of decisive military victory by pursuing instead a negotiated settlement.[20] In allowing public authority to become diluted they enabled private voices to proliferate. Discussing the Earl of Strafford's impeachment and attainder, a crucial moment in the lead-up to civil war, Hobbes offers a version of the Hydra myth:

> B. You have read, that when Hercules fighting with the Hydra, had cut off any one of his many heads, there still arose two other heads in its place; and yet at last he cut them off all.

[13] B, 1. [14] B, 3. [15] DC, 133.
[16] B, 17. [17] B, 109. [18] B, 3–4.
[19] B, 4. [20] B, 116–117.

> A. The story is false. For Hercules at first did not cut off those heads, but bought them off; and afterwards, when he saw it did him no good, then he cut them off, and got the victory.[21]

This sardonic telling of the tale points not just to what Hobbes takes to have been a crucial tactical mistake on the king's part – trying to buy off the opposition instead of taking it on. It also reveals Hobbes's view of the causes of decline. Just as the Hydra's heads multiply, so the multiplicity of voices in the public realm causes the commonwealth to spin out of control. Decisive force, well applied, is the one thing that can stop it.[22]

Behemoth shows how a ragbag of factions spouting fictions brought down a commonwealth. Disagreement, Hobbes suggests, has a tendency to *cascade*.[23] Theological questions seep into questions of political authority. What universities teach impacts on parliament. Elite behaviour is copied by the people. Such cascades are neither predictable nor easily controllable. Situations of confusion make perfect breeding grounds for manipulation. Hobbes often uses the language of seduction to capture this phenomenon. As we saw, he first calls those who led the commonwealth astray the 'seducers'. Seduction is a two-way relationship. And Hobbes finds both seducer and seduced guilty. One for manipulating the other, the other for not resisting. One for being corrupt, the other for being so weak. *Behemoth* is full of such dangerous liaisons. Universities seduce the impressionable. Classical authors lead young gentlemen astray. Orators lure the populace from its duty.

Once political speech moves beyond public control and becomes a matter of private enterprise and private judgement, as happened in the 1640s,[24] the demise of sovereign authority and the collapse of social order

[21] B, 72.

[22] Interestingly, Oliver Cromwell comes out pretty well in *Behemoth*. One reason for this was that Cromwell was precisely the kind of decisive leader that Hobbes found attractive.

[23] It may be possible to model Hobbes's conception of the state of nature in similar terms. The war of all against all results, that is, from a fear-driven cascade: the anticipation of one man being attacked causes them to attack the other because the first considers it a better option than waiting to be attacked.

[24] See David Zaret, *Origins of Democratic Culture: Printing, Petitions, and the Public Sphere in Early-Modern England* (Princeton University Press, 2000). This was a Europe-wide phenomenon. See, e.g., Noel Malcolm, *Reason of State, Propaganda, and the Thirty Years' War: An Unknown Translation by Thomas Hobbes* (Oxford University Press, 2007), 30: 'Since the outbreak of the Thirty Years' War in 1618, a flood of pamphlets, newsletters, and broadsheets, both informative and polemical, had poured from the presses … [C]onsiderable efforts were made by rulers and political leaders both to control the flow of such publications and to insert into it works supportive of their own policies.'

is imminent. This specific pathology of the death of the English body politic is of a piece with Hobbes's more general fascination with the dangers of language: 'man's tongue is a trumpet to war and sedition', as he put it in *De Cive*.[25] Disorder is not caused, as the Greeks taught, by the re-emergence of the beast in man. Rather it results from 'the unruliness of the world-made mind'.[26] Ideas and the words used to convey them matter profoundly to us as they are the stuff that we use to construct the worlds in which we live. But the human mind, as well as being a source of ingenuity, is at the same time tragically limited and as such a source of great danger. This is why Hobbes keeps returning to the failings of the universities. Within a mind-constructed world these institutions, quintessential centres of ideas, have immense influence. Hobbes places 'consistent emphasis on the public function of the universities as the places where the blank paper of the ruling classes' minds was imprinted with civil doctrine'.[27] They are, as we might say, a source of considerable soft power. But the 'Schoole-men' tend, so Hobbes claims, to use that power irresponsibly at best, treasonously at worst. 'When men write whole volumes of such stuffe, are they not Mad, or intend to make others so?'[28] These remarks, while aimed at the universities, have a wider significance. The proliferation of political tracts, penned by individuals for their own private ends, is either madness in itself or else designed to induce madness in others. Either way, to allow for such a plurality of competing voices means that the authoritative voice of sovereign command will be drowned out. With the loss of the public voice goes the commonwealth's standard of right reason. Also lost is the idea of a single judge and with it the possibility of justice. We are back in the state of nature, or something very much like it.

The problem posed by the resurgent 'sovereign' subject is discussed in *Leviathan* where the 'poyson of seditious doctrines' comes very high on the list of things that weaken a commonwealth. First among such doctrines is the idea that '*every private man is Judge of Good and Evill actions*'. The central error here is that it mistakes the civil for the natural

[25] DC, 71. DC, 4 (discussing the Latin maxims 'Man is a God to man, and Man is a wolf to Man'): 'men have a natural tendency to use rapacity as a term of abuse against each other, seeing their own actions reflected in others as in a mirror where left becomes right and right becomes left'.

[26] Pettit, *Made With Words*, 99.

[27] R.W. Serjeantson, '"Vaine Philosophy": Thomas Hobbes and the Philosophy of the Schools' in Conal Condren, Stephen Gaukroger and Ian Hunter (eds.), *The Philosopher in Early Modern Europe* (Cambridge University Press, 2006), 118.

[28] L, 59.

condition: 'This is true in the condition of meer Nature, where there are no Civill Lawes; and also under Civil Government, in such cases as are not determined by the Law. But otherwise, it is manifest, that the measure of Good and Evil actions, is the Civill Law.'[29] The lengths to which the civil authorities should go in order to stamp out behaviour of this sort is evident in the way Hobbes suggests Presbyterian ministers should have been dealt with before the civil war. Since their sedition was in his view a primary cause of civil war and the death of perhaps 100,000 people, would it not have been better had 'those seditious ministers, which were not perhaps 1000, had been killed before they had preached? It had been (I confess) a great massacre; but the killing of 100,000 is greater'.[30]

Killings of this (presumably extra-legal) sort are exceptional. In normal times, Hobbes envisages a structure in which the propagation of ideas is tightly controlled. It is essential that the commonwealth speak with one voice. This entails the absence of any division or restriction in the constitution of government.[31] It also means that the multiplicity of private wills must be subordinated to the sovereign's determination of the public interest.[32] This injunction plays out most strongly in respect of two institutions, the church and the universities, where ideas proliferate most readily. For the church, Hobbes espouses a statist ecclesiology according to which the 'sovereign would act as absolute lord of the commonwealth's spiritual life, an archbishop with his dominion as his diocese'.[33] The universities must likewise 'bend and direct their studies to … the teaching of absolute obedience to the laws of the King'.[34] Common to both is the imposition of the public interest as determined by the sovereign over private interests.

'By the laws, I mean, laws living and armed'

We can now more clearly specify the mischief that civil law is designed to cure. Stability, let alone peace, is impossible in the natural condition where rights-holding and self-adjudicating individuals are free to do as

[29] L, 223. [30] B, 95. [31] EL, 166–167.

[32] At least in public. Hobbes distinguished carefully between forbidding teaching and forbidding men to believe what they were taught: 'But what (may some object) if a King, or a Senate, or other Soveraign Person forbid us to believe in Christ? To this I answer, that such forbidding is of no effect; because Beleef, and Unbeleef never follow mens Commands' (L, 343).

[33] Jeffrey R. Collins, *The Allegiance of Thomas Hobbes* (Oxford University Press, 2008), 26.

[34] B, 56.

they please. Law provides an architectonic structure of rule that enables authority to be concentrated in the hands of the sovereign. Law gives the commonwealth its standard of right and measure of justice.[35] All laws need interpretation and enforcement, but the radical pluralism of the natural condition makes authoritative determination impossible. The advent of civil law ends this polyphonic confusion. Enabling the commonwealth to speak in one voice enables truly concerted action, action as a political community (*civitas*) rather than as disjointed groups of individuals (*multitudo*).[36]

Law circumscribes the ambit of the subject's duty of obedience. 'The virtue of a subject is comprehended wholly in obedience to the laws of the commonwealth.'[37] Liberty begins where the laws run out.[38] There are a few exceptional cases where Hobbes allows the subject to disobey a law without injustice, for instance where a man is commanded to harm or kill himself. But in general, liberties 'depend on the Silence of the Law. In cases where the Soveraign has prescribed no rule, there the Subject hath the Liberty to do, or forbeare, according to his own discretion'.[39] Since civil authority, the regulation of human conduct by law, does not and cannot prescribe the whole of man's conduct, Hobbes can argue that the purpose of laws is not to stop people from doing all that they want, but to prevent them from doing harm through rashness or their impetuous desires. Laws are 'as Hedges are set, not to stop Travellers, but to keep them in the way'.[40]

Hobbes's account of law's function is reflected in his analytical jurisprudence. Law (*lex*) is to be distinguished from right (*ius*), he insists, since 'right is that liberty which the law leaveth us'.[41] Nor should law be confused with covenant, which only binds in relation to the promise specifically covenanted for.[42] Nor is law counsel, which carries no obligation.[43] Rather, 'CIVIL LAWS (to define them) are nothing other than commands

35 DC, 79. 36 DC, 75–76. 37 B, 44.

38 This is consistent with his more general position on freedom. See Thomas Hobbes, *Treatise 'Of Liberty and Necessity'* in Vere Chappel (ed.), *Hobbes and Bramhall on Liberty and Necessity* (Cambridge University Press, 1999), 38: 'I conceive liberty to be rightly defined in this manner: Liberty is the absence of all the impediments to action that are not contained in the nature and intrinsical quality of the agent.'

39 L, 151–152. 40 L, 239–240.

41 EL, 179; also L, 200; D, 35.

42 EL, 178. Also EL, 166: 'law implieth a command; covenant is but a promise'. See also EL, 139: 'A Lawe bindeth, by a promise of obedience in general.'

43 EL, 178. The parallel passages in DC, chapter 14 distinguish laws from advice (*consilium*) and agreement (*pactum*).

about the citizens' future actions from the one who is endowed with sovereign authority'.[44] This succinct definition comes from *De Cive*. I will probe the more elaborate definitions he provided in later works shortly. But note here how the ability to enforce law is built into law's very definition: 'By the Laws, I mean, Laws living and Armed.'[45] Laws, if they are to count as such, must be effective.[46] The subject has no duty to obey a putative authority that does not operate a system of laws that provides for the subject's safety and protection.

The functional imperatives of law, as Hobbes sees them, are also realized in the systematic way he clears the jurisdictional terrain of other sources and systems of law that might compete with the civil law. The notion of fundamental law is dismissed, unless it refers to either the sovereignty principle or the safety of the people. 'I understand not how one law can be more fundamental than another, except only that law of nature that binds us all to obey him, whosoever he may be, whom lawfully and for our own safety, we have promised to obey; nor any other fundamental law to a King, but *salus populi*, the safety and well-being of his people.'[47] Custom is not a valid source of law, unless it receives the imprimatur of the sovereign.[48] Natural law is similarly discounted.[49] Hobbes sees the laws of nature as theorems of reason conducive to self-preservation, rejecting the classical natural lawyer's notion that legal obligation has its source in whatever specific means we identify for pursuing self-evident goods. 'For the Lawes of Nature ... are not properly Lawes, but qualities that dispose men to peace, and to obedience.'[50]

44 DC, 79. See also EL, 76: 'when the command is a sufficient reason to move us to the action [commanded], then is that command called a LAW.'

45 D, 59.

46 Stephen Holmes, 'Hobbes's Irrational Man' in Stephen Holmes, *Passions and Constraint: On the Theory of Liberal Democracy* (University of Chicago Press, 1995), 79. See also D, 14: ''Tis not therefore the word of a Law, but the Power of a Man that has the strength of the Nation, that makes the Laws effectual.'

47 B, 67–68. See also L, 199: 'There is another distinction of Laws, into *Fundamentall*, and *not Fundamentall*: but I could never see in any Author, what a Fundamentall Law signifieth.'

48 L, 184.

49 S.A. Lloyd talks about the 'self-effacing' quality of the natural law in Hobbes: 'Hobbes's Self-Effacing Natural Law Theory' (2001) 82 *Pacific Philosophical Quarterly* 285. See also Perez Zagorin, *Hobbes and the Law of Nature* (Princeton University Press, 2009), 49.

50 L, 185. See also L, 111: 'These dictates of Reason, men use to call by the name of Lawes, but improperly: for they are but Conclusions, or Theoremes concerning what conduceth to the conservation and defence of themselves; whereas Law, properly is the word of him, that by right hath command over others.'

As such they are counsel not command.[51] They are not laws unless the sovereign wills it. 'One can be obliged to follow the dictates of the laws of nature only in the context of a political society firmly ruled by a sovereign who will enforce them as *legal* laws.'[52] (This is not quite the end of the story as far as natural law is concerned, as we see below in our discussion of equity.)

Hobbes systematically downgrades forms of law other than civil law, and reserves the word 'law' for the public commands of the sovereign. What we might call the imperial quality of Hobbes's jurisprudence, with its seemingly insatiable harmonizing drive, flows directly from the polity-stabilizing functions that he ascribes to law. Authority is funnelled into a single channel – the civil law. The sovereign provides a single public voice for the commonwealth. His commands are the standards of right in relation to which the subjects are to organize their lives and resolve their conflicts. The dangers of allowing that public standard of right to become confused or challenged are so significant that no interference with those transmission cables of authority, the 'Artificiall Chains' of laws that link sovereign and subject, can be permitted: 'all Judicature is essentially annexed to the Soveraignty; and therefore all other Judges are but Ministers of him, or them that have the Soveraign Power'.[53]

The same centralizing instinct is evident in Hobbes's late work, the *Dialogue Between a Philosopher and a Student, of the Common Laws of England*, a central feature of which is its attack on the common lawyers. Throughout, Hobbes asserts the power of modern, scientific reason[54] over the medieval 'reason of the guild'.[55] He took aim at their claim to be stewards of a separate, near autonomous system of justice that some of them took to embody a fundamental constitution to which king and parliament

[51] We might say that natural laws are divine commandments. But even then, divine commands are binding in the commonwealth only insofar as the sovereign says that they are.

[52] Russell Hardin, 'Hobbesian Political Order' (1991) 19 *Political Theory* 156, 162.

[53] L, 168.

[54] D, 13: '*Ph.* See you Lawyers how much you are beholding to a Philosopher, and 'tis but reason, for the General and Noble Science, and Law of all the World is true Philosophy, of which the Common Law of *England* is a very little part.' Jean Bodin in *Iuris universi distributio* [1580] similarly argued that jurisprudence must be a science, for it permits men to distinguish the true from the false.

[55] Alan Cromartie, *The Constitutionalist Revolution: An Essay on the History of England, 1450–1642* (Cambridge University Press, 2006), 215. Donald R. Kelley refers to the 'guild sense' of the common lawyers in his *History, Law and the Human Sciences* (London: Variorum Reprints, 1984).

were subject.[56] This independent-mindedness could lead to instability in the operation of the laws, as events leading to the civil war proved.[57] Hobbes, who at the time of writing the *Dialogue* feared he might be charged with heresy,[58] also disliked the shrillness of the lawyers and the tendency to populist updrift in sentencing policy (especially for heresy) when they gave themselves freedom to manoeuvre beyond statute. So, when the Student, representing the common lawyers, tries the standard lawyer's move of opening up a space between the common law and statute, the Philosopher (Hobbes's alter ego) closes him down:

> Law. You speak of the Statute Law, and I speak of the Common Law.
> Ph. I speak generally of Law.[59]

The Philosopher then steals Sir Edward Coke's line about the common law being supreme reason to subvert Coke's message. Law is reason, agreed. Yet it receives its highest expression not in the pronouncements of judges but in the commands of the sovereign: 'the Kings Reason, when it is publickly upon Advice, and Deliberation declar'd, is that *Anima Legis*, and that *Summa Ratio*, and that Equity which all agree to be the Law of Reason, is all that is, or ever was Law in *England*'.[60] What is true for making laws should also be true for adjudicating on the basis of those laws: 'since therefore the King is sole Legislator, I think it also Reason he should be sole Supream Judge'.[61] This has to be the case given that our goal is the instantiation of the public reason of the sovereign and the eradication of 'any private Reason' of the type offered by the common lawyers. To do otherwise would mean that 'there would be as much contradiction in the Lawes, as there is in the Schooles'.[62] Hobbes's specification of the king's reason as *summa ratio* has a religious dimension or quality. In *Leviathan* ch. 37, discussing miracles and their use, he says that the question of

[56] The final pages of the final volume of Coke's Reports (on *Bagg's Case*) contain the assertion that 'no wrong or injury, either public or private, can be done but that it shall be here reformed or punished by due course of law' (Sir Edward Coke, *The Reports of Sir Edward Coke, Kt., In English, Compleat in Thirteen Parts. The Eleventh Part* (London: E. & R. Nutt, 1727), 98a). See also J.G.A. Pocock, *The Ancient Constitution and the Feudal Law* (Cambridge University Press, 2nd edn, 1987); Cromartie, *Constitutionalist Revolution*, chapter 7.

[57] Alan Cromartie, 'General Introduction' in Hobbes, *Writings on Common Law and Hereditary Right*, xxxv: 'Though common lawyers ranked behind the presbyterian clergy in Hobbes's private demonology, he was consistent in his fear of them and in his diagnosis of the ultimate source of the mischief.'

[58] John Parkin, *Taming the Leviathan: The Reception of the Political and Religious Ideas of Thomas Hobbes in England 1640–1700* (Cambridge University Press, 2007), 240.

[59] D, 10. [60] D, 19. [61] D, 27. [62] L, 187.

whether the report of a miracle is true or a lie is not one for 'our own private Reason, or Conscience, but the Publique Reason, that is, the reason of Gods Supreme Lieutenant, Judge; and indeed we have made him Judge already, if wee have given him a Soveraign power'.[63]

Law as command 'Publickly and plainly declar'd'

Law, when allied to sovereign power, is the solution to instability and insecurity. Since law itself is open to disagreement, particularly in its interpretation, it is essential that the structure of legal command is kept as clear as possible: 'all Judicature is essentially annexed to the Soveraignty'.[64] This applies to legislation and adjudication. In 'all Courts of Justice, the Soveraign (which is the Person of the Common-wealth,) is he that Judgeth'.[65] The sovereign, then, has virtually unlimited legal capacity. He is endowed with plenipotentiary authority, the open-ended power 'to legislate, potentially on any aspect of life, for the whole community'.[66] But this does not mean that the sovereign has licence to do what he wills. The commonwealth of laws, as well as framing the exercise of enormous power, also provides obstacles to the misuse of power. As the Philosopher observes in the *Dialogue*, some laws 'are in themselves very good for the King and People, as creating some kind of Difficulty for such Kings as for the Glory of Conquest might spend one part of their Subjects Lives and Estates, in Molesting other Nations, and leave the rest to Destroy themselves at Home by Factions'.[67]

There can be no legal limits to the sovereign's authority.[68] Yet law can provide some sort of brake on sovereign power. We can start to unravel this apparent paradox by exploring the notion of civil law as public command. That those commands need to be clear is elementary, otherwise they would be incapable of performing the stabilizing function that Hobbes envisages. This is evident even in the pithy definition of law Hobbes gives in his earlier writings. In *De Cive*, as we saw, law is defined as the sovereign's public commands concerning future actions of the citizen,

[63] L, 306. [64] L, 168. [65] L, 187.

[66] Noel Malcolm, 'Hobbes's Theory of International Relations' in Noel Malcolm, *Aspects of Hobbes* (Oxford University Press, 2002), 432, 443.

[67] D, 21.

[68] L, 184: 'The Soveraign of a Common-wealth ... is not Subject to the Civill Lawes. For having the power to make, and repeale Lawes, he may when he pleaseth, free himselfe from that subjection, by repealing those Lawes that trouble him, and making of new; and consequently he was free before.'

a formulation that contains implicit limits. The category 'law' would not seem to include the sovereign's non-public commands ('Will no one rid me of this turbulent priest?'). Nor can the term 'law' apply to sovereign acts relating to past behaviour. The subject is presumably free from retrospective criminalizing of his conduct.

Later definitions expand on the publicity requirement. The formulation in *Leviathan* is as follows: 'CIVILL LAW, Is to every Subject, those Rules, which the Common-wealth hath Commanded him, by Word, Writing, or other sufficient Sign of the Will, to make use of, for the Distinction of Right and Wrong; that is to say, of what is contrary, and what is not contrary to the Rule.'[69] Admittedly the limits here seem pretty trivial. All the more so as Hobbes in the same passage indicates that laws need not be general,[70] thereby seeming to accept for instance the legality of bills of attainder (the measure that did for Strafford). But there is still a requirement that the sovereign intends to create legal obligations and of some agreed public formality to signify that intention. The point is elaborated in the *Dialogue*. Law is defined as such 'when it is *publickly upon Advice, and Deliberation declar'd*'.[71] This statement, while suggestive, is ambiguous since it is not clear whether the two conditions – publicity and advice – are essential elements of law or whether they are aspirational or prudential, qualities that a good law should possess. The Philosopher's second attempt at a definition clarifies matters:

> *Ph.* Thus; A Law is the Command of him, or them that have the Soveraign Power, given to those that be his or their Subjects, declaring Publickly, and plainly what every of them may do, and what they must forbear to do.[72]

The advice requirement has now been dropped to the realm of prudence. This is consistent with the way advice is treated elsewhere in the work. The Student describes at one point the sovereign's failure to consult before making decisions about war and peace as a 'sin' – not, that is, something that renders his actions unlawful. The publicity requirement, by contrast, seems now to be firmly embedded within the concept of law. If anything, it has been strengthened. To count as a law the command must be declared both publicly and plainly. And the Philosopher indeed reasserts the requirement against opposition from the Student, who says 'whereas you make it *of the Essence of a Law* to be Publickly and plainly declar'd to the People, I see no necessity for that'.[73] The Philosopher then spells

[69] L, 183. [70] L, 183.
[71] D, 19 (emphasis added). [72] D, 31.
[73] D, 32 (emphasis added).

out what the publicity requirement might entail. When new statutes are passed, he says:

> the Knights of the Shires should be bound to furnish People with a sufficient Number of Copies (at the Peoples Charge) of the Acts of Parliament at their return to the Country; that every man may resort to them, and by themselves, or Friends take notice of what they are obliged to; for otherwise it were Impossible they should be obeyed: And that no Man is bound to a thing Impossible is one of Sir *Edw. Cokes* Maxims at the Common-Law.[74]

The content of the duty to promulgate reflects what Hobbes says elsewhere. 'Knowledge of the laws depends on the legislator, who has a duty to promulgate them', he writes in *De Cive*, 'for otherwise they are not laws'.[75] It is also consistent with his theory of political obligation. Unlike Machiavelli's Prince who manipulates allegiance personally, through his alertness, decisiveness and forcefulness as a ruler in the interests of securing his estate,[76] Hobbes's sovereign is a public and formal creation, a piece of legal artifice, albeit on the grandest scale. Subject to what I have to say later on prerogative power, the sovereign exists and exercises power through law. It speaks through the civil laws.[77] The Prince governs in his own interest; the sovereign exists for the security and well-being of the commonwealth. Hobbes's ideal is a state that provides a stable framework of laws in which people can seek the satisfaction of their desires, whatever those desires may be.[78] But if that ideal is to be realized, those subject to the laws must be clear about the legal boundaries in which they are meant to operate. If you want certainty about the laws, you want it all the way down. You cannot assume, as the Student does, that people should have knowledge of the laws that bind them.[79] You must do all that you can to

[74] D, 32.

[75] DC, 160. See also DC, 172 'a ruler's *precepts* are laws for the ruled. But they are not *laws* unless they are promulgated clearly, so that there can be no excuse for ignorance'.

[76] Cornelia Navari, 'Hobbes and the "Hobbesian Tradition" in International Thought' (1982) 11 *Millennium: Journal of International Studies* 203, 210–212.

[77] See DC, 161: 'By *written* law I mean law which requires the voice or some other sign of the will of the legislator to become law ... the requisite of *written law* is not *writing* but vocal expression [*vox*] ... *Unwritten law* is law which needs no promulgation but the voice of nature, or natural reason, such as are *natural laws*.'

[78] Malcolm, 'Hobbes's Theory of International Relations' in Malcolm, *Aspects of Hobbes*, 440.

[79] There is another dimension to the argument against the Student, namely that in the monarchical commonwealth Hobbes favours, parliament cannot consent to new laws on behalf of the people because it is not their representative.

make sure that they know. Only then can you engender certainty about the operation of the system of laws as a whole. Absent this and insecurity and lack of trust sneak back in, leading to precisely the problems Hobbes's commonwealth was set up to resolve.

But how is the publicity requirement supposed to be enforced in a context where sovereignty is 'power unlimited'?[80] Hobbes insists, after all, that there are no legal controls over the sovereign[81] and that the sovereign is not subject to the civil laws.[82] And yet it would seem that Hobbes expects the sovereign's judges, when faced with a putative law that was not properly promulgated, to decline to enforce it. So hostile to the questioning of sovereign authority in other quarters,[83] Hobbes is surprisingly open to legal challenges to the exercise of sovereign power. As he writes in *Leviathan*:

> If a Subject have a controversie with his Soveraigne, of debt, or of right of possession of land or goods, or concerning any service required at his hands, or concerning any penalty, corporall, or pecuniary, grounded on a precedent Law: he hath the same Liberty to sue for his right, as if it were against a Subject; and before such Judges, as are appointed by the Soveraign. For seeing the Soveraign demandeth by force of a former Law, and not by vertue of his Power; he declareth thereby, that he requireth no more, than shall appear to be due by that Law. The sute therefore is not contrary to the will of the Soveraign.[84]

This passage indicates not just that litigation against the sovereign is possible, but that the category of possible suits is in fact very wide. It includes the types of action a subject might bring against another subject (property, contract, tort, employment, etc.). But it goes further by allowing a series of actions in public law ('concerning any penalty, corporall, or pecuniary, grounded on a precedent Law'). If we read this passage alongside what Hobbes says about the duty to promulgate, then the subject ought to be able to argue in court that the 'precedent Law' under which you are charged is in fact no law at all.[85]

[80] L, 155. [81] L, 222; D, 76. [82] L, 224.

[83] Holmes, 'Hobbes Irrational Man', 69: 'Thomas Hobbes apotheosized unquestionable authority as the only practicable alternative to anarchy and disparaged political liberty in almost all its forms.'

[84] L, 153.

[85] Compare the following passage from DC, 85: 'There are indeed many things permitted to citizens by the commonwealth, and legal action may sometimes be taken against the holder of *sovereign power*; but such action is not a matter of *civil law* but of *natural equity*; and the question is not what the holder of *sovereign power may* rightly do, but what he

Hobbes also says that this type of action is not a challenge to the sovereign. But how can this be true if, in public law cases, the court will sometimes limit the sovereign's capacity to act? An answer might be found if we pay closer attention to the different types of limits that law can impose. Law can limit *substantively*. It can restrict the range of possible options open to a decision-maker. Constitutional law does this when it disallows action contrary to basic rights (e.g. imprison without cause). Hobbes rejects this kind of limit on the basis that sovereignty is plenitude of power. There is no law more fundamental than the idea of absolute sovereignty. Law can limit *institutionally*. One institution's room for action may be limited or checked by another institution (e.g. tax without the consent of parliament). Again, Hobbes explicitly rejects any such separation of powers arrangement.[86] But law can also limit in a way that is internal to itself. In this case, the limit stems from law's *form*. Law has enormous coordinating potential, but only if it has certain qualities. Only if law is publicly and plainly made known is it able to specify in advance the behaviour required of subjects. Clarity is vital here because what is at stake is the public command of the sovereign. Without such clarity there can be no real stability or security, and subjects would not be able to shape their lives sure in the knowledge of what the law expects of them.

The benefits that stem from the effective operation of the laws are considerable – peace, order and good government. These benefits come, though, at a price. And that price is paid to the integrity of the legal form. Sovereignty flows through legal channels. But the value of such channels diminishes if the sovereign neglects or bypasses them. The importance of form to legal order explains the need to police the formal integrity of laws through a body charged with that task. This is the scenario that Hobbes raises with the prospect of public law actions against the sovereign. These actions do limit sovereign power. They do

willed; hence he himself will be the judge, as if he could not give an unfair judgement, when equity is taken into account.' This is a problematic passage, not least because its meaning is not especially clear. It resembles the passage from *Leviathan* in that it allows legal challenges to the sovereign. It appears to differ in that it would require suits to be made in equity rather than (as the *Leviathan* passage suggests) at law ('he hath the same Liberty to sue for his right, as if it were against a Subject'; 'the Subject has the Liberty to demand the hearing of his Cause; and sentence, according to that Law'). I suspect the difference Hobbes imagines is primarily jurisdictional. Cases against the sovereign (in *De Cive*) should go through something like the Court of Chancery. Such cases (in *Leviathan*) should go through the ordinary courts. I discuss these jurisdictional differences below.

[86] See L, 225; EL, 166–167.

so, however, in a way that is internal to the formal structure of law and for reasons relating to the integrity of the system of laws. The judges who decide these cases unquestionably owe allegiance to the sovereign. But they fulfil their office by ensuring that the system of public command at the apex of which is the sovereign functions in the way that it should.

That Hobbes took legal form seriously is evident from the care with which he distinguished the private acts of the king in his natural capacity from the public commands of the king as sovereign. The difference marks the boundary between public command (law) and private wish (counsel), only the first of which carries an obligation. Those acts, he writes in the *Dialogue*, 'which are done by the King previously to the passing of them under the Great Seal of *England*, either by word of Mouth, or warrant under his Signet, or privy Seal, are done in his natural Capacity; but when they have past the Seal of *England*, they are to be taken as done in his politick Capacity'.[87] This is a particularly good example of the attention Hobbes paid to the public/private divide – and the especial importance of identifying and isolating the category of 'the public'. In this instance, the vital moment of transition from private to public is utterly formal and appears almost trivial. But it makes all the difference when it comes to specifying the duties of the subject. (No court, we are to presume, would enforce a mere wish, however kingly, as opposed to a proper legal command.) Why should form count for so much? We should not ignore the element of performance here. There is a theatricality of sorts at play here, after all, and Hobbes was always attuned to the role-playing dimensions of public life. But what is most at stake is clarity and publicity. All relevant actors – king, officials, judges, subjects – know that when something is done under the Great Seal it counts as law. It doesn't matter much what the proper form is, so long as it is generally accepted and sufficiently public. Reason of state writers of Hobbes's time revelled in the claim that political truths are always shrouded in mystery.[88] Hobbes insisted to the contrary that subjects should know the laws of the commonwealth and the reason why it exercises authority over them. The commonwealth, as he wrote in *De Cive*, 'does not want to take anything away from the citizen in underhanded ways, and yet is willing to take everything from him in an open fashion'.[89]

[87] D, 139.
[88] Malcolm, *Reason of State*, 122.
[89] DC, 86.

'By vertue of his power': the sovereign and the prerogative

But perhaps we have been a little hasty. So far, we have a reasonably benevolent, if rather austere, theory of rule through law. Yet Hobbes says repeatedly that the sovereign is not bound by civil law but only by the law of God. Does that mean that the sovereign can act outside the law? Is there anything (at least of this world) that prevents him from doing so? Even the passages I drew upon that envisage litigation against the sovereign seem to assume that the sovereign can act in this way. Hobbes tells us that such litigation is in order 'seeing the Soveraign demandeth by force of a former law, and not by vertue of his Power'. This seems to presuppose that the sovereign has a choice between exercising power in two ways, the legal and the extra-legal. This reading is supported by a later part of the same passage: 'But if he [the sovereign] demand, or take any thing by pretence of his Power; there lyeth, in that case, no action of Law.'[90] If the sovereign has free rein when it comes to acting in accordance with the law and its formal constraints, what becomes of the rule of law commonwealth that Hobbes has so painstakingly constructed?

There is no doubt that Hobbes was exercised by such questions. Whether the king had the capacity to act outside normal legal channels was the key constitutional question of the age. The issue usually came wrapped in the language of royal prerogative. The prerogative was generally understood as a bundle of powers that could be exercised by the monarch without parliament's consent and a source of reserve power for the king to use in times of need. Early-modern England was saturated with law, with a deep-rooted sense that public life should be governed by law.[91] The possibility of kingly rule outside the bounds of law was disturbing. There was little if any consensus on the relationship between law and prerogative, but legal writers tended to draw a distinction between 'ordinary' and 'absolute' prerogatives. The king had an ordinary, legal prerogative, they said, which he exercised through the common law because it was part of that law. But he also had an absolute prerogative, since he was also God's lieutenant on earth, and in this capacity he could act outside the common law at least in those instances where he believed that the safety of the public required it.[92]

[90] L, 153.

[91] Christopher W. Brooks, *Law, Politics and Society in Early Modern England* (Cambridge University Press, 2008), 135–138.

[92] Glenn Burgess, *The Politics of the Ancient Constitution: An Introduction to English Political Thought, 1603–1642* (London: Macmillan, 1992), 89.

Naturally it was the king's claims in respect of his absolute prerogatives that most troubled contemporaries. These claims were tested on a number of high-profile occasions in the decades preceding the civil war. Hobbes probably wrote *The Elements of Law* as a response to one such moment.[93] In a wider sense, his political theory can be read as a response to the questions of law, authority and obedience that such constitutional moments invoked. The burden of the theory was to defeat the tendentious claims of constitutionalists and believers in fundamental law and divided rule. It is strange, then, that in none of his major works on political theory is the prerogative a feature.[94] (Compare Locke's *Second Treatise of Government.* That slender work contains a chapter dedicated to king's prerogative.[95]) That does not mean that his position on the subject is unclear. His assertion in all the main works that the sovereign is not subject to the civil law is enough to put him clearly on one side of the debate.[96]

Elsewhere in his output, there is a little more to point. In *Behemoth*, as we have seen, Hobbes raises the option of killing a few thousand Presbyterian ministers – presumably an exceptional act outside the reach of normal law – to avoid the bigger slaughter that followed. Questions concerning the existence and scope of various prerogative powers crop up more frequently in the *Dialogue*, which deals directly with contemporary legal and political issues. When they do, Hobbes persistently advocates giving the king the widest degree of latitude in the exercise of those powers. His defence is often strident and derisive of supposed legal limits. On the subject of the king's power to levy soldiers and the money needed

93 Quentin Skinner, *Hobbes and Republican Liberty* (Cambridge University Press, 2008), chapter 3.

94 One possible reason for this silence is that Hobbes was trying to avoid saying too much too directly about contemporary flashpoints. DC, 6: 'I have paid careful attention through the whole length of my discourse not to say anything of the civil laws of any nation, i.e. not to approach shores which are sometimes dangerous because of rocks, sometimes because of current storms.'

95 John Locke, 'The Second Treatise of Government', Chap. XIV 'Of Prerogative' in Peter Laslett (ed.), *Locke: Two Treatises of Government* (Cambridge University Press, 1988). That chapter has generated a substantial literature: see, e.g., Pasquale Pasquino, 'Locke on Kings' Prerogative' (1998) 26 *Political Theory* 198; Clement Fatovic, 'Constitutionalism and Contingency: Locke's Theory of Prerogative' (2004) 25 *History of Political Thought* 276.

96 EL, 166: 'It is an error therefore to think: that the power which is virtually the whole power of the commonwealth, and which in whomsoever it resideth, is usually called supreme or sovereign, can be subject to any law but that of God Almighty.' L, 224: while it is true 'that Sovereigns are all subject to the Lawes of Nature', it is 'repugnant to the nature of the Common-wealth' to imagine that '*he that hath the Soveraign Power, is subject to the Civill Lawes*'.

to pay for them without parliament's consent, Hobbes writes: 'You may therefore think it good Law, for all your Books; that the King of *England* may at all times, that he thinks in his Conscience it will be necessary for the defence of his People, Levy as many Souldiers, and as much Money as he please, and that himself is Judge of the Necessity.'[97] The position entails that the king is entitled to ignore even Acts of Parliament that purport to limit his prerogative.[98]

The same type of argument recurs in relation to other prerogatives – the capacity to do justice in individual cases (equity),[99] the power to punish,[100] and the power to pardon (mercy).[101] In each case, Hobbes stakes a position at the far 'royalist' reaches of the spectrum of contemporary opinion. This is true even of the most significant of absolute prerogatives, the so-called dispensing power. At issue here was whether the sovereign had the power to override or ignore (dispense with) existing law.[102] Hobbes is clear that it does. The safety and well-being of the people, as determined by the sovereign, must trump ordinary norms of behaviour.[103] While there is nothing to stop a king agreeing to pass statutes that restrict his power, those grants are always subject to the more fundamental duty to protect his subjects. A prudent king will consult before dispensing with such a law. But Hobbes leaves us in no doubt that this is exclusively the province of the sovereign:

> But if a King find that by such a Grant he be disabled to protect his Subjects if he maintain his Grant, he sins: and therefore may, and ought to take no Notice of the said Grant: For such Grants as by Error, or false Suggestion are gotten from him, are as the Lawyers do Confess, Void and of no Effect, and ought to be recalled.[104]

Hobbes's analysis of prerogative often sees him slipping from the institutional plane (the institution of sovereign authority) to the individual (the prerogative of the king). Indeed, it is hard to escape the conclusion, on reading passages like this one, that we have moved from the realm of stable and public laws into a world once more beset by private judgement.

97 D, 22. 98 D, 18. 99 D, 55.

100 D, 91: where Hobbes suggests that in respect of exceptional acts that are sins, even where there is no law in place, 'surely the King has power to Punish him (on this side of Life or Member) as he please; and with the Assent of Parliament (if not without) to make the Crime for the future Capital'.

101 D, 127–129.

102 Kenneth Pennington, *The Prince and the Law, 1200–1600* (Berkeley: University of California Press, 1993).

103 Malcolm, *Reason of State*, 117.

104 D, 20.

Hobbes would deny this. In the body of the king, private interest and public interest are almost entirely coextensive.[105] Even if we accept this, the prerogative introduces a destabilizing, anti-formal element into a theory that is otherwise rigorous in its insistence on form and formality in law-making. We are left with something of a puzzle. The sovereign is legally constituted, but sovereign capacity is not exhausted by law nor is sovereign power constrained by law. Existing law can be ignored if the sovereign thinks that it needs to be.[106]

The prerogative opens up a fissure within Hobbes's theory that is not easily closed. One approach that might help us is to pay attention to the theory's self-description as a science of politics. The commonwealth should apply Hobbes's principles for the 'well governing of mens Actions' if it seeks peace and good order.[107] 'Sovereigns act, and the science on the basis of which they act is Hobbesian civil science.'[108] Civil science must be able to explain two things in respect of the prerogative. First, why in principle you need so much of this type of power (as per the *Dialogue*). Second, why in practice you expect prerogative powers – or at least the more serious of them – to be used very rarely (as per *Leviathan*). Answering the first question is straightforward. Sovereignty requires plenitude of power – power needs to be united in the hands of one authority.[109] Absent which a stable and well-ordered commonwealth is impossible: it takes Leviathan to subdue Behemoth. This position requires a sovereign with a capacity unlimited by other institutions or by existing laws for the sovereign to do what he thinks is necessary to preserve order.

The answer to the second question is more complicated. We can accept that Hobbes's project is a normalizing one that favours ordinary law over extraordinary prerogative. But it is still not clear what basis we have for

[105] L, 131.

[106] Hobbes's broad interpretation of what counts as the safety of the public serves merely to heighten the tensions here. See, e.g., EL, 172: '*Salus populi suprema lex*; by which must be understood, not the mere preservation of their lives, but generally their benefit and good.'

[107] See the Dedicatory Letter to *De Cive*. DC, 4. See also Thomas Hobbes, 'The Verse Life: A Contemporary Translation (Anonymous)' in *Human Nature and De Corpore Politico*, 257: 'To Various Matter and Various Motion brings/ Me, and the different Species of Things./ Man's inward Motions and his Thoughts to know,/ The good of Government, and Justice too,/ These were my Studies then, and in these three/ Consists the whole course of Philosophy:/ Man, Body, Citizen.'

[108] Ross Harrison, *Hobbes, Locke and Confusion's Masterpiece: An Examination of Seventeenth-Century Political Philosophy* (Cambridge University Press, 2002), 59.

[109] Denis Baranger, *Écrire la Constitution Non-Écrite: Une Introduction au Droit Politique Britannique* (Paris: Presses Universitaires de France, 2008), 228.

thinking that the sovereign, given the option of going outside the laws, would choose to remain within them. Why choose law, with its formal and institutional constraints, when you could enjoy the much freer style of rule through prerogative? The sovereign, then, seems to have a 'commitment' problem that persists so long as he can break the legal fetters whenever he chooses. Russell Hardin's reading of Hobbes as a proto-game theorist might offer a way forward.[110] The whole point for Hobbes of artificial virtues like law and justice, Hardin argues, is strategic. 'They are valued not per se but rather for their beneficial regulation of social interaction.'[111] If civil and political relations could be modelled as a series of one-off games between sovereign and his subjects, then we might well expect the sovereign to opt for the prerogative. The prerogative has less baggage (fewer formalities and constraints) and so lets him get what he wants done with a minimum of fuss. But Hobbes rightly sees the civil condition as an ongoing affair. And in repeated games law is to be preferred. We remarked earlier on the enormous coordinating capacity of law. Prerogative gives you no such pay-off over the long run, since it is anti-formal and unpredictable. The more recourse the sovereign makes to his prerogatives, the more he will undermine law's capacity to act as a stable framework for political and social obligations. The result is less efficiency in the operation of rule. And, since it would be less clear what the real obligations of the subjects are (and even less clear what they are likely to be in future), it would also result in less trust and less loyalty. Subjects would begin to see the sovereign as incapable of providing the benefits of efficient rule by law (order and security) and begin to treat him as a terribly powerful private enemy.

The sovereign chooses law because reason tells him to.[112] Does that mean that we can ignore prerogative power, or at least relegate it to a box marked 'only in case of dire need'? I don't think so. Although he is not terribly clear on this, Hobbes's insight may be that the prerogative is one of the operating conditions of effective law. Sovereign authority flows through law but prerogative power is needed to institute law. The

110 John Finnis, 'Law's Authority and Social Theory's Predicament' in John Finnis, *Philosophy of Law: Collected Essays, Vol. IV* (Oxford University Press, 2011), 55: 'Some theorists, like Hobbes, have thought to explain the point of legal regulation in terms of one of the paradigm games in game theory: the Prisoners' Dilemma', referring in particular to Hobbes's state of nature.

111 Hardin, 'Hobbesian Political Order', 163.

112 A decision made easier since, as Noel Malcolm reminds us, reason instructs the sovereign to be neither a warmonger nor a natural coloniser: 'Hobbes's Theory of International Relations' in Malcolm, *Aspects of Hobbes*.

sovereign must have at his disposal a spectrum of special legal and extra-legal capacities up to and including the power to dispense with particular laws and the power to act ruthlessly (the killing of Presbyterian ministers) where the public interest demands it. On this reading, prerogative acts as something like the dark matter of Hobbes's constitutional universe.[113] Rarely visible, its residual presence holds together the more prominent and, in the normal course of events, more important stuff of political life. The civil laws in particular cannot properly be understood without it. Law's stabilizing and harmonizing functions can only take effect in the shadow of this only partly legal framework of power. The possibility of overwhelming force, concentrated in the hands of the supreme law-maker, is what allows law to be law. Odd though it may seem, if our goal is peace, this concentration of force and law is essential. The availability of force on this scale, behind the operation of normal law, makes the sovereign feel secure and so more likely to exercise power through normal legal channels.[114] Beyond the specific (and presumptively reasonable) sanctions that individual laws may carry, it also inclines subjects towards obedience.

'Civill, and Naturall Law are not different kinds, but different parts of law'

The relationship between law and equity is another complicating feature of Hobbes's jurisprudence, and the last to be discussed here. The function of law is to reduce disagreement in the interests of stability and security. As such, laws ought to be clearly promulgated and honestly applied. It also entails, as we have seen, the harmonization of law, a process that involves among other things a denial of the autonomy of the common law. Yet apparently at odds with this trend towards jurisdictional hegemony, Hobbes adds an extra layer, equity, on top of the civil law. This arrangement

[113] In astronomy, dark matter is a currently undetermined type of matter which accounts for a large part of the mass of the universe (thought to be 83 per cent of the mass in the universe and 23 per cent of the mass-energy) but neither emits nor scatters light or other electromagnetic radiation and so cannot be directly seen with telescopes. Its existence is inferred from its effects on visible matter. Dark matter is what created the structure of the universe and is essentially what holds it together.

[114] Compare David Hume, 'Of Passive Obedience' in David Hume, *Essays – Moral, Political and Literary*, edited by Eugene F. Miller (Indianapolis: Liberty Fund, 1987), 492: 'Where the king is an absolute sovereign, he has little temptation to commit such enormous tyranny as may justly provoke rebellion: But where he is limited, his imprudent ambition, without any great vices, may run him into that perillous situation.'

has the potential to complicate the network of legal relationships within the commonwealth and so needs to be explained.

Equity plays an important, if ambiguous, role in Hobbes's theory. Equity is the law of reason given political form. It operates on two levels, the conceptual and the institutional, that is, both as a body of law and a jurisdiction. The relationship between equity and civil law at first seems straightforward. Equity is unwritten law and is subordinate to the civil law – it 'may by the Civill Law be abridged, and restrained'.[115] The subaltern position of equity is necessitated by Hobbes's theory of sovereignty. But this is not the end of the matter, for Hobbes clearly imagines the law and equity existing in a denser relationship: 'Civill, and Naturall Law are not different kinds, but different parts of Law; whereof one part being written, is called Civill, the other unwritten, Naturall.'[116] And, indeed, when we look more closely we find that the equity component of law is much more pronounced than we might have expected from a theory that pays so much attention to the formal elements of law.

Law is always open to interpretation, Hobbes acknowledges,[117] and should be interpreted according to the meaning or spirit rather than the letter of the law.[118] Equity has a direct role to play in statutory interpretation. The judge should try to interpret the law so that it accords with equity[119] and should always presume, absent an explicit command to the contrary, that the sovereign intends to legislate in accordance with the principles of equity.[120] Equity is important at the appellate level too. The

[115] L, 185. See also D, 25: equity is unwritten law and as 'Distinct from Statute-Law, [it] is nothing else but the Law of God … Natural Reason'. See also EL, 182: 'Written laws therefore are the constitution of a commonwealth expressed; and unwritten, are the laws of natural reason.'

[116] L, 185. In this, Hobbes was in line with Renaissance understandings of law and legal text. Ian Maclean, *Interpretation and Meaning in the Renaissance: The Case of Law* (Cambridge University Press, 1992), 87–88: 'The need for interpretation arises from a fundamental asymmetry in the law itself. The written law is, on the one hand, not the law; rather it embodies more or less directly and successfully the norms and force of the law … The law, on the other hand, *is* the spoken or written law.'

[117] Although sometimes through gritted teeth. D, 48: 'I believe that Men at this day have better learn't the Art of Caviling against the words of a Statute, than heretofore they had, and thereby encourage themselves, and others, to undertake Suits upon little Reason. Also the variety and repugnancy of Judgments of Common-Law do oftentimes put Men to hope for Victory in causes, whereof in reason they had no ground at all.'

[118] L, 190. 'For it is not the Letter, but the Intendment, or Meaning; that is to say, the authentique Interpretation of the Law (which is the sense of the Legislator) in which the nature of the Law consisteth.'

[119] L, 191. [120] L, 194.

interpretative openness of law means that there will inevitably be mistakes in the application of laws.[121] Two kinds of redundancies (or back-up systems) are introduced to take account of judicial fallibility. First, the sovereign is to handpick the judges. At least then there is a chance of consistency in the application of the laws.[122] There is no particular need to appoint legal specialists.[123] A judge, on Hobbes's account, does not work from precedents[124] but from his own sense of equity, a quality which depends 'on the goodnesse of a mans own naturall Reason, and Meditation'.[125] Second, there needs to be a jurisdiction capable of correcting mistakes that occur in the legal system. Subjects are entitled, for instance, to bring actions against corrupt or dishonest judges[126] (another aspect of the public law jurisdiction envisaged by Hobbes).

This second redundancy reveals the jurisdictional nature of Hobbes's use of the word 'equity'. Equity was not for Hobbes or his contemporaries a free-floating category of legal principles. It was rather a particular court – Chancery – and a particular body of law that stemmed from it. The Court of Chancery was originally part of a department of state, whose head, the chancellor, was a senior minister of the crown. As well as its administrative tasks, Chancery developed two judicial functions, the more important of which (the 'English side') evolved into a flexible jurisdiction handling cases about wrongs that the ordinary law could not or would not cure. Most chancellors were bishops and Chancery officials were mainly clerics, so naturally this jurisdiction was influenced by principles of equity derived from canon law and civil law (*ius civile*).[127] The justice practised in the Chancery was described earlier in its development as 'conscience', later as 'equity'. 'Conscience' meant (probably) the private knowledge or belief of legally relevant facts that had not been appropriately pleaded and proved according to the common law's rigid system of pleading.[128] The Chancery's role was to correct injustices that resulted

[121] L, 192: there is 'no Judge Subordinate, nor Soveraign, but may erre in Judgement of Equity; if afterward in another like case he find it more consonant to Equity to give a contrary Sentence, he is obliged to do it'.

[122] L, 190.

[123] In fact, he argues in the *Dialogue* that bishops would do a better job: 'but certainly they are, especially the Bishops, the best able to Judge of matters of Reason; that is to say … of matters (except of Blood) at the Common-Law' (31).

[124] L, 193. [125] L, 195. [126] L, 168.

[127] Ronald A. Marchant, *The Church under the Law: Justice, Administration and Discipline in the Diocese of York, 1560–1640* (Cambridge University Press, 1969), 2. See also Maclean, *Interpretation and Meaning in the Renaissance*, 185–186.

[128] Mike Macnair, 'Equity and Conscience' (2007) 27 *Oxford Journal of Legal Studies* 659.

from that system. Chancery decisions supplemented the common law – they did not alter common law rules. The Court 'behaved much more like a jury than a court of law'.[129] It could act in the way it did because of its proximity to the king. The king's duty to dispense justice required not just that the law was observed. It also meant providing redress in cases where the law itself was defective.[130] The Chancery's equitable jurisdiction was thus as much an expression of bureaucratic power, and an example of centralized control, as a particular brand of justice. As J.B. Post observes, it is 'much more important to regard the medieval Chancery as a supplementary jurisdiction than as a jurisdiction of supplementary law'.[131]

This contextual analysis reveals what precisely Hobbes is arguing here. Law and equity are conceptually distinct but exist in a symbiotic relationship. Law is central for structuring relationships of authority and obligation within the commonwealth, as we have seen. But those artificial chains of authority are to be oiled by equitable principles. His suggestion as to how this is to be done is radical and amounts almost to the swamping of civil (or common) law by equity. The common law judge should act like an equity judge, in fact just like a miniature version of the medieval chancellor. Each case is to be treated on its merits.[132] Accordingly, no legal training is required. The disposition of a case requires simply the application of natural reason and meditation ('conscience'). And the system of the common law as a whole is made subject to the equity jurisdiction of Chancery (or a court just like it). Why is this necessary, the Lawyer asks in the *Dialogue*, if equity is already part of the common law (as Hobbes in the guise of the Philosopher has suggested)? Were judges infallible then it would be unnecessary, the Philosopher replies. But they are fallible and so

[129] Timothy S. Haskett, 'The Medieval Court of Chancery' (1996) 14 *Law and History Review* 245, 270.

[130] J.L. Barton, 'Equity in the Medieval Common Law' in R.A. Newman (ed.), *Equity in the World's Legal Systems* (Brussels: Établissements Émile Bruylant 1973), 145–147.

[131] J.B. Post, 'Equitable Resorts before 1450' in E.W. Ives and A.H. Manchester (eds), *Papers Presented to the Fourth British Legal History Conference, University of Birmingham 1970* (London: Royal Historical Society Studies in History, no. 26, 1983), 68–9.

[132] By the early seventeenth century, Chancery judges had long been leading the way in treating cases on their merits rather than in accordance with established rules. In doing so, they quite regularly relied upon precedents as recorded in the Chancery Register's Books, although in looking at prior decisions they were usually looking for similar actions on similar facts and were not especially interested in what earlier judges had to say. See W.H.D. Winder, 'Precedent in Equity' (1941) 57 *Law Quarterly Review* 245; Neil Duxbury, *The Nature and Authority of Precedent* (Cambridge University Press, 2008), 53, n 96.

the king must find a way to remedy injustice caused by 'the Ignorance, or Corruption of a Judge'.[133]

So the relationship between law and equity, despite first appearances, fits Hobbes's harmonizing agenda. But it does so in a way that sheds light on his conception of law. Principles of equity give substance to the formal and strategic functions that are inherent to law and legal order. They must therefore be allowed to permeate the operation of law both in the resolution of individual cases and at the appellate level. Judges are appointed on the basis of their ability to operate effectively within an equity-dominated legal framework. Meanwhile, the task of ensuring that justice is done across the system is given to a court of equitable jurisdiction operated by officials situated as close as possible to the source of justice, the sovereign. To insist that the law is infused with equity in this way stems in part from Hobbes's recognition that law is not just a formal process, that the operation of law involves considerations of justice and fairness not spelled out in the laws themselves. But it is also about the strategic needs of sovereign authority requiring a streamlined, bureaucratic system of justice under law.

Conclusion

Civil life is fragile and only law conjoined with power can hold it together. Hobbes's proposal for peace within the commonwealth pivots around three key juridical themes.

1. Hobbes's rule of law sensibility flows from the conviction that stability and security are fundamental to peaceful coexistence. This perspective generates demands for certainty and clarity within the system of law. Law is civil law is the public command of the sovereign. Other potential forms of law – natural law, custom etc. – are declassified and relegated to subordinate categories. Law structures expectations and obligations, enabling the sovereign to rule effectively and citizens to plan their lives. The formal properties of law are important in this scheme. It is the use of a particular form that allows us to identify the public commands of the sovereign. Such an action turns a private wish of a powerful individual or body into the public command of the sovereign. And only these commands trigger public obligations that we are obliged to obey and that are enforceable by the sovereign's officials. Authority being both top-down and bottom-up, Hobbes insists that laws must be promulgated and publicized by the

[133] D, 31.

sovereign. The logic of this position entails that courts refuse to enforce a putative law that has not been properly publicized. And, indeed, Hobbes stakes out a public law jurisdiction that allows subjects to bring claims against the sovereign in the sovereign's courts. Such suits do not count as challenges to the sovereign largely because they turn on the formal qualities of the laws they challenge. Nor are the judges who refuse to uphold a sovereign command as law acting improperly. They are fulfilling their duty to uphold the system of rule by ensuring the integrity of the laws issued in the sovereign's name.

2. This structured and formal account of a rule of law system needs to be set against Hobbes's view of the sovereign's prerogatives. In one sense, it is self-evident that the sovereign must have an array of prerogative powers, including powers that Locke called *extra et contra legem*, since sovereignty is for Hobbes an absolute and legally unbounded condition. But there are two complications. The first is textual. Hobbes's main works are near silent on the specific issue. The *Dialogue*, by contrast, shows Hobbes defending full and extensive prerogative powers. The second is more substantial. How does this defence of a strong prerogative fit with Hobbes's rule of law theory? Clearly the formal presuppositions of the latter can be undermined by the anti-formal freedom of the former. The best way of reducing these complications is to take seriously the theory's self-description as civil science. Despite appearances to the contrary, the sovereign has only one rational option: to choose law in all but exceptional cases. To do otherwise would be to undermine the conditions in which the rule of law can operate and thus risk the viability of the commonwealth. Nonetheless, even if prerogative power is only rarely if ever put into operation, its existence is a precondition for the effective exercise of legal authority. The possibility of overwhelming and unconstrained force, concentrated in the sovereign's hands, is what allows law to be law.

3. The relationship between sovereign and law needs also to be explored through the prism of what Hobbes has to say about equity. Equity is how natural law enters the political realm. In a sense, then, it has to be subordinate to the civil law. As the public commands of the sovereign, these have superior legal status within the commonwealth. Yet Hobbes is also clear that law and equity exist in a complex relationship. Indeed, law is infused with equity in such a way as to make one wonder whether equity is not the superior partner. Judges are to decide legal cases in the manner of the equity judge. And the civil law jurisdiction is to be subject to an equity court. One reason for this arrangement is contextual and jurisdictional. Hobbes and his contemporaries associated equity with the Court

of Chancery and thus with the residual capacity of the monarch to do justice, particularly where none was available through the ordinary law. As such, to favour equity over law is to argue for a more centralized, even bureaucratized, system of justice. And centralizing and harmonizing the legal system is a central strand of Hobbes's theory of law. But it also shows that, for Hobbes, the exercise of sovereign authority (through civil law) is accompanied by an internal code (through natural law) by means of which the law is interpreted and applied. In its application, civil law is interpreted and applied through what we might call (although Hobbes didn't) canons of legality – including, for instance, the injunction that the judge must always suppose that the legislator intends to act in accordance with equity. Natural law wraps round and insinuates itself within positive law. Perhaps this is what Hobbes meant when he said that natural law and civil law 'contain each other, and are of equall extent'.[134] Positive law is the sovereign's, as are the courts, but the strictures of legality are not, at least not in any straightforward sense.

[134] L, 185.

6

Criminal law for humans

ALICE RISTROPH

Thomas Hobbes was a theorist of the human animal, and he forgot neither the fact that humans *are* animals nor the distinctive characteristics of *this* animal. It is easy to exaggerate the brutishness of Hobbesian man, especially when one compares Hobbes's account of the state of nature and his argument for a powerful sovereign to contemporary theories of divided, limited government. But it pays to look closely at the way Hobbes used his famous epithets. He never called his fellow humans nasty or brutish (or short); these words described instead the conditions of human life in the absence of civil society governed by an established sovereign. Humans themselves, whether within society or without, Hobbes appeared to view with understanding and respect.[1] His appreciation for the many dimensions of the human animal produces an account of criminal law and punishment both familiar and strange.

It is familiar, because Hobbes's view of the proper content and form of the substantive criminal law corresponds quite closely to contemporary Anglo-American law. Among other things, Hobbes advocated written statutes and impartial adjudicators; notice requirements and a prohibition of *ex post facto* laws; laws that punished action rather than intent alone; a special condemnation of physically injurious activity; an individual right of self-defence; excuses based on incapacity and duress; and a graded scale of crime seriousness that generates correspondingly graded punishments. In some respects, Hobbes simply adopted within his theory already existing features of English law, features that survive in contemporary

[1] According to George Kateb, Hobbes's writings display his 'passionate tenderness' for his fellow humans. George Kateb, 'Hobbes and the Irrationality of Politics' (1989) 17 *Political Theory* 355, 385. Slightly less sentimentally, Stephen Holmes suggests that 'Hobbes probably viewed most people as pitiable chumps. But he wrote sincerely on their behalf'. Stephen Holmes, 'Introduction' to Thomas Hobbes, *Behemoth, or the Long Parliament* (University of Chicago Press, 1990), xiii n. 16.

criminal law. In other respects, though, Hobbes was ahead of his time: his arguments for statutes over common law, for legislative rather than judicial determination of the content of criminal prohibitions, and for determinate sentencing, ran counter to seventeenth-century English practices but prefigured legal reforms that would be widely adopted long after he wrote.

And yet Hobbes's account is also startling and strange for its discussions of punishment. Hobbes asserted the sovereign's need and right to punish criminals, but he also insisted that punishment was an act of violence that the criminal had a right to resist. Scholars today devote considerable effort to the articulation and refinement of theories of justified punishment; very few express any doubt that some satisfactory justification of punishment exists. Hobbes's theory of punishment is surprising in its implication that punishment, while necessary, is at best imperfectly legitimate in a political system grounded in the consent of the subjects.

Both the familiar content of Hobbes's criminal law theory and his more surprising claims about punishment are, I suggest, the product of his unwavering attention to the humanity of the various persons who make, break and enforce the criminal law. His criminal law addresses and sometimes accommodates human frailty, but as or more importantly, it also reveals a commitment to equal human dignity. Be they victims or criminals, humans are physically vulnerable creatures whose passions may lead them astray but whose instinct for self-preservation is to be respected. Criminal law and punishment are necessary to steer men's actions towards peace and away from conflict. Punishment is not, however, an occasion for the law-abiding or the enforcer to engage in moral self-congratulation. It is instead an occasion for regret; it is evidence that the project of consensual government has failed in some way. Ultimately, then, Hobbes's account of criminal law and punishment offers broader lessons about the promise, and limits, of liberalism.

The content and form of the criminal law

To see how Hobbes offered a theory of criminal law for humans, it will help to remember what he viewed as the most important shared characteristics of human beings. Among political thinkers, and almost certainly among early liberal thinkers, he was unusually attentive to man's status as an animal: as a sentient, embodied and mortal being. Importantly, humans are animals with *vulnerable* bodies; each and every person is susceptible to injury and death. Common physical vulnerability is Hobbes's starting point for his description of the human condition. Although there are some variations in intellectual capacities and physical strengths, the degree of variation is limited. We all die eventually, and even more importantly, we all have the capacities to kill and be killed. 'For as to the strength of body, the weakest has strength enough to kill the strongest, either by secret machination, or by confederacy with others, that are in the same danger with himself.'[2] No one is so strong or so smart that he will avoid death, or that he can repel any and all physical assaults coordinated by other human beings.

And yet avoiding death is just what we (usually) want to do. Almost as undeniable as the fact that we live in physical bodies is the fact that we wish to keep living with those bodies intact. On Hobbes's account, this inclination is as self-evident and as natural as gravity: man avoids death 'by a certain impulsion of nature, no less than that whereby a stone moves downward'.[3] The 'necessity of nature' leads us to seek 'that which is good for themselves, and to avoid that which is hurtful; but most of all, the terrible enemy of nature, death, from whom we expect both the loss of all power, and also the greatest of bodily pains in the losing'.[4]

While an appreciation for humans' physical vulnerability proves central to Hobbesian criminal law, it is important to remember that Hobbes did not reduce the human animal to its corporeal body. Hobbes resisted the metaphysical claims of Cartesian dualism, in which mind and body are ontologically distinct. He scorned the 'gross errors' of the 'writers of metaphysics [who] consider thought without the consideration of body' and thus fail to conceptualize 'a thinking-body'.[5] Thinking is more than simple sentience; as thinking bodies, we do not merely suffer pain and eventual death. We are conscious of our own physical vulnerabilities, and we are capable of fear, anger, vengefulness, righteousness, and myriad other emotions and passions. We are also capable of rational thought and deliberation, and our thinking may sometimes address matters of little relation to our embodiment.[6] Corporeal vulnerability explains much

[2] Thomas Hobbes, *Leviathan* (Cambridge University Press, 1996), 87.

[3] Thomas Hobbes, *De Cive, or The Citizen* (New York: Appleton-Century-Crofts, 1949), 26.

[4] Thomas Hobbes, 'De Corpore' in *The English Works of Thomas Hobbes*, edited by Sir William Molesworth (London: Bohn, 1640/1839), vol. IV, 83.

[5] *Ibid.*, vol. I, 34. See Samantha Frost, 'Faking It: Hobbes's Thinking-Bodies and the Ethics of Dissimulation' (2001) 29 *Political Theory* 30, 33–34.

[6] Michael Oakeshott has similarly observed that Hobbes's view of humans emphasizes both their 'bodily structure' and their 'other endowments' such as memory, imagination and rationality. Michael Oakeshott, 'The Moral Life in the Writings of Thomas Hobbes' in *Hobbes on Civil Association* (Indianapolis: Liberty Fund, 2000), 85–89.

of the content of the criminal law, but as we will see, it does not explain everything.

From the very outset of his discussion of criminal law in *Leviathan*, Hobbes emphasized its distinctively human quality. In contrast to sin, a broad category of wrongdoing that includes evil thoughts detectable only by God, crime must be designated as such by a human legislator, charged by a human accuser, and adjudicated by a human judge.[7] In the absence of civil law and an established sovereign, nothing may be properly called crime.[8] Or as criminal law scholars put it, *nullum crimen sine lege*: no crime without [human] law. Law itself Hobbes defined in terms of a human relationship: 'Law in general is not counsel but command; nor a command of any man to any man; but only of him, whose command is addressed to one formerly obliged to obey him.'[9] (It is thus an oversimplification to categorize Hobbes as a 'command theorist' of law, since on his account obligation and authority are at least as essential to law as the command itself.) For reasons discussed in more detail below, in *Leviathan* Hobbes argued also that criminal prohibitions required a written statute rather than mere judicial decisions.[10]

In some tension with the account of crime in *Leviathan*, the 'Philosopher' in Hobbes's *Dialogue on the Common Laws of England* describes treason as a *malum in se* offence – a 'crime in itself', made criminal by reason rather than only by statute.[11] Elsewhere in the *Dialogue*, however, and at much greater length, the same Philosopher argues against a conception of common law that would allow the content of law to be determined by lawyers and judges. Against his interlocutor's suggestion that legal scholars possess special insights into the law, the Philosopher replies that '[i]t is not wisdom, but authority, that makes a law'.[12] To equate law with wisdom or reason would invite each individual to use his own reason to determine for himself what the law required, which would open the door to a

[7] Hobbes, *Leviathan*, 201–202.

[8] *Ibid.*, 202. [9] *Ibid.*, 183. [10] *Ibid.*, 190, 202–203.

[11] Thomas Hobbes, *A Dialogue Between a Philosopher and a Student of the Common Laws of England* (University of Chicago Press, 1971), 102. It is not entirely clear how to interpret the *Dialogue* as a statement of Hobbes's views. It is structured as a discussion, with some disagreements, between a 'Philosopher' and a 'Lawyer'. The Philosopher often expresses views consistent with Hobbes's arguments in other writings, but occasionally the Lawyer does the same, and each articulates some positions at odds with the claims Hobbes made elsewhere. Moreover, the work was published only posthumously and is almost certainly unfinished, with some speeches apparently assigned to the wrong speaker. See Joseph Cropsey, 'Introduction' to Hobbes, *Dialogue*, 2–8.

[12] Hobbes, *Dialogue*, 55.

plurality of interpretations that the Philosopher, and Hobbes in his own voice, clearly found objectionable. The common law was a 'disputable art' and thus inferior to the clear command of the sovereign found in a statute.[13] Indeed, much of the *Dialogue* is a critique of Sir Edward Coke's defence of common law reasoning. The Philosopher resists the general suggestion that lawyers or judges may determine law through the distinctive faculty of legal reason, and also occasionally mocks Coke's specific conclusions, such as the argument that to cut another man's wheat and throw it immediately into one's cart is not a felony, but to allow it to fall to the ground and then place it in one's cart is felony theft.[14] 'If [Coke's] definitions be the rule of law, what is there that he may not make felony, or not felony, at his pleasure? … [T]o me it seems so far from reason as I think it ridiculous.'[15]

To reconcile these seemingly inconsistent positions, one could read the discussion of 'crimes in themselves' in the *Dialogue* as an account of the 'minimum content' of a penal code.[16] In other words, Hobbes did not retreat from the principle that law should be statutorily rather than judicially determined, but certain harmful activities such as treason and killing must be banned in any rational legal system. Hobbes appeared to hold fairly conventional views about the kinds of acts that were *mala in se*: treason (since an assault on the king was an assault on the safety of the people as a whole); killing; robbery; theft.[17] And among those acts, Hobbes ranked offences, classifying those that inflicted the worst harm to the vulnerable human body, or the worst fear to the psyche, as the most serious. 'To kill against the law, is a greater crime, than any other injury, life preserved. And to kill with torment, greater, than simply to kill. And mutilation of a limb, greater, than the spoiling a man of his goods. And the spoiling a man of his goods, by terror of death, or wounds, than by clandestine surreption.'[18] One might contrast this emphasis on the distinct wrongfulness of physical injury to the writings of some later British thinkers, who would argue that property crimes required governmental

[13] *Ibid.*, 69, 71; see also 121 (a criminal jury ought not to consider the interpretation of the law from Sir Edward Coke or any 'private lawyer', but only 'the statutes themselves pleaded before them').

[14] *Ibid.*, 119. [15] *Ibid.*

[16] The reference is to Hart's discussion of 'the minimum content of natural law'. See H.L.A. Hart, *The Concept of Law* (Oxford University Press, 1961), 193–200.

[17] Hobbes, *Dialogue*, 111.

[18] Hobbes, *Leviathan*, 212. Hobbes said relatively little about rape or other sexual offences, but did specify that forcible rape was a more serious crime than seduction by flattery, and rape of a married woman worse than rape of an unmarried woman. *Ibid.*, 213.

action more than did interpersonal violence.[19] Hobbes's emphasis on physically injurious crimes is consistent with modern criminal codes, which usually treat crimes of violence as more serious offences than property crimes. More generally, Hobbes suggested that crimes should be scaled according to factors such as 'malignity of the source' (which may be a reference to culpable intent, as evidenced by the murder-manslaughter distinction discussed below), the harmful effect of the offence, and the risk that the offence would lead to copycat offences.[20]

Even within a single category of violent crime, Hobbes urged further delineations consistent with then-extant common law principles that have largely survived into the twenty-first century. For example, Hobbes identified secretive killings as particularly heinous, both because it was harder to identify the killer and because such killings left other humans acutely aware of their own mortality.[21] Similarly, many modern homicide statutes identify more secretive killings, such as those by poison or 'lying in wait', as forms of first degree murder. Hobbes also seemed to endorse the common law distinction between murder and manslaughter, in which 'a crime arising from a sudden passion, is not so great, as when the same arises from long meditation'.[22] This distinction was based on a concession to human weakness: crimes of passion, Hobbes suggested, arose from 'the common infirmity of human nature'. Still, sudden passion could at most reduce the penalty and could not serve as a total excuse; each person has an obligation to strive 'to rectify the irregularity of his passions continually'.[23]

[19] '[W]hen one man kills, wounds, beats or defames another, though he to whom the injury is done suffers, he who does it receives no benefit. It is otherwise with the injuries to property.' Adam Smith, *An Inquiry into the Nature and Causes of the Wealth of Nations* (London: Methuen, 1904), vol. II, 202–203. Smith argued that violent crimes were motivated by 'envy, malice, or resentment', passions of only limited influence on human behaviour. In contrast, 'avarice and ambition in the rich, in the poor the hatred of labour and the love of present ease and enjoyment, are the passions which prompt to invade property; passions much more steady in their operation, and much more universal in their influence'. *Ibid.*, 203. Similarly, David Hume suggested that of three 'species of goods' humans possess – 'the internal satisfactions of our minds, the external advantages of our body, and the enjoyment of such possessions as we have acquired by our industry and good fortune' – only the third was sufficiently threatened by others' wrongful acts to merit governmental protection. David Hume, *A Treatise of Human Nature* (Oxford: Clarendon Press, 1888), 487–488.

[20] Hobbes, *Leviathan*, 209.

[21] Hobbes, *Dialogue*, 112.

[22] Hobbes, *Leviathan*, 210.

[23] *Ibid.* The distinction between murder and manslaughter is also addressed in the *Dialogue*, where the Philosopher appears to raise some doubts about whether all crimes of passion lack 'malice aforethought'. Hobbes, *Dialogue*, 114.

The distinction between murder and manslaughter suggests that Hobbes was concerned not only with the humanity of potential crime victims, but also with the humanity of the criminal. The humanity of the Hobbesian lawbreaker is evident in at least three features of his work. First, Hobbesian criminal law is structured to give incentives to thinking-bodies – to rational and embodied beings capable of responding to incentives but also driven at times by irrational passions. Second, as we have already seen illustrated in the discussion of crimes of passion, Hobbes sometimes mitigated criminal liability according to certain recognized human limitations or weaknesses. Finally, and most interestingly, Hobbes believed each criminal to have a right to resist his lawful punishment.

The purpose of criminal law, Hobbes made clear, is to shape human behaviour and, more narrowly, to discourage harmful conduct. Accordingly, the law must keep its subjects in mind; it must be designed so that humans can, and likely will, understand it and adhere to it. Prior notice is thus essential to legal obligation. The law must be published and promulgated so that subjects will know of its commands. Hobbes did concede that some unwritten rules could bind – the laws of nature – because these rules are obvious to any rational human.[24] But for the vast majority of laws, Hobbes expected a prior, written (or otherwise 'published') promulgation of the sovereign's command.[25] Aside from the self-evident laws of nature, it is insufficient to rely on reason as a guide to the content of the law, because humans are capable of rational disagreement: 'the doubt of it is, of whose reason it is, that shall be received for law.'[26] These concerns led to Hobbes's preference, discussed above, for statutory law over judicially developed common law. Common law leaves greater uncertainty about the content of the law – and gives subordinate judges the opportunity to usurp the sovereign's lawmaking power. The requirement of prior notice prohibits *ex post facto* laws, of course, and Hobbes also endorsed the related principle that once a specific penalty has been published, an offender may not be punished in excess of that penalty.[27] Relatedly, Hobbes argued that penalties must be applied consistently: a criminal who violated a law that had previously gone unpunished (such as the prohibition of duels) should

[24] Hobbes, *Leviathan*, 188.

[25] *Ibid.*, 188 ('The law of nature excepted, it belongs to the essence of all other laws to be made known to every man that shall be obliged to obey them, either by word, or writing, or some other act, known to proceed from the sovereign authority'); see also *ibid.*, 203 ('[I]f the civil law of a man's own country be not sufficiently declared as he may know it if he will, nor the action against the law of nature, the ignorance is a good excuse').

[26] *Ibid.*, 189. [27] *Ibid.*, 203–204.

be at least partially excused, since the earlier failure to punish would have signalled the sovereign's tacit acceptance of the criminal activity.[28]

Attention to the humanity of the criminal is evident in Hobbes's discussion of a range of criminal law defences, including incapacity, duress, necessity, self-defence and ignorance of law. Those without capacity to know the law (such as 'natural fools, children, or mad-men', or one who has lost his mental faculties in 'any accident [not] proceeding from his own default') are not bound by it and are excused for any violation.[29] More broadly, Hobbes believed that the criminal law must accommodate the powerful drive for self-preservation. He recognized a defence akin to what modern legal systems call duress or compulsion: 'If a man by terror of present death, be compelled to do a fact against the law, he is totally excused; because no law can oblige a man to abandon his own preservation.'[30] For similar reasons, Hobbes recognized a defence of necessity. 'When a man is destitute of food, or other thing necessary for his life, and cannot preserve himself any other way, but by some fact against the law; as if in a great famine he take the food by force … which he cannot obtain for money nor charity … he is totally excused.'[31] And of course, Hobbes the theorist of self-preservation could not fail to recognize a strong claim of self-defence. 'A man is assaulted, fears present death, from which he sees not how to escape, but by wounding him that assaults him; If he wound him to death, this is no crime, because no man is supposed at the making of a commonwealth to have abandoned the defence of his life or limbs where the law cannot arrive time enough to his assistance.'[32] Notably, this account of self-defence reflects traditional common law restrictions on the right to use deadly force that survive in contemporary doctrinal rules. The threat must be imminent; it must be one of death or great bodily injury; and the force must be necessary (i.e. there must be no opportunity to seek official protection).[33] In sharp contrast to contemporary law, however, Hobbes did not restrict the right to use force in self-defence to those who faced *unlawful* threats of harm. The individual's right of self-preservation produces a right to resist even the duly authorized sovereign, or his agents, should they pose a threat of physical harm or injury – as they often do, for instance, when they seek to impose punishment. The right to resist

[28] *Ibid.*, 211.

[29] *Ibid.*, 187; see also 208 ('The want of means to know the Law, totally Excuseth').

[30] *Ibid.*, 208. [31] *Ibid.* [32] *Ibid.*, 206.

[33] These restrictions on the legally recognized right of self-defence – the right of self-defence in civil society – do not apply in the state of nature, where each individual has a right to use force whenever he thinks necessary, even in the absence of an imminent threat.

punishment is one of the most intriguing features of Hobbes's discussion of criminal law, and I address it in a separate section below.

In keeping with his insistence on notice as a condition of legal obligation, Hobbes endorsed a fairly broad ignorance of law defence. As we have seen, ignorance is no excuse to a violation of the law of nature, nor is one excused if he fails to know the civil law through mere 'want of diligence'.[34] But ignorance may excuse a violation of a civil law if the law is not 'sufficiently declared, as he may know it if he will'.[35] This language suggests the possibility that even a written law may be too obscure or imprecise to oblige subjects. Further, Hobbes argued that those who misunderstand the law thanks to the teachings of some public authority should be excused.[36] This defence appears similar to the modern 'reasonable reliance' defence suggested by the Model Penal Code and adopted in some jurisdictions.[37] For the most part, though, contemporary law recognizes only ignorance of the law as an excuse only in very narrow circumstances, and Hobbes's view appears to be more liberal than the current law.

If Hobbes's victims and criminals are all distinctively human, so are his enforcers. For all his emphasis on legal clarity and written rules, Hobbes did not imagine that a legal system could remove the human element from adjudication and enforcement. Indeed, he emphasized that penal laws (as opposed to distributive ones) were actually directly addressed to those who would execute the law. 'For though every one ought to be informed of the punishments ordained beforehand … nevertheless the command is not addressed to the delinquent (who cannot be supposed will faithfully punish himself,) but to public ministers appointed to see the penalty executed.'[38] In addition to human enforcers, laws need human interpreters. 'All laws, written and unwritten, have need of interpretation.'[39] Even the

[34] *Ibid.*, 208. [35] *Ibid.*, 203. [36] *Ibid.*, 209–210.

[37] The Model Penal Code, drafted and published by the American Law Institute as a model for state legislatures, provides that '[a] belief that conduct does not legally constitute an offence is a defense to a prosecution … when … [the defendant] acts in reasonable reliance upon an official statement of law, afterward determined to be invalid or erroneous', promulgated by statute, judicial decision, administrative order, or 'an official interpretation of the public officer or body charged by law with the responsibility for the interpretation, administration or enforcement of the law defining the offense'. American Law Institute, *Model Penal Code* § 2.04(3).

[38] Hobbes, *Leviathan*, 197. The distinction between distributive laws (addressed to subjects and defining their liberty or property interests) and penal laws (addressed to public officials) is similar to Meir Dan-Cohen's oft-cited distinction between conduct rules and decision rules. Meir Dan-Cohen, 'Decision Rules and Conduct Rules: On Acoustic Separation in Criminal Law' (1984) 97 *Harvard Law Review* 625.

[39] Hobbes, *Leviathan*, 190.

laws of nature, presumably self-evident to all rational humans, cannot be settled by appeal to abstract principles of moral philosophy. Laws need a human judge, one duly authorized by the sovereign authority.[40] Of course, human judges could err, both in their assessment of the law of nature and their interpretation of the sovereign's commands. Hence Hobbes was suspicious of the principle of stare decisis – 'No man's error becomes his own law, nor obliges him to persist in it. Neither (for the same reason) becomes it a law to other judges, though sworn to follow it.'[41] In general, Hobbes viewed judges as essential to a legal system but also as potential usurpers of sovereign authority, and his mistrust of the judiciary can be viewed as a precursor to twentieth and twenty-first century criticisms of 'judicial activism'.

So much of Hobbesian criminal law is consistent with modern Anglo-American criminal jurisprudence that one suspects his work deserves more attention from contemporary legal theorists than it typically receives. Of course, it is not likely that Hobbes's writings were themselves a direct influence on contemporary law; instead, both Hobbes and modern doctrine were influenced by legal traditions already in place, or developing, by the time Hobbes wrote.[42] But Hobbes did not merely parrot existing rules. He was a sharp critic of Coke in particular, as we have seen. Hobbes's preference for statutory law, and some of his narrower arguments such as that in favour of determinate sentencing, reflect concerns about fair notice and a suspicion of judicial discretion that were hardly mainstream in the seventeenth century. The same sorts of concerns, of course, have become increasingly prevalent in the twentieth century and into the present, providing further reason to believe that Hobbes's criminal law theory is worth our study today.[43]

Finally, one might note that Hobbes avoided two sorts of overgeneralization that all too often plague criminal law theory. The various features of the substantive criminal law discussed above assume the humanity of criminals and their victims, but they do not depend on a criminological portrait of 'the' typical offender. Hobbes identified several frequent

[40] *Ibid.*, 191. [41] *Ibid.*, 192.

[42] At the outset of the *Dialogue*, Hobbes's Philosopher explains that he has read Littleton's Book of Tenures and Sir Edward Coke's commentaries. Hobbes, *Dialogue*, 54.

[43] I have focused on Hobbes's discussion of the substantive criminal law, but it is worth noting that he endorsed several procedural protections for criminal defendants, such as a right to present evidence and a right to a jury trial. See Hobbes, *Leviathan*, 193, 195. Even more radically, he appeared to recognize the jury's right to 'nullify' the law by reaching a verdict inconsistent with the judge's legal instructions. *Ibid.*

causes of crime, but he also emphasized the great variety of criminals and offences.[44] Nor does the substantive content of the criminal law depend on a theory of the justification of punishment. As discussed below, it is doubtful that Hobbes viewed punishment as 'justified' at all, at least in the way that modern criminal law theorists use that term. Hobbes's criminal law is firmly grounded in his political theory, shaped by the conditions of, and constraints on, sovereign power. It is an account of criminal law that keeps firmly in view the shared humanity of criminals, victims and enforcers.

Interlude: a note on sovereign power

I have just claimed that Hobbes's criminal law reflects his broader political theory's constraints on sovereign power. Since Hobbes is widely known as a theorist of absolute and undivided sovereignty, the notion of a constrained sovereign requires some explication. Put differently, we could ask whether the various principles of criminal law identified in the previous section, especially those that mitigate punishment or otherwise protect criminal defendants, are mandatory. Suppose the sovereign simply declines to recognize a defence of duress, or refuses to promulgate written laws. What then?

Hobbes made clear that the social contract that creates the sovereign does not itself bind the sovereign in any way. The sovereign is not a party to the social contract, and could not be, since he does not exist qua sovereign until the moment the contract is made. Instead, the sovereign is a kind of third-party beneficiary to a contract that is made among private individuals. 'Because the right of bearing the person of them all, is given to him they make sovereign, by covenant only of one to another, and not of him to any of them; there can happen no breach of covenant on the part of the sovereign.'[45]

Under one standard interpretation of Hobbes, the sovereign's authority is unlimited, or else he (or it) is not properly called a sovereign. There is considerable textual support for this reading: for example, Hobbes claimed

[44] *Ibid.*, 204–207.

[45] *Ibid.*, at 122. Even if the office of the sovereign is occupied by a single natural person, we should not think that this natural person covenants with the subjects. He cannot contract with all subjects as a single party, because 'they are not yet one Person' before the sovereign has been appointed, and if the natural-person-who-will-become-sovereign contracts with each future subject individually, those contracts will be void once sovereignty is established.

that the sovereign power 'is as great, as possibly men can be imagined to make it', and adds, 'though of so unlimited a power, men may fancy many evil consequences, yet the consequences of the want of it … are much worse'.[46] Hobbes rejected mixed government as unstable – 'a kingdom divided in itself cannot stand' – and insists that a single, undivided sovereign must have ultimate authority to make, interpret, and enforce the laws of the commonwealth.[47] Some of these tasks may be delegated to subordinates, as we have already seen with respect to the judiciary, but Hobbes insisted that the subordinates stay *subordinates*, not independent agents with the authority to check the sovereign power. And Hobbes was explicit that the sovereign is not himself bound by the laws he makes: 'Nor is it possible for any person to be bound to himself; because he that can bind, can release; and therefore he that is bound to himself only, is not bound.'[48]

We should add some nuance to this account, though, for Hobbes's endorsement of absolutism is easily exaggerated. Perhaps most importantly for legal theorists, Hobbes distinguished between power and law. Though a sovereign may sometimes act 'by virtue of his power' without establishing a prior law, we have seen Hobbes claim repeatedly that the preferable form of rule is the promulgation of written laws.[49] Like modern constitutionalists and champions of the rule of law, Hobbes emphasized consistency and predictability as virtues of a stable legal system. Moreover, even if the sovereign is not subject to *civil* law, he or it is bound by the *laws of nature*.[50] It is, for example, against the law of nature to punish the innocent; such punishment is an injury to God (not to the innocent subject).[51] To be sure, the laws of nature are subject to problems of uncertainty (or contested interpretive authority) and enforcement. Subjects of the sovereign have no means to enforce the sovereign's obligations to honour the

[46] *Ibid.*, 144–145. [47] *Ibid.*, 124–127. [48] *Ibid.*, 184.

[49] E.g., *ibid.*, 152–153 (distinguishing between sovereign acts 'grounded on a precedent law' and those 'demand[ed] or take[n] by pretense of his power'). For further discussion, see David Dyzenhaus, 'Hobbes's Constitutional Theory' in Ian Shapiro (ed.), *Leviathan* (New Haven: Yale University Press, 2010); David Dyzenhaus, 'How Hobbes Met the "Hobbes Challenge"' (2009) 72 *Modern Law Review* 488.

[50] *Leviathan*, 224 ('It is true, that Sovereigns are all subject to the Laws of Nature; because such laws be Divine, and cannot by any man, or Commonwealth be abrogated').

[51] *Ibid.*, 148, 192. To understand Hobbes's claim that punishment of the innocent does no injury to the punished individual, it is important to remember Hobbes's specific understanding of the term *injury*. An injury is a breach of a covenant; the sovereign cannot injure his subjects (though he may certainly damage or harm them) because he is party to no covenant with them. E.g., *ibid.*, 104.

laws of nature, and for that reason some have questioned the status of these laws as true law.[52] But Hobbes himself maintained that the laws of nature were 'actual' and 'proper' laws once a commonwealth was established.[53] Additionally, he claimed that these laws were binding on the sovereign, even if it is only God that can address the sovereign's violations.[54]

A number of scholars have recently explored the ways in which legal restrictions, and rights, generate a more complex account of political power in Hobbes than the simple model of an all-powerful sovereign.[55] Of special interest here is the individual right to self-preservation, the right that generates the right to resist punishment. This right to resist imposes practical and moral constraints, if not legal ones, on the Hobbesian sovereign. And it demonstrates that Hobbes's account of punishment, like his account of the substantive criminal law, is one grounded in an appreciation of the humanity of all involved.

Punishment by and for humans

Hobbes began his discussion of punishment with 'a question to be answered, of much importance; which is, by what door the right, or authority of punishing in any case, came in'.[56] As soon as he posed the question, Hobbes rejected the possible answer that any individual gives the sovereign the right to punish him as part of the social contract: 'no man is supposed bound by covenant, not to resist violence; and consequently it

[52] E.g., John Deigh, 'Reason and Ethics in Hobbes's Leviathan' (1996) 34 *Journal of History of Philosophy* 35.

[53] Hobbes, *Leviathan*, 185.

[54] *Ibid.*, 224, 231. It is also worth noting that those who dismiss Hobbes as unduly absolutist may exaggerate the degree to which alternative arrangements have actually imposed limits on penal power. While Hobbes was clearly wrong about the (im)possibility of stable divided government, the ostensible limits on the substantive criminal law and on the power to punish in some modern societies – the United States in particular – are much weaker than they may first appear. I have explored the difficulties of limiting penal power in several articles. E.g., Alice Ristroph, 'Proportionality as a Principle of Limited Government' (2005) 55 *Duke Law Journal* 263; Ristroph, 'State Intentions and the Law of Punishment' (2008) 98 *Journal of Criminal Law & Criminology* 1353; Ristroph, 'Covenants for the Sword' (2011) 61 *University of Toronto Law Journal* 657.

[55] Eleanor Curran, *Reclaiming the Rights of the Hobbesian Subject* (London: Palgrave, 2007); Dyzenhaus, 'Hobbes's Constitutional Theory'; Dyzenhaus, 'How Hobbes Met the "Hobbes Challenge"'; Alice Ristroph, 'Respect and Resistance in Punishment Theory' (2009) 97 *California Law Review* 601; Susanne Sreedhar, *Hobbes on Resistance: Defying the Leviathan* (Cambridge University Press, 2010).

[56] Hobbes, *Leviathan*, 214. The following account of Hobbes's theory of punishment is a revised version of my discussion first published in Ristroph, 'Respect and Resistance'. Material is used here with the permission of the California Law Review.

cannot be intended that he gave any right to another to lay violent hands upon his person.'[57] Accordingly, the commonwealth's right to punish 'is not grounded on any concession … of the subjects'.[58]

The concept of self-preservation is a familiar one, but Hobbes's unusual view of that concept merits further scrutiny. For Hobbes, a strong right of self-preservation is central to what it means to be human. In other passages, Hobbes held that an individual could not renounce this right: '[T]here be some rights, which no man can be understood by any words, or other signs, to have abandoned, or transferred. As first a man cannot lay down the right of resisting them, that assault him by force, to take away his life.'[59] Again, the claim is not a prediction of what men will do (i.e. no one would renounce the right) or a word of advice (i.e. no one should renounce the right), but a claim of impossibility: no one can abandon the right of self-preservation. If one does promise to give up the right of self-preservation, the covenant is void.[60] This right is truly inalienable. And the right to resist applies to all violent assaults, not simply those of immediate death: 'The same may be said of wounds, chains, and imprisonment; both because there is no benefit consequent [to suffering such harms]: as also a man cannot tell, when he sees men proceed against him by violence, whether they intend his death or not.'[61]

The strong and inalienable right to self-preservation means that individuals contracting to create a sovereign do not grant the sovereign a right to punish them. So where does the sovereign power to punish come from? Hobbes depicted it as an expression of the *sovereign's own* right to self-preservation. In other words, the punisher is human, too:

> before the institution of commonwealth, every man had a right to every thing, and to do whatsoever he thought necessary to his own preservation; subduing, hurting, or killing any man in order thereunto. And this is the foundation of that right of punishing, which is exercised in every commonwealth. For the subjects did not give the sovereign that right; but only in laying down theirs, strengthened him to use his own, as he should think fit, for the preservation of them all: so that it was not given, but left to him, and to him only[.][62]

Thus, in Hobbes's view, an individual's natural right to do violence as he judges necessary for his own security becomes, in civil society, the sovereign's right to punish. More precisely, the natural right to use violence preemptively, even against someone who does not pose an imminent threat,

[57] Hobbes, *Leviathan*, 214.
[58] *Ibid.* [59] *Ibid.*, 93. [60] *Ibid.*, 98.
[61] *Ibid.*, 93. [62] *Ibid.*, 214.

becomes the right to punish. Everyone but the sovereign renounces this right when they agree to the social contract. Only the sovereign – who is not a party to the social contract – retains the broad discretion to use force as he thinks necessary, and so only the sovereign may punish. Notice that Hobbes did not claim that every lawbreaker poses an immediate threat to the life or bodily well-being of the sovereign, but as noted above, the natural right of self-preservation (distinguished from the civil right of self-defence) is not limited to imminent threats. A ruler might judge that his own long-term security, and the security of society as a whole, requires him to use force to punish those who break the law.

The social contract does not itself create the right to punish, but neither is it irrelevant to that right. Though subjects do not give the sovereign the right to punish, they consent to a world in which he will have that right: the right is 'not given, but left to [the sovereign], and to him only'. Put differently, it is not as though punishment never crosses the mind of Hobbes's contracting subjects. Each may well contemplate, and agree to support, the punishment of *other* subjects. 'In the making of a commonwealth, every man gives away the right of defending another, but not of defending himself. Also he obliges himself, to assist [the sovereign] in the punishing of another, but of himself not.'[63] This clarification is important, for in many other passages, Hobbes described subjects as 'authors' of all the sovereign's actions, including, presumably, acts of punishment.[64] Punishment is authorized, in some senses; the critical question will become the extent to which a subject can be said to authorize *his own* punishment and the normative significance of any such authorization.

The sovereign's right to punish, on this account, is a distinctive manifestation of the right of self-preservation that belongs to all natural, mortal humans. The sovereign punishes to preserve himself (and his obedient subjects). But this produces a new puzzle. Even if the office of the sovereign is held by a natural person, as would be the case in Hobbes's preferred form of government (an absolute monarchy), the right to punish as a natural right could only belong to the natural person, the man who happens to be king, and not to the artificial person of the sovereign. The sovereign is a creation of the social contract, an artificial man springing into existence by fiat ('Let us make man') at the moment

[63] *Ibid.*; but note that a subject may refuse a command to *kill* another, *ibid.*, 151.

[64] See, e.g., chapter 18, 120; chapter 20, 148 ('[N]othing the sovereign representative can do to a subject ... can properly be called injustice, or injury; because every subject is author of every act the sovereign does').

of covenant.[65] If no commonwealth, and thus no sovereign, exists in the state of nature, it makes little sense to say the sovereign keeps rights that he possessed in the state of nature.

This tension can be alleviated, if not entirely dispelled, by examining more closely Hobbes's state of nature. 'State of nature' is a term of art that refers to neither a discrete historical moment nor a purely hypothetical construct. Instead, the state of nature is the always-possible situation in which political authority is absent. Because political authority might appear, disappear and reappear, the state of nature is a recurrent circumstance. Indeed, one could identify various kinds of states of nature. For example, one could distinguish between the state of nature in which no political authority has ever been established ('the original state of nature') and a state of nature in which political authority has been established but has failed or been destroyed ('a recurrent state of nature').[66] One could also distinguish between a state of nature in which political authority exists nowhere ('a universal state of nature') and a state of nature in which political authority, otherwise intact, has been rejected only by a single individual ('a specific state of nature').[67]

Conceptually, we could understand punishment as a distinctive species of violence that takes place in a recurrent, specific state of nature, not an original or universal one. Once a subject has disobeyed the sovereign, he and the sovereign are in the state of nature vis-à-vis each other. The sovereign, a uniquely political and artificial construct, now exists in a version of the state of nature, and he possesses the broad right of mortal beings to do whatever he thinks necessary to preserve himself from imminent or future threats.[68] But if this is all punishment is – a conflict between

[65] *Ibid.*, Introduction, at 10.

[66] Hobbes did not use these names for various states of nature, but he clearly contemplated the possibility that subjects could return to a state of nature after an established political authority collapsed. *Ibid.*, 154 ('if a monarch shall relinquish the sovereignty, both for himself, and his heirs; his subjects return to the absolute liberty of nature').

[67] Again, these are not Hobbes's phrases. But one may find support for this conceptualization in Hobbes's discussion of criminals who, having resisted the sovereign and drawn the threat of punishment, may band together to defend themselves collectively against the still-existing sovereign. The sovereign remains a sovereign for his law-abiding subjects, but vis-à-vis the band of criminals the sovereign is simply an aggressor in a state of nature. See *ibid.*, 152.

[68] Even with this elaboration of the states of nature, the claim that the right to punish is a manifestation of a natural right to self-preservation is perplexing. I noted above that Hobbes seems to view the fact of mortality, and the desire for self-preservation, to imply in humans a right to self-preservation. But it is not clear why sovereigns – who are not obviously mortal beings – would have a similar right.

two mere mortals in the state of nature – then both the sovereign and the criminal will have equal rights of self-preservation, and the criminal has as much right to resist punishment as the sovereign has to impose it. In fact, this is exactly Hobbes's claim. Hobbes's radical egalitarianism committed him to the claim that in the absence of a reciprocally recognized third party to adjudicate disputes, each individual has an equal claim to preserve himself by whatever means he believes necessary. This gives the sovereign a right to punish, but it also gives any individual facing punishment a right to resist.

When Hobbes imagined the general covenant by which individuals authorize the sovereign, he did not include any explicit reservations other than the condition that others also grant authority to the sovereign: 'I authorize and give up my right of governing my self, to this man, or to this assembly of men, on this condition, that you give up your right to him, and authorize all his actions in like manner.'[69] But there is a further, *implicit* reservation in this grant of authority: the right to defend one's body from immediate harm. And this inalienable right is the basis of the right to resist punishment.[70] Perhaps Hobbes considered this reservation so obvious that it did not need to be stated expressly, and perhaps he was correct. To state the reservation expressly, the subject would have to say, 'I authorize you to do whatever you think necessary to preserve me, but I reserve the right to resist should you attempt to destroy me'.[71]

On at least two occasions, Hobbes imagined a more specific authorization – the manner in which subjects would authorize punishment. Each time, he was explicit that this authorization must include a reserved right to resist. Hobbes states in *Leviathan*, 'For though a man may covenant thus, *unless I do so, or so, kill me*; he cannot covenant thus, *unless I do so,*

[69] *Ibid.*, 120.

[70] For a similar reading, and a detailed argument for the inalienability of the right to resist force, see Yves-Charles Zarka, 'Hobbes and the Right to Punish' in Hans Blom (ed.), *Hobbes – The Amsterdam Debate* 71 (Hildesheim: Georg Olms Verlag, 2001).

[71] Of course, Hobbes does not allow the subject to say to the sovereign, 'I think your national security policy is lunacy and surely inadequate to protect me, so I am going to resist you violently', or 'These tax rates are killing me; I am going to rebel'. But we can distinguish between a strategy of long-term self-preservation on one hand and preservation of the body from immediate threats on the other hand. We give the sovereign complete authority over the former; we are not allowed to second-guess his strategy. Since protection from immediate threats is necessary to long-term preservation, we expect the sovereign to protect us from immediate threats as well. But if he fails to do so, we are free to do our best to ensure our own immediate self-preservation. Cf. Hobbes, *Leviathan*, 206 ('[N]o man is supposed at the making of a commonwealth to have abandoned the defense of his life, or limbs, where the law cannot arrive time enough to his assistance').

or so, I will not resist you, when you come to kill me'.[72] This right to resist belongs to the guilty as well as the innocent.[73] Hobbes makes the same point at greater length in *De Cive*: 'No man is obliged by any contracts whatsoever not to resist him who shall offer to kill, wound, or any other way hurt his body … It is one thing, if I promise thus: if I do it not at the day appointed, kill me. Another thing, if thus: if I do it not, though you should offer to kill me, I will not resist.'[74] If it seems impossible that one person should have a right to kill and the second should have a right to resist, note that this is exactly the situation of the state of nature. When an individual promises to obey a sovereign, he removes himself from the state of nature. If he later rejects the sovereign's authority and disobeys the sovereign's commands, all bets are off; the individual and the sovereign are in the state of nature again vis-à-vis each other – what I have called the 'specific state of nature'.

Sovereign and disobedient subject are not, of course, the only persons with a stake in punishment. Recall that in forming the social contract, the subjects leave the sovereign his natural right to use violence in self-preservation 'as he should think fit, *for the preservation of them all*'.[75] Arguably, each subject contemplates, and accepts (or even actively desires), the possibility that the sovereign will exercise his natural right of self-preservation to punish *other* people. David Gauthier explained the status of punishment in these terms: 'Each man authorizes, not his own punishment, but the punishment of every other man. The sovereign, in punishing one particular individual, does not act on the basis of his authorization from that individual, but on the basis of his authorization from all other individuals.'[76]

Moreover, one should remember that the criminal's right to resist punishment is not a legally enforceable right; it is not a right that implies a correlative duty to refrain from punishing on the sovereign's part.[77] The right of resistance is instead a 'blameless liberty', an act 'not against reason' that merely reflects the vulnerable human's rational efforts at

[72] *Ibid.*, 98. [73] *Ibid.*, 152.

[74] Hobbes, *De Cive*, 39–40.

[75] Hobbes, *Leviathan*, 214 (emphasis added).

[76] David Gauthier, *The Logic of Leviathan: The Moral and Political Theory of Thomas Hobbes* (New York: Oxford University Press, 1969), 148.

[77] Eleanor Curran has argued that Hobbes's work reveals inadequacies in Wesley Hohfeld's influential conception of rights as necessarily implying correlative duties. Eleanor Curran, 'Lost in Translation: Some Problems With a Hohfeldian Analysis of Hobbesian Rights' (2006) 19 *Hobbes Studies* 58.

self-preservation.[78] Alternatively, we can understand this right as an absence of obligation: on the Hobbesian account, even the guilty have no obligation to submit to punishment. And yet obligation is central to Hobbes's account of law: law is a sovereign command 'addressed to one formerly obliged to obey him'.[79] Thus there seems to be a fissure between the law itself and the remedies for its violation. Subjects have an obligation to obey the criminal law, but should they violate that obligation, they have no further obligation to cooperate in their own punishments.

Given that the sovereign has no duty to refrain from punishing, and indeed has a right to punish, one may wonder whether the criminal's right to resist has much practical significance. After all, we can expect that in most cases the sovereign will possess superior physical force and will be able to subdue even a resisting subject. The right to resist does have some implications for the substantive criminal law – for what should be criminal – but more importantly, it suggests a minimalist approach to punishment. With respect to the substantive criminal law, the right to resist punishment counsels against the separate criminalization of efforts to avoid punishment. In both *Leviathan* and the *Dialogue*, Hobbes sharply criticized the common law principle that an accused felon who flees trial must forfeit his property as penalty for his flight, even if he is later found to be innocent of the underlying felony. Flight from trial is perfectly understandable, especially given that judges (being human) are frequently corrupt and partial.[80] The imposition of punishment for the flight itself was, in Hobbes's words, an 'unchristian and abominable doctrine'.[81] Hobbes's critical vitriol was directed at the common law rule; he acknowledged that a *written* law could forbid flight from prosecution and impose punishment on violators.[82] But his discussion suggests that such a written law is not advisable, and it certainly does not violate natural law to flee criminal prosecution. Modern statutes criminalize flight from prosecution along with various other efforts to avoid punishment such as resisting arrest or escape from confinement. Perhaps such statutes help ensure the efficacy of the criminal justice system, but Hobbes would endorse them only grudgingly, it seems. One cannot get too enthusiastic about statutes that make the criminal justice system more effective if one has underlying doubts about the system itself.

[78] '[T]hat which is not against reason, men call right, or *jus*, or blameless liberty of using our own natural power and ability.' Hobbes, *Elements of Law*, 71.

[79] Hobbes, *Leviathan*, 183. [80] *Ibid.*, 192.

[81] Hobbes, *Dialogue*, 151.

[82] Hobbes, *Leviathan*, 192.

As just noted, it remains unclear whether legal principles or institutions could restrain the penal power, in Hobbes's theory or in our time. But if law cannot effectively curtail the power to punish, perhaps it is all the more important to endorse penal minimalism as a matter of policy. Hobbes's conception of punishment as an act of violence which even the guilty may resist is much more conducive to penal minimalism than theories that justify punishment. Hobbes urged that punishment be imposed only when necessary, and his assessment of necessity was fairly narrow. He also claimed that mercy was required by natural law; any offender who showed repentance and who could give assurances of future obedience should be pardoned.[83] Similarly, natural law proscribed revenge; the correction of the offender or general deterrence were the only permissible purposes of punishment.[84] A penal minimalist would also urge less severe punishments, and Joseph Cropsey has suggested that the final section of Hobbes's *Dialogue* reveals a concern that the criminal law has become too punitive and vengeful.[85] The arguments there are not altogether clear, but Hobbes's Philosopher does advise that laws must impose no more than the people can endure.[86]

Hobbes's discussion of punishment and the right to resist it might be fairly read to suggest that punishment is, at best, imperfectly legitimate. The right to punish is not derived from the subject's consent; it is a manifestation of the natural right to do violence in self-preservation. Nor is punishment universally and unequivocally authorized. Each subject either fails to authorize his own punishment, or cabins the authorization so as to avoid a duty to submit. Punishment remains an act of violence that the condemned individual has a right to resist. Hobbes, the great champion of absolute sovereignty and political stability, seems to have left a chink in the sovereign's armour – an opportunity for the re-emergence of the violent conflict of the state of nature.

Or is Hobbes himself to blame for this chink? Perhaps it was simply Hobbes's honesty that stopped him from claiming that people consent to be imprisoned or executed.[87] Perhaps the chink is the inevitable

[83] *Ibid.*, 106. [84] *Ibid.*

[85] Cropsey, 'Introduction', 40–41.

[86] Hobbes, *Dialogue*, 166.

[87] George Kateb has claimed that Hobbes offers a powerfully emancipatory theory notwithstanding his efforts to defend absolute sovereignty. 'He emancipates, to some degree, in spite of himself, when his honesty gets in his way.' Kateb, 'Hobbes and the Irrationality of Politics', 356.

consequence of a theory of legitimacy that takes consent seriously. Though I do think ruthless honesty would have kept Hobbes from claiming that criminals willingly submit to punishment, we should not forget the normative dimension of the right to resist. The right to resist is not simply a descriptive claim about human psychology. To see this, imagine a world in which the condemned do submit: the criminal gives up and places his own head in the noose. What would Hobbes say of such a world? It might be more stable, but I suspect Hobbes would find it regrettable. Hobbes does not try to solve the problems of the state of nature by convincing anyone to give up on self-preservation, and indeed, he betrays great sympathy for those who seek to preserve themselves. In this, he is deeply egalitarian and deeply individualist. Every person – even the rebel who has attacked the sovereign – can and should seek to preserve himself. But to honour these egalitarian and individualist commitments within a voluntarist account of obligation, we must sacrifice an account of punishment as fully legitimate. Ultimately, Hobbes recognized the limits of consent-based authority, and his account of criminal law and punishment is correspondingly chastened.

7

Hobbes's relational theory

Beneath power and consent

EVAN FOX-DECENT

> I know not how the world will receive [*Leviathan*], nor how it may reflect on those that shall seem to favour it. For in a way beset with those who contend, on one side for too great liberty, and on the other side for too much authority, 'tis hard to pass between the points of both unwounded.
>
> Thomas Hobbes, *Leviathan,* Letter Dedicatory.[1]

Introduction

The social contract rests on the consent of the contractors, so it is not surprising that many scholars view Hobbes, a pioneer in the social contract tradition, as a consent theorist of one stripe or another.[2] Others, however, view Hobbes as either a royalist or a royalist who later became a de facto theorist so as to make peace with the commonwealth after the execution of Charles I in early 1649.[3] Royalists are committed to the principle of indefeasible hereditary succession and therefore uphold the right to rule

For helpful comments, I thank Matt Finn, Dennis Klimchuk and Lars Vinx.

[1] Subsequent references to *Leviathan* are indicated by 'L' and are to chapter (or 'R&C' for the Review & Conclusion), paragraph and page number from the Curley edition: *Leviathan with selected variants from the Latin edition of 1668*, edited by Edwin Curley (Indianapolis: Hackett Publishing, 1994). Unless otherwise indicated, italics are from the original.

[2] See, e.g., Gregory Kavka, *Hobbesian Moral and Political Theory* (Princeton University Press, 1986) (Hobbes as hypothetical consent theorist); Kinch Hoekstra, 'The *de facto* Turn in Hobbes's Political Philosophy' in *Leviathan after 350 Years*, edited by Tom Sorell and Luc Foisneau (Oxford University Press, 2004), 33–73 (Hobbes as attributed consent theorist).

[3] See, e.g., James Hamilton, 'Hobbes the Royalist, Hobbes the Republican' (2009) 30 *History of Political Thought* 411 (Hobbes as royalist); Richard Tuck, 'Introduction' in Thomas Hobbes, *Leviathan*, edited by Richard Tuck (Cambridge University Press, 1991) (Hobbes as royalist then de factoist); Deborah Baumgold, 'When Hobbes needed History' in

of a vanquished monarch. De facto theorists maintain that even if the possessor of sovereign power is a usurper, mere possession of effective power is sufficient to ground the subject's duty to obey and/or the power holder's authority. Royalist and de facto theories diverge in their treatment of usurpers, but agree that consent is not a necessary condition of authority or obligation.

In the years leading up to the publication of *Leviathan* in 1651, British intellectual culture was marked by pamphlet wars in which the various participants defended royalist, de facto, or consent theories.[4] On the one side were the Levellers and less radical parliamentarians who insisted that authority and obligation could rest only on the consent of the people. On the other side were supporters of the Rump Parliament (a parliament set up by the army in December of 1648) who took a de facto line, as well as royalists who still supported the defeated son of Charles I (later Charles II). The central issue was whether the consent of the people was a necessary condition of *de jure* rule. To be heard in this debate, Hobbes had to structure his argument around the question of consent.

While Hobbes's social contract theory and his account of authorization trade explicitly on consent, he notoriously held that submission to a battlefield victor 'to avoid the present stroke of death' (L xx.10, 130) was a valid form of consent. Elsewhere he suggests that irresistible power is a sufficient basis for authority (L xxxi.5, 236). And in the final paragraph of *Leviathan*, he claims that his argument is presented 'without other design than to set before men's eyes the mutual relation between protection and obedience' (L R&C.17, 497). This thesis was a lodestar for de facto theorists following the regicide in 1649.

In his discussion of sovereignty by acquisition or conquest, Hobbes offers a way to reconcile consent and de facto theories. He claims that if consent is not expressly given to the conquering sovereign, it nonetheless can be presumed or attributed where the subject enjoys natural liberty and lives openly under the protection of the conqueror (L xxi.10, 141; R&C.7, 491). Since 'every man is presumed to do all things to his own benefit' (L xv.31, 98), and because submission to an effective sovereign

G.A.J. Rogers and Tom Sorell (eds.), *Hobbes and History* (New York: Routledge, 2000), 25 (Hobbes as royalist then de factoist).

4 Quentin Skinner, 'The Proper Signification of Liberty' in Quentin Skinner, *Visions of Politics: Hobbes and Civil Science*, vol. III (Cambridge University Press, 2002), 209, 228–31; Quentin Skinner, 'Conquest and Consent: Hobbes and the Engagement Controversy' in Quentin Skinner, *Visions of Politics: Hobbes and Civil Science*, vol. III (Cambridge University Press, 2002), 287.

is of benefit to all, tacit consent can be presumed, and consent plus liberty yields both authority and obligation.[5] While this account appears to reconcile Hobbes's commitments to consent and de facto theory, we shall see that it stands in tension with Hobbes's reasons for thinking that the original covenant must be between the subjects themselves, and not between the subjects and the sovereign. Hobbes's commitment to consent also compels him to make the controversial claim that parental authority rests on the child's consent. This view in turn seems to contradict claims he makes elsewhere about children not being the authors of their actions nor subject to law because they are incapable of covenanting. The only way to save Hobbes from inconsistency, I argue, is to rethink the role and meaning of consent in Hobbes's overall argument. Hobbes, we shall see, ultimately relies on a wider model of authority than the social contract, a model that can incorporate consent (as it is usually conceived, as voluntary submission) but that can survive without it as well.

My argument is that within Hobbes's account of sovereignty, express and tacit consent are just particular expressions of an underlying and unifying model of authority. The underlying model is premised on the sovereign enjoying de facto power while standing in a morally significant relationship to his people, a relationship that authorizes him to impose legal obligations on them as part of a broader authorization to secure legal order and external defence on their behalf.[6] Under this model, the sovereign has authority and the subject a duty to obey if and only if the sovereign is morally required to respect the terms of his authorization, and generally does so. Crucially, the authorization remains in place whether individuals submit voluntarily or not, as it can arise and be sustained over time by the confluence of de facto power, the position of trust occupied by the sovereign and his officials, and compliance with the constitutional requirements of Hobbes's legal order. We shall see that the sovereign's morally significant relationship to his people is one of agency and mutual trust, and that 'the mutual relation between protection and obedience' is a moral relationship all the way down. Hobbes is

[5] For nuanced defence of this interpretation, see Hoekstra, 'The *de facto* Turn', 58–73.

[6] For ease of exegesis I will follow Hobbes and refer to the sovereign in the masculine throughout. A. John Simmons defends the idea that for authority to exist there must be a moral relationship of the appropriate kind between sovereign and subject, though he claims that only a relationship based on actual consent can satisfy this requirement. See A. John Simmons, *Justification and Legitimacy: Essays on Rights and Obligations* (Cambridge University Press, 2001), ch. 7.

therefore best understood as a relational rather than a consent or de facto theorist.

I begin with a sketch of Hobbes's consent-based accounts of sovereignty by institution and acquisition, and discuss some of the difficulties Hobbes invites by relying on tacit consent. I then argue that Hobbes thought the sovereign and his officials occupied positions of trust in the service of the people. The trust-like or fiduciary position of the sovereign discloses a compelling model of authority that operates independently of consent. In the final section I argue that the sovereign has an overarching duty to govern in accordance with the rule of law, which for Hobbes is drawn from a sophisticated account of legal order in which structural and normative legal principles – the laws of nature – figure prominently. Once we see that the sovereign is bound by laws of nature of a moral and determinate character, the last necessary condition of the fiduciary model of authority is in place.

Consent

Hobbes says that sovereignty may arise in one of two ways, through institution or acquisition. Sovereignty by institution arises when a multitude, by mutual covenants of one with another (the 'original covenant'), agrees to authorize and own all the public actions of the person or assembly they appoint to represent and govern them (L xviii.1, 110). By appointing a sovereign representative, the multitude becomes unified as an artificial person – a commonwealth – through (and not before) the sovereign's representation of the commonwealth (L xvii.13, 109). This follows from Hobbes's theory of attributed action according to which a 'multitude of men are made *one* person, when they are by one man, or one person, represented so that it be done with the consent of every one of that multitude in particular' (L xvi.13, 104). It is thus through the original covenant that the state, 'as a real unity of them all', is born (L xvii.13, 109).

Importantly, Hobbes's account of the state and the sovereign's authorization allows him to insulate the sovereign from complaints of injustice. While the sovereign's public actions are attributed to the state, his subjects are the authors of those actions, 'and consequently he that complaineth of injury from his sovereign complaineth of that whereof he is the author, and therefore ought not to accuse any man but himself' (L xviii.6, 112). Hobbes admits that the sovereign may commit iniquity, 'but not injustice, or injury in the proper signification' (L xviii.6, 113).

Moreover, the sovereign cannot forfeit his authority through a breach of the original covenant because he is not a party to it; the original covenant is between the members of the multitude alone (L xviii.4, 111). Hobbes offers the following arguments to show that the sovereign does not acquire power through a covenant with his subjects. The sovereign cannot covenant with 'the whole, as one party … because as yet they are not one person' (*ibid.*). The reasoning behind why the sovereign cannot be understood to covenant with every person separately is less straightforward. Hobbes writes:

> That he which is made sovereign maketh no covenant with his subjects beforehand is manifest, because … if he make so many several [separate] covenants as there be men, those covenants after he hath the sovereignty are void, because what act soever can be pretended by any one of them for breach thereof is the act both of himself and of all the rest, because done in the person and by the right of every one of them in particular. (*ibid.*)

Hobbes's basic claim here is that sovereignty by institution cannot arise from 'so many several covenants [with the sovereign] as there be men'. His argument presupposes that an existence condition of any covenant is that it is susceptible to breach. The possibility of breach implies that there must be more than one party to a contractual relationship, since a person cannot be in nor breach a contract with herself. Once sovereignty is instituted, and the subject is author of the sovereign's actions, as a conceptual matter the sovereign cannot breach a covenant with his subjects, since any allegedly breaching action is really the action of his subjects. Pre-commonwealth covenants with the sovereign that purport to grant sovereignty are therefore void in civil society because they are not susceptible to breach. While Hobbes was anxious to avoid sovereign–subject covenants so as to eliminate a source of complaint against the sovereign, arguably he also worried that if such founding covenants were void, then they could not ground the subject's obligation, even if the sovereign still retained authority to rule.

In the next paragraph Hobbes reaffirms that it is 'in vain to grant sovereignty by way of precedent covenant [with the sovereign]', this time because there would be no judge to adjudicate any alleged breach of covenant, leading back to 'the sword again' (L xviii.4, 112–13). Hobbes again targets subject–sovereign covenants that purport to establish sovereignty.

This presents a puzzle. When Hobbes discusses sovereignty by acquisition he seems to suggest that the subject does covenant directly with the sovereign. Hobbes says that the victor acquires dominion over the vanquished 'by covenants of the vanquished to the victor' (L xxi.11, 141). Such individuals 'hath covenanted to obey the civil law … with the representative itself one by one' (L xxvi.8, 175). The question, then, is how to square these covenants with conquering sovereigns with Hobbes's assertions that such covenants are 'void' and made 'in vain', as well as with his abiding worry that making the sovereign a party to founding covenants opens the door to sovereignty-weakening claims that he has breached them.

Sovereignty by acquisition can be brought in line with sovereignty by institution by interpreting the covenant with the sovereign on submission as really a legitimating covenant with the sovereign's subjects akin to the original covenant. Because every subject is author of all the sovereign's public acts, when a conquering sovereign covenants with a vanquished party who is yet in the state of nature vis-à-vis the sovereign, the sovereign's subjects are the authors of the sovereign's covenant with the vanquished. In effect, the sovereign opens the original covenant on behalf of his people to admit willing individuals into the 'unity of them all', which is to say, into the commonwealth. While some outsiders may submit out of fear 'to avoid the present stroke of death', Hobbes avers that this form of sovereignty 'differeth from sovereignty by institution only in this, that men who choose their sovereign do it for fear of one another, and not of him whom they institute' (L xx.2, 127). Furthermore, Hobbes emphasizes that 'the rights and consequences of sovereignty are the same in both' (L xx.2, 128). If the founding covenant with the vanquished failed to bring them into the original covenant, Hobbes could not make this claim without running afoul of his earlier objections to covenants with sovereigns. As it turns out, all of these objections can be granted, since the conquering sovereign covenants with outsiders in his public capacity and as his people's representative. It remains to consider how the state can maintain its legitimacy over time, as new generations are born into it who do not expressly enter into an original covenant nor submit to a conquering or existing sovereign.

One candidate solution is tacit or presumed consent. If a subject is living within a commonwealth under the authority of an effective sovereign, and she enjoys natural liberty, she is presumed to consent tacitly. Hobbes makes this claim most explicitly in his discussion of sovereignty by acquisition (L xx.5, 130; xx.10, 130; R&C.7, 491). If this form of sovereignty can rest on tacit consent, and if sovereignty by acquisition implicates sovereignty by institution, as I have claimed, then arguably tacit consent can serve as an equally effective legitimating basis of sovereignty by institution. Hobbes admits this possibility in his discussion of the liberty of subjects. Without reference to the particular form of sovereignty at issue, he says that submission can be derived 'from the express words *I authorize all his actions*, or from the intention of him that submitteth himself to the power (which intention is to be understood by the end for which he so submitteth)' (L xxi.10, 141). Put another way, in the absence of express words, submission implies tacit consent to the original covenant because the intention of everyone is peace, and peace is only possible in a commonwealth.

Yet there is good reason to believe that consent as voluntary submission is not the whole story for Hobbes, or even a necessary part of the story. At times Hobbes's use of consent seems especially contrived, no more so than in his discussion of parental authority. Hobbes claims that parental authority over a child is not derived 'from the generation [of the child] as if therefore the parent had dominion over his child because he begat him, but from the child's consent, either express or by other sufficient arguments declared' (L xx.4, 128).[7] The parent's dominion over the child is by covenant of the 'child to the parent' (L xxi.11, 141). Speaking to circumstances where the mother abandons the child and someone else takes him in, he says that 'it ought to obey him by whom it is preserved, because preservation of life being the end for which one man becomes subject to another, every man is supposed to promise obedience to him in whose power it is to save or destroy him' (L xx.5, 130). The child, in other words, is presumed to consent to the authority of 'him in whose power it is to save or destroy him'.

That this is a theoretical contrivance is suggested by what Hobbes says about children elsewhere. In his discussion of persons, Hobbes says that 'children, fools, and madmen that have no use of reason … can be no authors (during that time) of any action done by them' (L xvi.10, 103). Likewise, Hobbes claims that '[o]ver natural fools, children, or madmen there is no law, no more than over brute beasts … because they had never power to make any covenant … and consequently, never took upon them to authorize the actions of any sovereign as they must do that make to themselves a commonwealth' (L xxvi.12, 177). If children are not subject to law because 'they never had any power to make any covenant', it is

[7] Lars Vinx has pointed out to me that one could attempt to avoid this difficulty by distinguishing dominion over someone from authority over someone. If dominion is relevantly distinct from authority, then the puzzle with parental dominion may not be a problem for political authority. Hobbes, however, at this juncture of *Leviathan*, appears to treat dominion as a synonym for authority, and as he uses parental dominion to set up his discussion of '[d]ominion by conquest' (L xx.10, 130).

hard to see how the child can be subject to the parent's dominion on the basis of a covenant. One could save Hobbes from inconsistency by interpreting what he says about parental authority to apply only to children mature enough to have the 'use of reason'. But then parental dominion over infants is left unexplained, and his discussion of parental authority is plainly intended to explain the origin of parental authority from the birth of the child onward, since it begins with a defence of the mother's superior right of first dominion over the child vis-à-vis the father.

A more promising way to resolve the inconsistency is to take seriously that in this context consent as voluntary submission *is* a contrivance. Hobbes's reference to consent is a shorthand way for him to refer to the more fundamental idea that authority must rest on a moral relationship of authorization between the holder of irresistible power and the subject. The nature of this relationship, I argue now, is one of mutual trust.[8]

From de facto to entrusted power

A necessary condition of the subject's duty to obey the law is that 'the victor hath *trusted* him [the captive] with his corporal liberty', which is why slaves in chains or prison are not under obligation (L xx.12, 131, emphasis added). A subject is one that 'hath corporal liberty allowed him, and upon promise not to run away, nor do violence to his master, is *trusted* by him' (L xx.10, 131, emphasis added). So there is a plain sense in which the sovereign trusts the subject: the subject is trusted with his life and liberty on condition that he obeys the sovereign and does not do violence to him. The sense in which trust flows in the other direction (and is not consent by another name) will take more careful elaboration to disclose. I begin with some of the ways Hobbes characterizes the sovereign's offices as positions of trust.

When Hobbes posits equity as a law of nature, he describes the judge or arbitrator as one who is '*trusted to judge between man and man*' (L xv.23, 97). Having received this trust from the parties, the adjudicator must '*deal equally between them*', since without equal treatment 'the controversies of

[8] The main alternative in the literature is hypothetical consent, where Hobbes is taken as saying that anyone subject to effective power would consent to subjection and the original covenant to avoid the state of nature. See, e.g., Kavka, *Hobbesian Moral and Political Theory*, 398–407. I will not discuss this interpretation further than to point out that even defenders of hypothetical consent accounts admit that its appeal as a basis of obligation is really an inference to the best explanation due in part to a lack of alternatives. See, e.g., David Gauthier, 'Public Reason' (1995) 12 *Social Philosophy and Policy* 19, 38.

men cannot be determined but by war' (*ibid.*). Similarly, Hobbes says that the arbitrator who distributes 'to every man his own' is someone who can be said to 'perform his trust' (L xv.15, 95). The arbitrator could not be said to 'perform his trust' unless he in fact held in trust, for the parties, the power of adjudication. Trust also surfaces in Hobbes's justification of the law of nature regarding impartial dispute resolution. If the judge or arbitrator would gain from one side's victory in the dispute, such a gain would be equivalent to a bribe, and therefore 'no man can be obliged to trust him' (L xv.32, 98). Hobbes implies here that there is a good sense in which the office of the judge is constituted by the judge's trustworthiness in relation to his role: for the parties to be bound by the judge's decision, there cannot be any reason for them to believe that the judge will decide their case on the basis of an interest he may have in the outcome rather than on the merits. In other words, a person subject to judicial authority cannot be obligated to take the judge's decision as binding if the judge has a conflict of interest. The consequence of such a conflict is that 'the condition of war remaineth' (*ibid.*).

Hobbes is equally explicit in his discussions of the relationship between the sovereign and the people. 'Monarchs or assemblies', Hobbes claims, are 'entrusted with power enough for [their people's] protection' (L xx.15, 132). The office of the sovereign itself arises from the people's trust: 'The office of the sovereign ... consisteth in the end, for which he was trusted with sovereign power, namely, the procuration of *the safety of the people*' (L xxx.1, 219). In the same vein, he says that a monarch with authority to appoint a successor 'is obliged by the law of nature to provide, by establishing his successor, to keep those that had trusted him with the government from relapsing into the miserable condition of war' (L xix.11, 123). Hobbes elsewhere acknowledges that 'a sovereign monarch, or the greater part of a sovereign assembly, may ordain the doing of many things in pursuit of their passions, contrary to their own consciences', and qualifies such action as 'a breach of trust, and of the law of nature' (L xxiv.7, 162). While Hobbes insists that such a 'breach of trust' would not justify rebellion or accusations of injustice, the sovereign could not be said to have committed a *breach* of trust unless he had violated a duty intrinsic to the constitution of public offices held in trust.

Hobbes may have adopted the language of trust because, once sovereignty is established, trust may persist seamlessly over time, whereas express consent marks a discrete event, while presumed consent smacks of an overly convenient theoretical construction. Hobbes's use of trust signals an appreciation of the idea that for the ongoing relationship between the sovereign and his subjects to be more than an unstable modus vivendi, it must be a moral relationship in which the subjects' legal obligations are matched by a commitment on the part of the sovereign to respect the constitutive requirements of offices held in trust. I explain now in more general terms how an authority relationship based on trust is possible where consent is unavailable, and then turn to consider the fit between Hobbes's view of authority and this model.

A significant advantage of trust over consent as a basis of authorization is that relations of trust can arise without the beneficiary doing anything (or being presumed to do anything) to bring them about. In law the classical example is the trust, a legal institution in which a settlor establishes a trust in favour of a beneficiary that is administered by a trustee. Trustees often hold essentially irrevocable power over the trust's assets vis-à-vis their beneficiaries, though they are bound to exercise their authority with due regard for the beneficiary's best interests.[9] In yet other cases, trust-like fiduciary relationships arise merely by operation of law. This occurs, for example, when a shipmaster contracts without prior authorization with a third party on behalf of a cargo owner to save the owner's goods from perishing in an emergency.[10] The shipmaster is said to act as an 'agent of necessity', and as such may contract with third parties so as to place the cargo owner under new legal obligations without the owner's prior consent. Agency law's authorization of the master is legally equivalent to an express authorization: both entail that the cargo owner must own the actions performed on her behalf by the shipmaster. And in both cases the shipmaster may be thought to act on the basis of the owner's trust because in both she is in fact entrusted to act on behalf of the owner. As Annette Baier rightly observes, '[w]hereas it strains the concept of agreement to speak of unconscious agreements and unchosen agreements … there is no strain whatever in the concept of automatic and unconscious trust, and of unchosen but mutual trust'.[11] For most sovereigns and their subjects, in practice, the relationship is one of 'unchosen but mutual trust'.

9 Cf. Norberto Bobbio, 'Hobbes Political Theory' in Norberto Bobbio, *Thomas Hobbes and the Natural Law Tradition*, translated by Daniela Gobetti (University of Chicago Press, 1993) ('By holding that the sovereign power is irrevocable, Hobbes opposes the theory of trust'), 53; Jean Hampton, *Hobbes and the Social Contract Tradition* (Cambridge University Press, 1988), 124–6 (arguing against reading Hobbes as an agency theorist because sovereign power is irrevocable).

10 See, e.g., *The Gratitudine* (1801) 3 CH Rob 240; *Australasian SN Co* v. *Morse* (1872) LR 4 PC 222; *China-Pacific SA* v. *Food Corporation of India: The Winston* [1982] AC 939, [1981] 3 All ER 688.

11 Annette Baier, 'Trust and Antitrust' (1985) 96 *Ethics* 231, 244–5.

The point is that relationships of trust and authorization can arise without prior consent. Elsewhere I have argued that they arise as a matter of law whenever the entrusted party possesses discretionary power of a certain kind over the beneficiary or her interests, and the beneficiary is in principle or in practice unable to exercise this power.[12] The discretionary power at issue must be other-regarding, purposive and institutional. It must be other-regarding in the strictly factual sense that another person is subject to it. The power must be purposive in that it is held for certain purposes, such as an agent's power to contract on behalf of her principal. Lastly, the power must be institutional in that it is situated within a legally permissible institution, such as the family. Indeed the parent–child relationship is paradigmatic: the child cannot consent to the relationship, so the law sets the terms and entrusts the parent with authority over the child. In these and other fiduciary circumstances, the main duty of the power holder is to act without regard to her own interests and in what she reasonably perceives as the best interests of the beneficiary. When there are multiple beneficiaries subject to the same power, the basic duty is to act selflessly, even-handedly, and with due regard for the beneficiaries' legitimate interests. In the common law tradition, understood broadly to include the historical jurisdiction of courts of equity, these kinds of relations are known generally as fiduciary relationships.

The legislative, judicial and administrative branches of the state all possess powers that are other-regarding, purposive and institutional. Moreover, private parties as such are not entitled to exercise these public powers, since no private party is entitled to set unilaterally the terms of interaction with another. It follows that the state and its institutions are in a fiduciary relationship to the people subject to their powers. Plausibly, the state's overarching fiduciary duty is to govern in accordance with the rule of law. On this model, the subject has a defeasible duty to obey the law that rests on the combination of the state's duty to abide by the rule of law, its compliance with this obligation, and the prohibition on private unilateralism. The state's duty is a necessary feature of the fiduciary model because it explains the fiduciary principle's authorization of state power on behalf of everyone subject to it: public power is authorized to protect individuals from unilateralism, and no such protection is universal

[12] I defend this characterization of trust-like or fiduciary relations, and the fiduciary model of public authority subsequently set out in the text, in Evan Fox-Decent, *Sovereignty's Promise: The State as Fiduciary* (Oxford University Press, 2011).

unless every legal actor in the state, including the sovereign, is subject to law. Does Hobbes's theory reflect this model of authority?

With respect to Hobbes's conception of sovereign power, we can readily see that it is other-regarding, purposive and institutional. It is other-regarding as it is exercised by the sovereign acting in his 'politic' or public capacity, as representative of his subjects (L xxiii.2, 156). It is purposive in that it is to be exercised as the sovereign '*shall think expedient, for their peace and common defence*' (L xviii.13, 109). By 'laying down' their right of nature (save the inalienable right to self-preservation), the subjects 'strengthened him to use his as he should think fit, *for the preservation of them all*' (L xxviii.2, 204, emphasis added). Sovereign power is also institutional in that the sovereign's will is to be channelled through law: 'the commonwealth only prescribes and commandeth the observation of those rules which we call law' (L xxvi.5, 173). Taken literally, this proposition implies that Hobbes forswears reliance on extra-legal exercises of power against the commonwealth's subjects (enemies are another matter), notwithstanding that at times he seems prepared to grant the sovereign such powers (e.g. L xxi.19, 143–4). We return to this point in the next section. Furthermore, all law is subject to an 'authentic interpretation' by a legal institution, a subordinate judiciary, so in this way too sovereign power is institutional (L xxvi.20, 180).

Finally, legal subjects, as private parties, are not entitled to exercise sovereign power, precisely because this would constitute unilateralism. Hobbes make this clear in chapter 5, where he states that in the event of a dispute 'the parties must by their own accord set up for right reason the reason of some arbitrator or judge to whose sentence they will both stand, or their controversy must either come to blows or be undecided, for want of a right reason constituted by nature, and so it is also in all debates of what kind soever' (L v.iii, 23). The last clause of this statement suggests that Hobbes took the prohibition on unilateralism to be a foundational premise in his general argument for sovereignty. He subsequently describes unilateralism as 'intolerable', and later posits the principle that '*no man is fit arbitrator in his own cause*' as a law of nature (*ibid.*; L xv.31, 98). While Hobbes says that the parties themselves must agree to arbitration, he also implies that the agreement can be through a forced submission akin to sovereignty by acquisition, since an individual in the state of nature who is not part of the multitude that establishes a commonwealth must either 'submit to their decrees or be left in the condition of war he was in before, wherein he might without injustice be destroyed' (L xviii.5, 112). In other words, such individuals must either appear before a judge if summoned or face being treated as enemies.

So Hobbes's understanding of sovereign power, and the subject's position in relation to it, appears to satisfy the criteria of fiduciary relationships. The next step is to consider in what sense, if any, the sovereign is bound to govern in accordance with the rule of law. We have seen already that Hobbes intends the sovereign to rule through law and legal institutions. The question now is whether there are any limits on the form or content law can assume, which is to say, whether there is any meaningful sense in which Hobbes's laws of nature constrain the sovereign. It bears emphasizing that under the fiduciary theory it is not the benefit of security within legal order per se that gives rise to the subject's duty to obey, but rather the duty of the power holder to supply legal order combined with his success in doing so. Thus, only if there is some sense in which the sovereign is under obligation – is subject to law – will Hobbes's theory of sovereignty count as a fiduciary theory of the kind sketched above.

From validity to legality

I argue now that Hobbes thinks the sovereign is subject to the laws of nature in the sense that their violation would subvert his authority and the subject's duty to obey. The dominant understanding of these laws in the Hobbes literature, to the extent they are discussed at all,[13] is that they pose no real constraints on the sovereign. Norberto Bobbio has developed a sophisticated account of this interpretation, one that even counts Hobbes as a natural law theorist of sorts on the grounds that the legitimacy of positive law rests on the validity of the natural law injunction to seek peace by way of the original covenant.[14] But Bobbio is adamant that the laws of nature have no purchase against the sovereign. I review and criticize the major steps of Bobbio's analysis, showing how he misinterprets Hobbes at various junctures and draws unwarranted conclusions at others. A better interpretation of Hobbes's laws of nature is that they

[13] Quentin Skinner, for example, makes no reference to the laws of nature in his discussion of authorization, and concludes that the original covenant 'is not a means of limiting the powers of the crown; properly understood, it shows that the powers of the crown have no limits at all'. Quentin Skinner, 'Hobbes and the Purely Artificial Person of the State' in Quentin Skinner, *Visions of Politics: Hobbes and Civil Science*, vol. III (Cambridge University Press, 2002), 177, 208.

[14] Norberto Bobbio, 'Natural Law and Civil Law in the Political Philosophy of Thomas Hobbes' in Norberto Bobbio, *Thomas Hobbes and the Natural Law Tradition*, translated by Daniela Gobetti (University of Chicago Press, 1993) [*Natural Law*].

supply moral principles and structures for legal institutions that resist encroachment by the sovereign.

For Hobbes, a law of nature is 'a precept or general rule, found out by reason, by which a man is forbidden to do that which is destructive of his life or taketh away the means of preserving the same, and to omit that by which he thinketh it may be best preserved' (L xiv.14, 79). Hobbes's conception of natural law, Bobbio claims, is distinctive. For other natural law theorists, such laws have indicated what is good and evil in itself, while for Hobbes 'reason indicates what is good or bad in relation to a given end'.[15] The fundamental end is self-preservation, and the means to secure it is peace. Thus the first and fundamental law is to seek peace when others are so willing, from which is derived a second law: '*to lay down [the right of nature] to all things, and be contented with so much liberty against other men, as he would allow other men against himself*' (L xiv.5, 80). Hobbes reinforces this requirement in the tenth law of nature, which commands that '*at the entrance into conditions of peace, no man require to reserve to himself any right which he is not content should be reserved to any one of the rest*' (L xv.22, 97). This law is said to follow from the ninth, which requires '*that every man acknowledge other for his equal by nature*' (L xv.21, 97). Hobbes's argument for the ninth law is that individuals will not enter into conditions of peace except on equal terms. But this and every other law, Bobbio says, is derived from the first and fundamental law to seek peace.[16] The 'derived' laws are thus instrumentally valuable as prudential norms in relation to peace, but have no intrinsic moral value.

Now, it is far from clear that the second, ninth and tenths laws in fact follow from the first. The terms on which individuals would actually agree to enter into 'conditions of peace' are contingent matters. Some may insist on equal terms and others may not, while others still may demand preferential treatment. If the state of nature is as inhospitable as Hobbes contends, some may be more desperate to leave than others, while those others, being more tolerant of risk and sensing desperation, may hold out for special status. One could speculate that creating a commonwealth on anything but equal terms will plant seeds of discontent or increase the risk of this transpiring. But history is littered with long-lived commonwealths the stability of which was never threatened by inequality. What is more, in a given multitude it may be the case that compelling some to accept equal terms causes greater upheaval than forcing others to accept inequality. These are all highly contingent matters that cannot plausibly

[15] *Ibid.*, 118–21. [16] *Ibid.*, 120.

be effaced by the imperative to seek peace if others are so willing. If the state of nature is as bad as Hobbes says, and if peace through a commonwealth is the only way out, what follows *from the perspective of rational self-interest alone* is that individuals should be prepared to enter into civil society as quickly as possible on virtually *any* terms, and not just on equal terms.

There is, however, a way to interpret the equality-demanding laws of nature that does not rely on dubious empirical claims. We can make sense of Hobbes's call for the recognition of equality if we interpret him as claiming that to enter civil society on equal terms is the most anyone can *justly* demand. It may or may not be destabilizing to one's future civil society to hold out for preferential treatment, but it would always be morally 'intolerable' to do so. Hobbes's argument against being judge and party to the same cause (the seventeenth law of nature) supports this reading.

He says that equity gives 'to each party equal benefit', and so 'if one is to be admitted to be judge, the other is to be admitted also; and so the controversy, that is, the cause of war, remains, against the law of nature' (L xv.31, 98). While Hobbes's justification of this particular law of nature traces back to its contribution to peace, he does not get to that justification without relying first on the equitable principle of equality before the law. This principle can have application, however, only if the subjects are understood to have entered the commonwealth on equal terms or otherwise enjoy equality before the law. If, for example, one of the parties is a slave or second-class citizen barred from seeking redress through legal institutions, the principle of equal benefit will never apply to her. The same is true with respect to Hobbes's other laws of nature that structure legal institutions around equality before the law, including equity itself (dealing equally between the parties) as well as laws that bear on resource distribution, impartiality in adjudication, and witnesses (L xv.26–9, 32–3, 97–9). All of these presuppose (or assert outright) that the sovereign and his delegates must regard the parties as equals. Moreover, as in the case of the law requiring entrance into civil society on equal terms, if the rationale for equality before the law were based entirely on self-interest, the argument would fail against those who believe (even if irrationally, by Hobbes's lights) that they could do better by relying on self-help rather than public institutions.

In other words, the problem of the fool would resurface and infect all the laws of nature. The fool keeps his covenants when he believes it is in his interest to do so, but breaches them if he thinks he can (L xv.4–5, 90–2). Hobbes calls this person a fool because he relies on others failing to apprehend that he is taking advantage of them, and it is imprudent to rest one's security on such errors (L xv.5, 92). This argument is unconvincing because there may be circumstances in which, on balance, the reward from breaching outweighs the risk and penalty of apprehension. Even if the penalty is to be treated as an enemy or killed, as Hobbes recommends, it is implausible to think that in all cases it is irrational (from the standpoint of self-interest) to chance death if the risk is negligible and the reward is significant. Pedestrians crossing a moderately busy street run such risks. The better argument for Hobbes trades on his claim that 'it is not against reason' to perform one's covenants even if, on balance, doing so is against self-interest. We can interpret Hobbes to be saying that acting out of a sense of justice is 'not against reason' and is itself a sufficient reason for action, so one is not a sucker for doing so.[17] This is supported by Hobbes's claim that an 'unrighteous man' does not 'lose his character for such actions as he does or forbears to do for fear, because his will is not framed by justice, but by the apparent benefit of what he is to do' (L xv.10, 93). The implication is that the just man is just because his will, unlike the will of the fool, is 'framed by justice'. The moral interpretation of the laws of nature essayed above is buttressed by the possibility of the just man, notwithstanding that such men are 'rarely found' (*ibid.*).

To sum up thus far, while Bobbio's instrumental and prudential explanation of the laws of nature is supported by much of Hobbes's text, the presupposition of equality within many of these laws suggests that Hobbes intended them to bear a moral as well as prudential construction. The prudential argument is that everyone can do better in a civil society than the state of nature, so following the laws of nature to enter civil society, when others are willing to do so, is in everyone's interest. The moral argument is that one cannot in justice seek preferential treatment, since to do so is to revert to unilateralism. Only the moral construction can explain the laws of nature as general requirements that can apply even if there is some cost to self-interest.

For Bobbio, the implication that morality can sometimes trump self-interest within Hobbes's theory would be tantamount to a *reductio ad absurdum* against the moral interpretation. He interprets Hobbes as saying that although the laws of nature always bind on conscience or a desire they should take place (*in foro interno*), they bind on action (*in foro externo*) only in civil society. The laws of nature 'are not binding in the

[17] I am indebted to Robert Shaver for this idea.

state of nature, because human beings cannot comply with them without harming themselves', whereas 'they are binding in civil society, because the sovereign is held to enforce them if they are violated'.[18] The idea here is that the laws of nature do not require individuals to make themselves 'a prey to others'; they have a conditional structure in that they apply to an actor only if there is assurance that others will also comply with them (L xv.36, 99). The sword of the commonwealth supplies the requisite assurance. Therefore, the laws of nature are fully binding in civil society, where individuals can comply with them 'without harming themselves'.

It does not follow, however, that the laws of nature are binding on action *only* in civil society, as Hobbes's discussion of covenants makes plain. Hobbes's third law of nature is '*that men perform their covenants made*,' but it applies only if there is no reasonable cause to believe that others will breach, such as when the parties are in civil society and able to call on the sovereign for enforcement (L xv.1, 89). Nonetheless, the reason covenants are binding in civil society is not the presence of security per se, but because security removes the fear of non-performance, a fear that only *sometimes* obtains in the state of nature (L xv.3, 89). It is 'reasonable suspicion' of non-performance that renders state-of-nature covenants invalid, not the fact that they are made in the state of nature (L xiv.18, 84). Moreover, Hobbes says that the 'cause of fear which maketh a covenant invalid must be always something arising after the covenant made', since 'that which could not hinder a man from promising, ought not to be admitted as a hindrance of performing' (L viv.20, 85). This implies that if one enters into a covenant in the state of nature, the mere fact of being in the state of nature is not enough to render the contract invalid. For the contract to be void, something has to happen *after* the contract is made that gives rise to a 'reasonable suspicion' that the other party will breach.

Various passages in *Leviathan* refer directly to valid state-of-nature covenants. In the discussion of the fool, Hobbes implies that covenants are valid 'where one of the parties has performed already', and the fool is chided when, in the state of nature, 'he breaketh his covenant' (L xv.5, 92–3). Hobbes at one point flatly states that '[c]ovenants entered into by fear, in the condition of mere nature, are obligatory', and gives the example of someone who is obligated to pay a ransom to an enemy with whom he has covenanted to save his life (L xiv.27, 86). This example follows from Hobbes's theory of contract: if there is no fear of non-performance, as there never can be if the other party has performed already, then the

[18] Bobbio, *Natural Law*, 133.

contract is valid and binding on the second performer. Gregory Kavka summarizes nicely the considerable extent to which covenants are binding in the state of nature: 'All second parties, and any first parties without new evidence about the untrustworthiness of their second parties, are obligated to perform their state-of-nature covenants, and they act unjustly if they do not.'[19] Furthermore, the fact that these parties are under obligation means they must perform their covenants even if breaching would leave them better off. Hobbes thus overstates the extent of his nominalism when he claims that 'injustice actually there can be none till the cause of such fear [of non-performance] be taken away, which, while men are in the natural condition of war, cannot be done' (L xv.3, 89), or that in the state of nature 'nothing can be unjust' (L xiii.13, 78). His own theory of contract shows that injustice in the state of nature is possible. What remains impossible in 'the natural condition of war' is the authoritative resolution of purported cases of injustice, since public institutions alone can make such determinations.

Consider what this means for the sovereign's relationship to other sovereigns. Hobbes thought that international relations between sovereigns mirror the relations between individuals in the state of nature (L xiii.12, 78). It follows that all sovereigns who covenant with other sovereigns and who are second-performers, or first-performers without a new reason to mistrust, are obligated to perform. Hobbes says as much: 'if a weaker prince make a disadvantageous peace with a stronger, for fear, he is bound to keep it, unless (as hath been said before) there ariseth some new and just cause of fear, to renew the war' (L xiv.27, 86). So in principle the sovereign can be bound *in foro externo* by the laws of nature.[20]

Valid state-of-nature covenants show that, *pace* Bobbio, the binding force of the laws of nature does not necessarily depend on the existence of an absolute sovereign and a regime of positive law. They bind *in foro interno* always, and *in foro externo* when there are no reasonable grounds to fear that others will take advantage of the law-of-nature-abiding actor. This implies something of a paradox. Because the absolute sovereign occupies a position of de facto ascendancy in relation to his subjects, in the ordinary case he will not have reasonable grounds to fear that his subjects will take advantage if he complies with the laws of nature. His monopoly

[19] Kavka, *Hobbesian Moral and Political Theory*, 351.

[20] For an insightful anti-realist interpretation of Hobbes's view of international relations, see Noel Malcolm, 'Hobbes's Theory of International Relations' in Noel Malcolm, *Aspects of Hobbes* (Oxford University Press, 2002), 432–56.

on coercive force ensures that he can comply with and enforce the laws of nature against those whose will is not 'framed by justice'. Therefore, in the ordinary case, the laws of nature bind the sovereign vis-à-vis his subjects, both in *foro interno* and *in foro externo*. The paradox is that it is the sovereign's ascendant power that makes this so. Rather than free the sovereign to rule in any manner he pleases, the sovereign's possession of awe-inspiring power enables the laws of nature to apply to him. This is of a piece with the fiduciary model of authority under which the sovereign is bound by the requirements of the rule of law as a consequence of his possession of irresistible power.

Hobbes confirms this interpretation numerous times in *Leviathan*. He says that violation of the laws of nature 'can never be made lawful. For it can never be that war shall preserve life, and peace destroy it' (L xv.38, 100). In comparing subordinate public bodies to the sovereign, he asserts that the latter has 'no other bounds but such as are set out by the unwritten law of nature' (L xxii.7, 147). Elsewhere he lays down that 'sovereigns are all subject to the laws of nature, because such laws are divine, and cannot by any man or commonwealth be abrogated' (L xxix.9, 213). He says essentially the same thing in his chapter on civil law, chapter 26: 'whatsoever is not against the law of nature may be made law in the name of them that have sovereign power' (L xxvi.41, 188).

Bobbio dismisses these passages as something Hobbes said merely 'in passing'.[21] He claims that with the institution of the commonwealth, the laws of nature are 'completely replaced by positive laws', so much so that natural law as such 'no longer exists in civil society'.[22] The sole function of natural law in Hobbes's account of sovereignty, according to Bobbio, is to provide the *Grundnorm* of the positive legal order. The fundamental law of nature prescribes that individuals seek peace, and the only way for them to do this is by agreeing to institute a commonwealth authorized to issue legal norms. The positive laws of the commonwealth thus derive their validity from the law of nature that requires individuals to 'perform their covenants made', which itself is deduced from the imperative to seek peace. But once the commonwealth is set up, 'there is no other valid law than positive law'.[23]

Some familiar passages from Hobbes appear to support this reading. Hobbes says at one point that the laws of nature are 'but conclusions and theorems concerning what conduceth to the conservation and defence

[21] Bobbio, *Natrual Law*, 138.

[22] *Ibid.*, 141. [23] *Ibid.*, 148.

of themselves, whereas law, properly, is the word of him that by right hath command over others', though he allows that these 'theorems' are 'properly called laws' if they are considered 'as delivered in the word of God, that by right commandeth all things' (L xv.41, 100). In chapter 26 Hobbes sets out the 'mutual containment thesis' according to which '[t]he law of nature and the civil law contain each other, and are of equal extent', so that the laws of nature are 'actually laws' only once a commonwealth is settled, 'as being then the commands of the commonwealth, and therefore also civil laws; for it is the sovereign power that obliges men to obey them' (L xxvi.8, 74).

All of this, however, is consistent with the laws of nature having a relatively determinate content and conditional binding force in the state of nature, as Hobbes confirms in his discussion of covenants. What happens with the advent of the commonwealth is that the fear of non-performance (or the fear that someone will take advantage) is removed, so the conditional obligation to obey the laws of nature becomes absolute. Hobbes's discussion in *Leviathan* of the role and efficacy of the laws of nature within legal order further suggests that they are not simply swallowed up and extinguished by the positive legal regime.

Hobbes thought that positive law had to be published to be binding. But once we are in civil society the laws of nature are binding without 'any publishing, nor proclamation', since they can be known 'not upon other men's words, but every one from his own reason' (L xxvi.13, 177). On much the same grounds, Hobbes concludes that '[i]gnorance of the law of nature excuseth no man', and that if an unwritten law discloses no iniquity and is generally observed, it must be a law of nature 'equally obliging all mankind' (L xxvii.4, 191; xxvi.9, 175). These passages are at odds with Bobbio's contention that the laws of nature disappear when the commonwealth is settled, since their content is apparent through reason alone.

Also in tension with Bobbio's position is the role Hobbes assigns the judge in legal order. We have seen already that in resolving disputes the judge is bound by equity to treat the parties equally. Hobbes also claims that when the judge interprets the sovereign's legislation, 'the intention of the legislator is always supposed to be equity; for it were a great contumely for a judge to think otherwise of the sovereign' (L xxvi.26, 183). Therefore, if the letter of the law does not 'authorize a reasonable sentence', the judge is to 'supply it with the law of nature' (*ibid.*). Similarly, if a judge has no positive law to go on, the laws of nature will fill in the gaps and provide the required legal principles, for in those circumstances the judge's sentence 'ought to be according to the reason of his sovereign (which being always understood to be equity, he is bound to it by the law of nature)' (L xxvi.14, 177–8).

Bobbio's reply to the gap-filling role of the laws of nature is essentially Hart and Raz's reply to Dworkin. He claims that 'it is entirely at the judge's discretion to identify and specify the law of nature'.[24] The judge, Bobbio says, 'has the same power of manipulating the laws of nature that the sovereign exercises [through his legislative power] in determining their content'.[25] Here is the passage from *De Cive* he relies on for this latter claim:[26]

> *Theft, Murder, Adultery* and all *wrongs* [*injuriae*] are forbidden by the laws of nature, but what is to count as a *theft* on the part of the citizen or as *murder* or *adultery* or a *wrongful act* is to be determined by the *civil*, not the *natural*, *law*. Not every taking of an object which is in the possession of another is *theft*, but only the taking of something *that belongs to another*; what counts as *ours*, what as *another's* is a question of the *civil law*. Similarly, not every killing of a man is *Murder*, but only the killing of someone whom the *civil law* forbids us to kill; and not every act of intercourse is *adultery*, but only what the civil laws forbid.

Bobbio takes this passage to show that in *De Cive* the 'laws of nature are empty formulas, which civil power alone can fill with specific content'.[27] This is misleading. The central terms have *some* meaning that is intelligible independently of civil law, but the civil law is necessary to narrow the scope of the terms so as to make them applicable to particular cases. Even then some indeterminacy will remain and be left for judges to resolve on a case-by-case basis. But neither the abstractness of the laws of nature nor the indeterminacy of their civil law counterparts implies that they are unintelligible. Hobbes's view that they are knowable through reason and not in need of publication points the other way.

Interestingly, Hobbes dropped the passage above when he came to write *Leviathan*. One reason he may have done so is that if the laws of nature are 'empty formulas', then Hobbes's argument for sovereignty is in jeopardy. At the end of chapter 13, Hobbes calls the laws of nature 'convenient articles of peace, upon which men may be drawn to agreement' (L xiii.14, 78).

[24] *Ibid.*, 136. [25] *Ibid.*

[26] Thomas Hobbes, *On the Citizen*, edited by Richard Tuck and Michael Silverthorne (Cambridge University Press, 1997), vi.16, 86. Bobbio cites from the Molesworth edition of *De Cive*, so the text quoted here is differs slightly from the text Bobbio quotes, but the meaning is the same.

[27] Bobbio, *Natural Law*, 130.

The expression 'articles of peace' refers to the terms of a peace treaty. The only plausible candidate for this treaty, at this juncture in *Leviathan*, is the agreement that will keep people out of the state of nature, i.e. the original covenant. But if the terms of the covenant are meaningless 'empty formulas', it is unclear why anyone would be drawn to agree on *them* rather than on other terms, or no terms at all. Additionally, we have seen that Hobbes's considered view in *Leviathan* is that, under a considerable range of circumstances (e.g. second-performers, first-performers with no new fear of non-performance), the laws of nature bind on action as well as conscience in the state of nature. This alone implies that those laws must be determinate enough to be intelligible to the persons they are binding. If so, the laws of nature quite plausibly provide the judge with a meaningful store of independent principles to guide interpretation of the sovereign's legislation, a point we turn to momentarily.

As for the sovereign's relationship to the subject, Hobbes allows that if 'a subject have a controversy with his sovereign … grounded on a precedent law, he hath liberty to sue for his right as if it were against a subject, and before such judges as are appointed by the sovereign' (L xxi.19, 143–4). Nonetheless, Hobbes maintains that 'if he [the sovereign] demand or take anything by pretence of his power, there lieth in that case no action of law, for all that is done by him in virtue of his power, is done by the authority of every subject' (*ibid.*). One way to read this passage is as approval of the sovereign's use of extra-legal power. This Schmittian interpretation, however, is in tension with the claim Hobbes makes later on in *Leviathan*, cited above, that 'the commonwealth *only* prescribes and commandeth the observation of those rules which we call law' (L xxvi.5, 173, emphasis added). The tension is resolved if by 'power' we read Hobbes to mean the sovereign's legislative power, which the sovereign can exercise at will to amend or repeal positive law. Hobbes contemplates elsewhere the possibility of the sovereign issuing a command that is 'contrary to a former law' (L xxvii.27, 198). He builds into the sovereign's law-making power a doctrine of implied repeal specifically designed to address such cases: 'when the sovereign commandeth anything to be done against his own former law, the command, as to that particular law, is an abrogation of the law' (*ibid.*). So even when the sovereign exercises power contrary to a precedent law, he seems to think he can do so only through law.

This raises the question of in what sense, if any, the law of nature binds a sovereign who possesses apparently omnipotent legislative power. Bobbio claims that to assign a 'legal meaning' to any sense in which the laws of nature bind the sovereign vis-à-vis the subject, 'we must admit that the subject has the right not to obey, that is, to resist any command of the sovereign that is contrary to the laws of nature'.[28] He rejects this hypothesis on now familiar grounds: the subject has authorized the sovereign 'to determine what is just and unjust', and so the subject cannot complain of injustice because he must acknowledge the sovereign's actions as his own.[29] Thus, if the sovereign violates equity and other laws of nature by sentencing an innocent man to death – Hobbes gives the example of David and Uriah (L xxi.7, 139) – he wrongs God but not his subject. And from this Bobbio concludes that the subject has no right of resistance, 'since no wrong has been committed against the subject'.

However, in the case of a subject condemned to death, whether innocent or not, the subject would have a right of resistance, one grounded on her inalienable right of self-preservation. It is significant that Hobbes uses an example such as this where the subject owes the sovereign no *ex ante* duty of obedience. The facts of the case let Hobbes uphold the formal validity of the inequitable punishment while not committing himself one way or the other on whether violating the laws of nature undermines the subject's duty to obey. I will argue that it does. Bobbio stacks the deck in his favour by framing the issue as whether the subject acquires a right of disobedience and resistance. The subject need acquire no such right for us to see a tangible sense in which the laws of nature bind the sovereign. Roughly, what happens when the sovereign violates the laws of nature is that he subverts his authority, to a greater or lesser degree depending on the extent and severity of the violation, and thereby correspondingly weakens or extinguishes his subject's duty to obey. The details of how badly the sovereign would have to behave so as to lose some or all authority over some or all of his people, and third-party effects (the effects of a breach of a law of nature on the sovereign's authority over subjects who are not directly wronged by the breach), are beyond the scope of this chapter. But it is important to see that on the fiduciary theory the sovereign can lose authority over individuals, as well as over his people generally, inasmuch as he breaches the laws of nature in his dealings with them. His position of trust is a position he occupies vis-à-vis every individual subject to his power, and so his authority over particular individuals depends directly on his treatment of them, as does their duty to obey.

To answer Bobbio's argument persuasively, though, we need to explain how the laws of nature bind the sovereign when he commands in his public capacity, since Hobbes's frequent contention that the sovereign can

[28] *Ibid.*, 139. [29] *Ibid.*

commit iniquity though not injustice presupposes that the sovereign is acting on the subjects' authorization and within his public capacity even when he commits iniquity. That is, we need to explain how the laws of nature can bind the sovereign when his commands are formally valid.

They can bind because they provide an independent reservoir of principles capable of guiding the interpretation of law, and because, according to Hobbes, 'all laws, written and unwritten, have need of interpretation' (L xxvi.21, 180). The institution charged to make authoritative interpretations of law is a subordinate judiciary (i.e. a judiciary that is subordinate to the sovereign, who is the supreme judge). Because the judge is required to interpret the sovereign's decrees in light of equity, offending laws must be read down, or words must be read in, such that they supply a 'reasonable sentence' that conforms to principle. In *Behemoth* Hobbes gives a powerful example that illuminates how equity can play this role. The example arises from a discussion of Charles I's passing of the bill that purported to grant parliament authority to decide the timing of its dissolution:[30]

> And I think that even by the law of equity, which is the unalterable law of nature, a man that has the sovereign power cannot, if he would, give away the right of anything which is necessary for him to retain for the good government of his subjects, unless he do it in express words, saying that he will have the sovereign power no longer. For giving away that, which by consequence only, draws the sovereignty along with it, is not (I think) a giving away of the sovereignty; but an error, such as works nothing but an invalidity in the grant itself.

Hobbes uses equity here as an 'unalterable' criterion for assessing and denying the validity of an explicit grant of power entrenched in valid legislation. Equity, in other words, constrains what the sovereign can do through clear and valid legislation. Even using express words, the sovereign cannot, 'if he would', transfer a power of sovereignty that 'by consequence only, draws sovereignty along with it'. If he really wishes to transfer his sovereignty to another person he can do so, with an express grant in which his purpose is made clear. But he cannot validly grant away through law an element of sovereign power that is constitutive of it. Hobbes is clearly of the view that a judge tasked with interpreting this

[30] Thomas Hobbes, *Behemoth or The Long Parliament* [1668], edited by Ferdinand Tönnies (University of Chicago Press, 1990), 118. See also 74, where Hobbes laments that parliament was able to obtain 'a continuance of their own sitting as long as they listed: which amounted to a total extinction of the King's right, in case that such a grant were valid; which I think it is not, unless the Sovereignty itself be in plain terms renounced, which it was not'.

legislation would have to read it down consistent with equity, and declare the grant invalid.

In *Leviathan*, Hobbes had previously set out the principle that sovereignty could be renounced only with 'direct terms', but without any reference to equity (L xviii.17, 116). It is noteworthy that in *Behemoth*, his account of the English Civil War, he calls on equity not so much to buttress an abstract philosophical argument, but to justify a constraint on a monarch who was contending with a constitutional crisis, if not an outright state of emergency. Although the constraint is intended to maintain the king's sovereignty, Hobbes would have known that Charles I signed the relevant bill (along with an execution order signed the same day against his closest advisor, the Earl of Strafford) because he thought doing so was necessary to save his regime, and possibly his life. The prospective effect of Hobbes's principle is that sovereigns under siege cannot use law in this way to attempt to save themselves and their regimes. If the sovereign wishes to grant away sovereignty, equity requires that he express his will clearly and publicly, and so in this sense legal order constrains the sovereign.

Notice that equity limits the sovereign's legislative power here in much the same way the common law of judicial review limits parliamentary sovereignty: in both cases the sovereign must use express words if the intent is to compromise principle. And in both Hobbes's legal order and commonwealth jurisdictions, where equity and other legal principles are called on to fills gaps in positive law and supply reasonable sentences, the subjection of legislation to principled interpretation provides subjects with a bulwark against arbitrary executive action.

What if, however, the sovereign passes explicit legislation that violates a law of nature but does not put the whole of his sovereignty in jeopardy? Suppose, for instance, the sovereign legislates that the testimony of 'democraticals' in judicial proceedings is not to be taken at face value, in violation of equity understood as the law of nature that requires judges to deal equally between the parties. A judge who understands her role should treat the command as an error similar in kind to the error contained within a purported grant of an essential right of sovereignty. Just as the purported grant of an essential right unravels the whole, a command to deal unequally between the parties to a dispute unravels the office of the judge. Because the constitutive requirements of her office are laws of nature, the judge knows them through reason. She should also know that as a judge she cannot give effect to the offending command, but rather must treat it as an error. To give it effect would subvert the rationale of her office by compromising her ability to render an impartial judgment, which is, Hobbes says, 'the cause of war' (L xv.23, 97).

Hobbes of course does not say that judges in this position can disobey their sovereigns through artful interpretation. But as noted above, he clearly states throughout *Leviathan* that the civil law cannot abrogate the laws of nature, and that the former must be read in light of the latter. Nowhere does Hobbes suggest that the sovereign or his judges may disregard the laws of nature. In practice a judge may bend when confronted with a direct and unequivocal command to breach a law of nature, but the judge and those subject to her authority would still know that, in bending, the judge had abdicated her responsibility as a judge.

Now, under Hobbes's theory, the sovereign can sit in judgment himself. Yet were he to do so and attempt to discriminate against democraticals, he could not expect them to treat his sentence as binding. By treating them unequally, he forsakes the condition of equality on which they entered civil society and authorized sovereign power. Assuming for the sake of argument that his judgment is formally valid such that the subject cannot complain of injustice per se, the fact that the laws of nature are knowable through reason and relatively determinate implies that the subject will know that the judgment in inequitable. Even if this is not a wrong against the subject, on Hobbes's terms, it is a plausible basis for the subject to question whether the sovereign is serving the ends of sovereignty. That is, the subject will have good grounds to consider whether the sovereign is in fact providing her protection. If the sovereign does not offer arbitration on equal terms, the subject's only recourse to resolve her controversies is through force, where by definition protection is absent. If the sovereign deliberately withholds protection in this manner, his relationship to the subject is perilously close to the circumstances in which the subject's obligation ceases because the sovereign has lost his power to protect her (L xxi.21, 144; R&C.6, 490). In both cases the subject is effectively thrust into the state of nature to fend for herself. The 'mutual relation between protection and obedience' is dissolved.

I conclude that the laws of nature, as moral as well as prudential precepts of reason, can be understood to bind the sovereign in a number of ways. First, they bind the sovereign whenever he occupies a position of ascendancy vis-à-vis his subjects or another sovereign. Second, they provide determinate and independent principles through which his commands are to be interpreted for the equal benefit of his subjects, by judges and subjects alike. Third, they supply the constitutive requirements of public offices that must be respected to function as such. Because the laws of nature have a moral character and bind the sovereign in his relations with his subjects, the sovereign is subject to binding moral requirements that frame his authorization to establish legal order. It follows from this and from what has been said above that Hobbes's theory of sovereignty, properly understood, is a relational and fiduciary theory.

Conclusion

I have argued that the sovereign and his delegates, in their public capacity, occupy positions of trust on behalf of the people. Sovereign authorities are essentially public agents of necessity, and as such they are authorized to exercise public powers on behalf of the people, whether particular individuals consent or not. Just as the shipmaster may act as an agent of necessity for cargo owners who are unable to contract for themselves, the sovereign and his delegates may act as agents of necessity for subjects who, as private parties, are not entitled to exercise public powers. The sovereign must exercise his powers in accordance with the laws of nature because his subjection to those laws justifies the fiduciary authorization he enjoys as a public agent of necessity to establish legal order. A failure to abide by these laws would subvert his authority and the moral claim he could otherwise make to his subjects' obedience.

While for rhetorical purposes at least, Hobbes used consent to explain the *origins* of sovereignty, the ongoing justification and stability of sovereignty, and so its *nature*, rests on the 'mutual relation' of reciprocal trust that his conception of legal order makes possible. In the passage cited in the epigraph, Hobbes implies that his purpose in writing *Leviathan* was to find a middle ground between 'those who contend, on one side for too great liberty, and on the other side for too much authority'. The relational interpretation of his theory makes good on this promise.

8

Hobbes on civic liberty and the rule of law

LARS VINX

Hobbes is often taken to have argued that we need to be willing to accept subjection to arbitrary sovereign power in order to enjoy social peace. In recent years, neo-republican authors like Philip Pettit and Quentin Skinner have adopted this reading and have used Hobbes as a foil against which to develop an account of the importance of the principle of non-arbitrary rule. I will show that Hobbes, far from providing the foil neo-republicans want, developed his own conception of non-arbitrariness, through his account of government according to law. This conception of non-arbitrariness differs in important respects from that put forward by neo-republican authors. But it might well provide a more plausible and realistic picture of the scope of the ideal of non-domination.

The chapter will proceed by examining Philip Pettit's perceptive account of Hobbes's theory of political freedom. Pettit has argued that Hobbes was concerned to defend two main claims about liberty.[1] The first is the thesis that 'it is only the exercise of a power of interference that reduces people's freedom, not its (unexercised) existence – not even its existence in an arbitrary, unchecked form'. The second is the view that 'the exercise of a power of interference always reduces freedom in the same way, whether it occurs in a republican democracy, purportedly on a "non-arbitrary" basis, or under a dictatorial, arbitrary regime'.[2]

I will argue that it is doubtful whether these two theses can be attributed to Hobbes, and I will show that, to the extent that they can, they do not carry the implications Pettit associates with them. Hobbes was

The author would like to thank Olli Koistinen, Juha Räikkä, Simon Wigley and Bill Wringe for their helpful comments on draft versions of this chapter.

[1] See Philip Pettit, *Republicanism. A Theory of Freedom and Government* (Oxford University Press, 1997), 35–41 and Philip Pettit, 'Liberty and Leviathan' (2005) 4 *Politics, Philosophy, and Economics* 131. I will be concerned here with the more recent and more elaborate statement in 'Liberty and Leviathan'.

[2] See Pettit, 'Liberty and Leviathan', 131, 148–149.

concerned about the unexercised existence of powers capable of arbitrarily interfering with our freedom and he did not believe that a sovereign is free to exercise his authority in completely arbitrary ways. Rather, Hobbes developed a distinctive conception of civic liberty which expresses the demand that all political rule must abide by rule-of-law standards. The chapter analyses this conception of civic liberty through a comparison of the different forms of freedom discussed in *Leviathan*.

Constitutional indifferentism and non-domination

According to Pettit's neo-republican conception of political freedom, we are subject to domination, even while we are not experiencing any actual interference with our negative liberty, as long as we have to live under a power that could interfere, and do so arbitrarily, i.e. without having to give consideration to our legitimate interests.[3] To be dominated is morally corrupting, for it forces us to 'bow and scrape'[4] in the face of superiors to prevent them from exercising their powers of arbitrary interference. Non-domination, non-subjection to powers of arbitrary interference, is therefore an essential prerequisite for enjoying the dignity and respect that is afforded to citizens but that is denied to mere subjects.

Hobbes, in Pettit's view, refuses to recognize non-domination as a distinct dimension of political freedom.[5] Our interest in freedom, for Pettit's Hobbes, boils down to an interest in avoiding actual interference. According to the first thesis Pettit attributes to Hobbes, our subjection to a power of interference that would interfere arbitrarily if it were to interfere does not reduce our freedom as long as that power does not in fact interfere. Our interest in freedom therefore does not provide us with any reason to be concerned about the mere existence of an arbitrary power of interference. According to the second thesis, it does not matter whether a power interferes arbitrarily or non-arbitrarily if it interferes. The restriction of freedom that one suffers will be equally bad in either case. Our interest in freedom, therefore, does not provide us with any reason to prefer subjection to a non-arbitrary power to subjection to an arbitrary or dictatorial power. Hobbes's explicit support for constitutional indifferentism, the view that we have no deep reason to prefer one of the three

[3] See Pettit, *Republicanism*, 51–109.

[4] See *ibid.*, 87.

[5] See *ibid.*, 37–38; Pettit, 'Liberty and Leviathan', 148–149. See also Quentin Skinner, *Liberty Before Liberalism* (Cambridge University Press, 1998), 59–77; Quentin Skinner, *Hobbes and Republican Liberty* (Cambridge University Press, 2008), 138–177.

constitutional forms (monarchy, aristocracy, democracy) to another,[6] is taken by Pettit to confirm this interpretation.[7]

This account of Hobbes's constitutional indifferentism gets off on the wrong foot. Hobbes does not hold that we have no reason to prefer non-arbitrary to arbitrary, dictatorial rule. He claims, rather, that no form of government is in itself more or less arbitrary than any other. In Hobbes's view, *any* form of organized social control, in order to qualify as a form of political rule or of sovereignty, will have to be non-arbitrary in a number of morally important respects relating to the form in which public power is exercised. But *no* constitutional system, whether democratic or not, can guarantee that its subjects will never have to live with political decisions that they have reason to regard as unreasonable or unfair.[8] The political decisions taken in a democracy will therefore not necessarily be less substantively arbitrary than those taken in a monarchy or aristocracy.

Note that constitutional indifferentism, so understood, does not entail that we have no reason to be interested in the difference between arbitrary and non-arbitrary forms of rule. It will lead us to that conclusion only once we identify one of the constitutional forms recognized by Hobbes, presumably democracy, with fully non-arbitrary and the others, like monarchy and aristocracy, with completely arbitrary or dictatorial rule.[9] But of course, Hobbes never endorses this identification, and there are good reasons for avoiding it. A monarchy might clearly succeed in living up to the requirements of legal governance identified in Lon Fuller's internal morality of law.[10] Nor is there any reason to think that a democratic government could never act arbitrarily. Constitutional indifferentism, then, does not by itself conflict with the idea that any form of sovereign power, be it democratic, aristocratic or monarchic, will have to be non-arbitrary in some respects in order to qualify as an instance of political authority.

[6] See Thomas Hobbes, *Leviathan*, edited by Richard Tuck (Cambridge University Press, 1991), 129–138.

[7] See Pettit, 'Liberty and Leviathan', 145.

[8] I will focus here on the first of these two elements of indifferentism. For discussion of the other see Lars Vinx, 'Constitutional Indifferentism and Republican Freedom' (2010) 38 *Political Theory* 809.

[9] Pettit seems to attribute this view to Hobbes in 'Liberty and Leviathan', 132, where he claims that Hobbes persuaded later authors 'that the exercise of a power of interference always reduces freedom in the same way, whether it occurs in a republican democracy, purportedly on a "non-arbitrary" basis, or under a dictatorial, arbitrary regime'.

[10] See Lon L. Fuller, *The Morality of Law* (New Haven: Yale University Press, rev. edn, 1964), 33–94.

As has been pointed out by other authors, Hobbes puts surprising emphasis on developing an ideal of the rule of law.[11] He evidently holds that some degree of respect for the ideal of the rule of law on the part of the sovereign is constitutive of the relationship between sovereign and subject (as opposed to the relationship between two enemies in a state of nature or the relationship of master and slave). And Hobbes's claim that any form of social control which is to count as a form of political rule will have to be non-arbitrary, in the sense of abiding by rule-of-law standards, stems precisely from his understanding of the nature of our interest in political freedom.

Pettit helpfully draws attention to the fact that Hobbes distinguishes between two different forms of freedom or liberty: liberty as non-obligation and liberty as non-obstruction. He also claims that these two are the only forms of freedom Hobbes recognizes.[12] I believe that what Hobbes says about these two forms of freedom does not support the attribution of the two theses or of their purported implication – that we have no reason to be concerned with the danger of arbitrary rule – to Hobbes. It is wrong, moreover, that liberty as non-obstruction and liberty as non-obligation are the only two forms of freedom recognized by Hobbes. To defend these points, I will discuss liberty as non-obstruction in the second section of this chapter and liberty as non-obligation in the third section. The fourth section will deal with a third kind of liberty acknowledged by Hobbes, the liberty of subjects, and explain why it is distinct from the two forms of liberty Pettit recognizes in Hobbes.

Hobbes on liberty as non-obstruction

Liberty as non-obstruction is a body's freedom to move around unimpeded by external physical obstacles. A body is free, Hobbes claims, as long as its local movement is not blocked or obstructed.[13] Liberty

[11] See David Dyzenhaus, 'Hobbes and the Legitimacy of Law' (2001) 20 *Law and Philosophy* 461; Noel Malcolm, 'Hobbes's Theory of International Relations', in Noel Malcolm, *Aspects of Hobbes* (Oxford University Press, 2002), 432.

[12] Pettit, 'Liberty and Leviathan', 139.

[13] Hobbes, *Leviathan*, 145–146: 'Liberty, or Freedome, signifieth (properly) the absence of Opposition; (by Opposition I mean externall Impediments of motion;) and may be applyed no lesse to Irrationall, and Inanimate creatures, than to Rationall. For whatsoever is so tyed, or environed, as it cannot move, but within a certain space, which space is determined by the opposition of some externall body, we say it hath not Liberty to go further. And so of all living creatures, whilest they are imprisoned, or restrained, with walls, or chains; and of the water whilest it is kept in banks, or vessels, that otherwise

as non-obstruction, then, has a very wide sphere of application. It can be attributed to rational and irrational creatures or even to inanimate physical objects. To cite one of Hobbes's examples: the liberty of the water in my mug is restricted by the wall of the mug, since the water would otherwise flow down. Likewise, Hobbes argues, the liberty of an animate creature is restricted if it is imprisoned, walled in, or put in chains.[14]

Hobbes's conception of liberty as non-obstruction is beset by an ambiguity that arises from the fact that the movement of animate creatures, including human beings, causally depends on their desires and on their beliefs about the external environment. Hobbes expresses this fact by saying that the external movement of animals is voluntary, that it proceeds from their own will, which is in turn defined as the last appetite in deliberation that immediately precedes action.[15] Needless to say, an animal's will, as formed by deliberation, will often reflect the animal's perception of external obstacles to motion. A prudent and experienced animal will avoid movement likely to bring it into collision with an external obstacle. The ambiguity in Hobbes's definition of liberty as non-obstruction concerns the question whether an animal that so adapts to external obstacles can be said to suffer a restriction of its liberty.

According to the reading of Hobbes's definition of liberty adopted by Pettit, we may call it the actualist reading, an external obstacle restricts my freedom only if it actually interrupts some voluntary motion of mine, i.e. only if I have decided to act in a certain way, have embarked upon the chosen course of action, and then find my movement frustrated by an external impediment.[16] According to this understanding of liberty as non-obstruction, my liberty will not be obstructed by some obstacle if I never form the will, in Hobbes's technical sense of the term, to do what the obstacle would prevent me from doing. And this result holds despite the fact that my deliberative processes are conditioned by my knowledge of the existence of the obstacle, even if I would form a will to act in the way the obstacle prevents me from acting if the obstacle didn't exist. This interpretation, Pettit points out, seems to fit well with Hobbes's definition of a 'free man' as 'he, that in those things which by

would spread it selfe into a larger space, we use to say, they are not at Liberty, to move in such a manner, as without those externall impediments they would.'

[14] See *ibid.*, 145–146.

[15] See *ibid.*, 37–38, 44–45.

[16] See Pettit, 'Liberty and Leviathan', 137–139.

his strength and wit he is able to do, is not hindred to do what he has a will to do'.[17]

Now clearly, this view of liberty as non-obstruction implies patently absurd consequences. It entails that I might enjoy complete freedom of non-obstruction even while being imprisoned in a windowless cell in the bowels of Alcatraz with my feet in thick chains. According to the actualist reading, I am suffering a restriction of liberty only as long as I make an actual attempt to break out of my cell. As soon as I stop hammering the walls with my bare fists, in recognition of the obvious fact that I won't be able to break them down, I am free, no matter how intensely I desire to get out of my cell. I am free since I no longer have the will (in Hobbes's technical sense of the term) to escape. The actualist interpretation, I conclude, openly contradicts Hobbes's official definition of liberty, which claims that a human being that is 'imprisoned, or restrained, with walls, or chains' suffers a restriction or loss of its liberty as non-obstruction.[18] As charitable readers, we therefore have reason to reject it if there is another interpretation that is exegetically defensible.[19]

One obvious alternative interpretation is to take Hobbes's definition of liberty to say that an agent is free to φ if and only if he is internally capable of φ-ing and no external impediment would prevent him from φ-ing if he were to form the will to φ. Since I am taken to suffer a restriction of

[17] Hobbes, *Leviathan*, 146. Pettit also points to a passage in the *Questions Concerning Liberty, Necessity, and Chance* in *English Works of Thomas Hobbes*, edited by William Molesworth, vol. V (London: John Boon, 1841), 351–352 to support the actualist reading. Hobbes discusses a scenario where someone deliberates whether to play tennis or not, not knowing that the door to the tennis court is locked, so that he won't be able to play should he decide to do so. Bramhall had used this example to argue that there is an inconsistency between Hobbes's claim that a man is free 'that hath not yet made an end of deliberating' and his claim that liberty is 'an absence of outward impediments': if liberty is an absence of outward impediments, then the man is not a free man since he is not at liberty to play tennis, which contradicts the claim that he must be free because he is still deliberating. Hobbes responds that 'it is no impediment to him that the door is shut, till he have a will to play; which he hath not till he hath done deliberating whether he shall play or not'. This reply seems to lend support to Pettit's actualist reading. However, the scenario assumes that the man doesn't know that the door is locked. Hence, it is unclear what Hobbes would have said about a scenario where the man desires to play tennis, and would form a will to do so, if it weren't for his knowing that the door is locked. I am therefore disinclined to regard the passage as decisive evidence for the actualist interpretation.

[18] Hobbes, *Leviathan*, 145–146.

[19] In a recent paper, Pettit acknowledges the absurdity of the actualist view, but nevertheless continues to attribute it to Hobbes, as though it didn't matter that the attribution conflicts with Hobbes's definition of liberty. See Philip Pettit, 'The Instability of Freedom as Noninterference: The Case of Isaiah Berlin' (2011) 121 *Ethics* 693, 699–701.

liberty whenever there is an obstacle that bars me from doing something that it would be in my power to do if it weren't for the obstacle, we can no longer infer that prisoners are free once they cease to try to escape, in recognition of the futility of the attempt. Another alternative interpretation that would likewise allow us to avoid the embarrassing implications of the actualist view, and that is perhaps closer in line with the text, holds that my freedom is restricted if and only if one of the following two conditions is met: either an action I have chosen to perform is obstructed by an external obstacle; or my awareness of an external obstacle stops me from forming the will to do something that I would choose to do if it weren't for my awareness of the obstacle.[20] Under this view, my freedom is not restricted by obstacles that would prevent me from doing things that I do not wish to do. But under the plausible assumption that those who are imprisoned or in chains typically wish not to be so constrained, we will still be able to save Hobbes's claim that prisoners or slaves suffer a restriction of liberty of non-obstruction.

The only textual passage in *Leviathan* that seems to favour the actualist reading over these alternatives is the definition of the free man, since it explicitly claims that we lack liberty only if we are blocked from doing what we have a will to do. However, to say that a free man is a man who is not hindered to do what he has a will to do might, in this context, be a shorthand way of saying that I am free to φ if I would not encounter an obstacle if I were to form the will to φ. It might be a way, alternatively, of expressing the point that someone who is not imprisoned, in chains, or under someone else's direct physical control will usually not encounter external obstacles in doing what he wishes to do.[21]

As I pointed out above, Pettit adopts the actualist interpretation of liberty as non-obstruction. He also holds that it entails that there is no reason to be concerned with the mere existence of a power of arbitrary

[20] Hobbes frequently suggests that our freedom is not restricted if an obstacle blocks actions that we do not desire to perform. In Hobbes, *Leviathan*, 146 he speaks of 'the Liberty of the man; which consisteth in this, that he finds no stop, in doing what he has the will, desire, or inclination to doe'. In the context of the tennis example, Hobbes explains: 'nor can any man be said to be hindered from doing that, which he had no purpose at all to do' (Hobbes, *Questions Concerning Liberty, Necessity, and Chance*, 352). On the plausible assumption that having a desire or inclination to φ is not the same thing, for Hobbes, as having a will (in Hobbes's technical sense of the term) to φ, these passages speak against the actualist reading.

[21] Hobbes repeatedly draws a simple contrast between people who are free to move about at will and those who have lost their freedom of movement since they are imprisoned or in chains. See Hobbes, *Leviathan*, 141, 147.

interference, a claim I do not wish to dispute. After all, it is hard to see why one should be concerned about the mere existence of a power of arbitrary interference if one is taken to be perfectly free until one literally runs up against a physical obstacle. If Matthew Kramer is right to argue that we can always choose to refrain from actively resisting a physical obstacle[22] the actualist interpretation will imply that we can always choose to be perfectly free, regardless of what others are doing to us. Why bother, in that case, with the existence of a power capable of arbitrary interference?

But how does the view that Hobbes is unconcerned with arbitrary rule hold up if we adopt one of the alternative and less absurd interpretations of liberty as non-obstruction? At first glance, the switch might seem to make little difference. Even if we agree that one of the alternative interpretations must be correct, it will still be the case that it is only the actual exercise of a power of physical interference, not its mere existence, which can reduce our freedom of movement. It still holds true, moreover, that a reduction of our freedom of movement will be equally bad regardless of how it comes about. A reduction of liberty of non-obstruction that is undesirable for the person who suffers it, insofar as it stops her from doing something she wishes to do or might come to wish to do, is not made any better by the fact that it results from a non-arbitrary interference. What I would like to argue, nevertheless, is that it doesn't follow from these observations, however true, that a Hobbesian interest in liberty as non-obstruction provides us with no reason to care whether we are subject to an arbitrary or a non-arbitrary power of interference.

Hobbes holds that the obstruction of their movement must be the prime evil for human beings. According to Hobbes's view of the good, our supreme interest is to live, and to live contentedly, for as long as possible.[23] And life, according to Hobbes, is nothing but continuous internal vital motion; a motion that is dependent on external resources that humans can only obtain through unimpeded external and voluntary motion.[24] Actual collision with other human beings, or physical confinement within a very narrow space at their hands, is not just inconvenient. It is typically inimical to the preservation of our life. We therefore have an overriding interest in avoiding such collision or confinement, to be able to perform such movements as are necessary for us to live and to live contentedly.[25]

[22] See Matthew Kramer, *The Quality of Freedom* (Oxford University Press, 2003), 17–20.

[23] Hobbes, *Leviathan*, 69–70.

[24] See *ibid.*, 37–40.

[25] That non-obstruction is our primary interest explains why Hobbes claims that non-obstruction is the proper signification of liberty. See *ibid.*, 91, 145.

Individual adaptive behaviour, in the state of nature, cannot reliably avoid obstruction at the hands of others. In the state of nature it is not in my own power, due to the unpredictability of the behaviour of others, to ensure that I will avoid potentially lethal or confining conflict. While moving around trying to procure the external resources I need to sustain my internal motion, I am very likely to find myself in situations, through no fault of my own, where I am forced to fight with others, and to hazard my life and my physical liberty on the guess that I will be strong enough to prevail.[26] In the state of nature I am threatened by everyone else's possession of a 'Right to every thing; even to one anothers body'.[27] This right is clearly an arbitrary power in Pettit's sense,[28] and Hobbes quite obviously thinks that we have to be concerned about the mere existence of that power in someone else's hands, even if we have not so far suffered any loss of liberty of non-obstruction from any actual exercise of that right.[29]

Our fundamental aim, Hobbes concludes, should be to put ourselves into a condition that makes it possible for us *unilaterally* to avoid collision with others or obstruction at their hands, while enjoying enough freedom of movement to maintain our life and to live contentedly. The crux of Hobbes's argument for civil society is that unilateral avoidance of physically obstructing conflict will become possible in civil society. Civil society provides the assurance that I will very likely be able to continue to move around unobstructedly, while doing what is necessary to satisfy my interest in survival and contentment, as long as I obey its laws.

The obvious reply for Pettit to make to this line of reasoning is to admit that Hobbes was concerned about the mere existence of private powers of arbitrary interference, but that he did not think we should be concerned about the mere existence of governmental powers of arbitrary interference. This reply overlooks that civil society, if it is to allow us unilaterally to avoid obstructing conflict, cannot take the form of an arbitrary dictatorship. In order to provide us with a reliable idea of what kinds of actions we will be able to perform without having to face interference by others, the sovereign will have to govern his subjects through a system of laws and not in a purely discretionary fashion. People must be in a position to know what rules to follow in order to have assurance that they will not

26 See *ibid.*, 86–90. 27 *Ibid.*, 91.

28 See Pettit, *Republicanism*, 52–58.

29 Hobbes, *Leviathan*, 147, in a revealing turn of phrase, calls the right of nature the liberty 'by which all other men may be masters of their lives'.

find themselves caught up in physically obstructing conflict.[30] Laws, to fulfil this function, will have to exhibit the features which theorists of the rule of law associate with legal governance: they will have to be public, prospective, sufficiently clear, and consistent with each other, they must not demand the impossible, and so on.[31]

Of course, compliance with law will allow me to avoid collision or confinement only if I can expect others to comply as well. This expectation cannot be wholly based on the sovereign's power to sanction transgressions of the law. The sovereign cannot credibly threaten all of us, or a majority of us, at the same time. The standard motive for obedience, then, will have to be some form of shared insight into the reasonableness of mutual compliance with the law.[32] This is why Hobbes strives to show that it is rational to obey the laws, even apart from any consideration of the threat of incurring a legal sanction, if others can be counted upon to do the same.[33] While this insight is unlikely to be perfectly effective, due to the influence of passion and irrationality, it will at least have to be available to all of us, which is another way of saying that it must be possible to see the laws as serving *everyone's* interest and as serving it *equally*.[34]

Finally, the idea of legal governance implies that the sovereign himself will treat his subjects in accordance with principles of legality.[35] To be authoritative, a sovereign's demands must be expressed in legal form and

[30] *Ibid.*, 231 Hobbes claims that sovereigns should govern 'by a generall Providence, contained in publique Instruction … and in the making, and executing of good Lawes, to which individuall persons may apply their own cases'. Also *ibid.*, 239–240: 'For the use of Lawes … is not to bind the People from all Voluntary actions; but to direct and keep them in such a motion, as not to hurt themselves by their own impetuous desires, rashnesse, or indiscretion; as Hedges are set, not to stop Travellers, but to keep them in the way.'

[31] See *ibid.*, 214–219, 239–241.

[32] Hobbes consequently argues *ibid.*, 232 that his views on sovereignty 'have the rather need to be diligently, and truly taught; because they cannot be maintained by any Civill Law, or terrour of legall punishment'.

[33] See *ibid.*, 96–97, 101–103.

[34] *Ibid.*, 108: 'if a man be trusted to judge between man and man, it is precept of the Law of Nature, that he deale Equally between them'. Hobbes consequently demands 'that Justice be equally administred to all degrees of People; that is, that as well the rich, and mighty, as poor and obscure persons, may be righted of the injuries done them; so as the great, may have no greater hope of impunity, when they doe violence, dishonour, or any Injury to the meaner sort, then when one of these, does the like to one of them' (*ibid.*, 237).

[35] This requirement does not rule out that a sovereign might, in cases of open rebellion, choose to treat a person as an enemy. But of course, a person so treated will no longer be a subject or have duties of obedience to sovereign authority. See *ibid.*, 216, 219.

be applied through the legal system.[36] Most importantly, subjects must have assurance that – as long as they do not rebel – the sovereign is not going to deprive them of their freedom of movement unless they have been found, in a fair trial, to have violated a known law. If the point of subjection to the laws is to put one in a position unilaterally to avoid collision and confinement, then the sovereign must refrain from using obstructing violence against his subjects in any other way than by punishing them for acknowledged breaches of known laws.[37]

The observation that sovereign authority must treat its subjects in lawful ways provides a reply to Pettit's basic claim that Hobbes was uninterested in the distinction between arbitrary and non-arbitrary rule. Sovereign authority must be non-arbitrary in a number of crucial respects since it would otherwise fail to allow us unilaterally to avoid physical collision with others or confinement at their hands, and safely to do what we need to do to survive and to live contentedly. Our interest in liberty of non-obstruction thus requires a government committed to the rule of law. In Hobbes's view, this is a claim about the nature of all government that applies regardless of constitutional form. It never makes sense, hence, to distinguish between arbitrary and non-arbitrary government. But it does not follow that Hobbes was uninterested in the distinction between arbitrary and non-arbitrary forms of social control.

Hobbes on liberty as non-obligation

Let us now come to the second understanding of liberty Pettit attributes to Hobbes. Liberty as non-obligation consists in 'one's freedom to choose between certain alternatives, uncommitted by prior … obligation'.[38] In the state of nature, we are typically free of all obligation, due to 'the liberty each man has, to use his own power, as he will himselfe, for the preservation of his own nature'.[39] Here, my actions depend exclusively on my own present will. I am not subject to anyone else's command and I am not bound to intentions that I may have formed or even declared in the past. Freedom as non-obligation can be lost only through the making of contracts by which one binds oneself to another. The most important of

[36] In a case of controversy with the sovereign, a subject 'hath the same Liberty to sue for his right, as if it were against a Subject' if the sovereign's claims are 'grounded on a precedent Law' (*ibid.*, 152–153).

[37] See the discussion of punishment, *ibid.*, 214–219.

[38] See Pettit, 'Liberty and Leviathan', 133–137.

[39] Hobbes, *Leviathan*, 91.

these contracts, of course, is the social contract, in which we give up our freedom to use our own power as we see fit to the sovereign, and thus bind ourselves to obey the sovereign's laws.

Pettit is certainly correct in pointing out that Hobbes recognizes freedom of non-obligation as a category of freedom distinct from non-obstruction. According to Hobbes, one can enjoy freedom of non-obligation, for example as a slave or prisoner of war, while finding one's freedom of movement obstructed.[40] On the other hand, where one is obligated, as a subject of a sovereign's laws, one will typically not be obstructed from violating one's legal obligations, though one must expect to face punishment should one decide to break the law.[41]

In Pettit's view, however, the acknowledgement of freedom of non-obligation does not soften Hobbes's attitude towards the problem of domination. Pettit argues that the two theses apply to freedom of non-obligation in exactly the same way they apply to freedom of non-obstruction. Hence, our interest in freedom as non-obligation, like our interest in freedom as non-obstruction, does not, according to Pettit's Hobbes, provide us with a reason to prefer non-arbitrary government.[42] What is more, the fact that subjection to the law will usually go along with possession of freedom as non-obstruction does not ease the burden of subjection in any meaningful way. According to Pettit, Hobbes held that people who are subject to physical chains or imprisonment and people who are tied by legal bonds 'are equally unfree', and that the commonwealth may therefore treat its subjects in just the same way as slaves without forfeiting its authority over them.[43]

Pettit's account of freedom of non-obligation and its relation to political power is mistaken on two counts. The first has to do with Pettit's understanding of freedom as non-obligation. Upon entry into civil society, Pettit assumes, our freedom of non-obligation is not altogether given up but merely restricted. Even in civil society, we retain a residue of liberty as non-obligation: the liberty to decide for ourselves where the laws are silent which Hobbes calls the liberty of a subject.[44] The possession of

[40] See *ibid.*, 141.

[41] See *ibid.*, 146–147. Also Quentin Skinner, 'Hobbes on the Proper Signification of Liberty', in Quentin Skinner, *Visions of Politics, Volume III: Hobbes and Civil Science* (Cambridge University Press, 2002), 209, 210–225.

[42] See Pettit, 'Liberty and Leviathan', 148.

[43] *Ibid.*, 141, 145.

[44] See Pettit, 'Liberty and Leviathan', 144. See also Skinner, 'Hobbes on the Proper Signification of Liberty', 233.

this residual freedom of non-obligation is clearly desirable, and since the residue may be smaller or larger, depending on how the sovereign chooses to exercise his legislative powers, it is desirable that the sovereign interfere as little as possible with it. Once we accept this picture of liberty as non-obligation, it is not hard to see how the two theses would apply to liberty as non-obligation. The mere unexercised existence of a governmental power entitled arbitrarily to restrict our residual freedom as non-obligation does not in fact restrict that freedom, and if that freedom is restricted, the restriction will be equally bad regardless of whether it came about arbitrarily or non-arbitrarily.

One clear exegetical reason to think that this must be an inaccurate portrayal of Hobbes's views is provided by the way Hobbes introduces the liberty of subjects in chapter 21 of *Leviathan*.[45] Hobbes declares that, in the rest of the chapter, he will speak exclusively about the liberty of subjects, and not about two other forms of freedom: the liberty of non-obstruction, which people so manifestly possess as law-abiding subjects of a sovereign, and the liberty that is an 'exemption from Lawes', a liberty 'by which all other men may be masters of their lives'.[46] The implication of this passage is clearly that there are three forms of freedom, but that it is not necessary to discuss the latter two after the commonwealth has been established, since people evidently possess the first of these latter two freedoms, as subjects of a sovereign, while they shouldn't at all want to have the second. That second freedom people shouldn't want to possess, the exemption from laws, can only be the complete freedom from obligation we enjoy in the state of nature. People shouldn't want to possess it because it entails a right to all things that permits everyone to kill or enslave everyone else. Hobbes's suggestion here must be that this natural form of non-obligation cannot be enjoyed within civil society.[47] But if this

[45] Hobbes, *Leviathan*, 147: 'In relation to these Bonds [legal obligations, L.V.] only it is, that I am to speak now, of the *Liberty* of *Subjects* … For if wee take Liberty in the proper sense, for corporeall Liberty; that is to say, freedome from chains, and prison, it were very absurd for men to clamor as they doe, for the Liberty they so manifestly enjoy. Againe, if we take Liberty, for an exemption from the Lawes, it is no lesse absurd, for men to demand as they doe, that Liberty, by which all other men may be masters of their lives.'

[46] *Ibid.*, 147.

[47] See *ibid.*, 200: 'But Civill Law is an Obligation; and takes from us the Liberty which the Law of Nature gave us. Nature gave a Right to every man to secure himselfe by his own strength, and to invade a suspected neighbour, by way of prevention: but the Civill Law takes away that Liberty, in all cases where the protection of the Law may be safely stayd for.' Admittedly, Hobbes sometimes slips into language that suggests a residual natural freedom. See for instance *ibid.*, 185.

is the case, the liberty of subjects, what we might call civil non-obligation, cannot be a simple residue of the natural freedom of non-obligation. It must be a different kind of freedom.

This point can also be defended on a systematic basis. Hobbes argues that it is impossible for us to incur any partial normative commitment of mutual trust to another private person without taking on a prior commitment of (almost) unconditional obedience to the sovereign.[48] Natural liberty as non-commitment, then, cannot be partially abdicated. As long as there is no sovereign, all individuals fully retain it. Once we are subject to a sovereign, by contrast, we retain none of it.[49] The liberty of subjects cannot be construed as a simple absence of obligation or an exemption from the laws. Rather, it is of the nature of an implicit permission. We enjoy the freedom of the subject at the sufferance of the sovereign who has chosen not to exercise his legislative power in a certain area, but who is entitled to modify or further restrict our sphere of freedom without our renewed consent.[50] It is wrong, then, to think of the liberty of a subject as a residue of our natural freedom as non-obligation.

If we have to distinguish between two different forms of non-obligation, we must inquire separately into how each relates to Pettit's two theses. Since I will return to the liberty of subjects in the next section, I will focus on natural non-obligation for now. As far as natural non-obligation is concerned, it should be clear that Pettit's two theses do not apply to it. If natural non-obligation can only be retained or be given up altogether, and if we ought to give it up to avail ourselves of the benefits of civil society, it simply makes no sense to think of natural non-obligation as a freedom that we should have an interest to keep. Nor does it make sense to think of it as a freedom that could be possessed to larger or lesser degree, depending on how a government chooses to exercise its powers.

This, however, is not the only thing that is wrong with Pettit's analysis of the natural freedom of non-obligation. Hobbes did not take the view that people who are subject to legal bonds are as unfree as people who are enslaved or imprisoned by physical obstacles. To see why this parallel is

[48] See *ibid.*, 96.

[49] Hobbes claims, of course, that there are 'some Rights, which no man can be understood by any words ... to have abandoned, or transferred' (*ibid.*, 93), such as the right to defend oneself against attack or to resist 'Wounds, and Chayns, and Imprisonment'. But these reservations will only apply where a sovereign and a former subject have already re-entered a state of war. They do not constitute limitations internal to the relationship of subject to sovereign and should therefore not be confused with a liberty that a subject enjoys under the laws of the sovereign.

[50] See *ibid.*, 152.

misleading is also to see why our natural freedom of non-obligation can only be given up to a power that is in important respects non-arbitrary.

In the context of his discussion of the right of conquest in *Leviathan*, Hobbes draws a clear distinction between servants or subjects and slaves. He explains that 'by the word Servant ... is not meant a Captive, which is kept in prison, or bonds'. Rather, a servant is someone who 'being taken, hath corporall liberty allowed him; and upon promise not to run away, nor to do violence to his Master, is trusted by him'.[51] Consequently, Hobbes emphasizes that it is not the fact of victory that gives the conqueror authority, but rather the voluntary subjection of the vanquished.[52]

This passage is difficult to square with Pettit's interpretation of Hobbes's discussion of the right of conquest. In Pettit's view, this discussion implies that a Hobbesian government has 'the same dominion over individuals that would hold if it constrained them by physical or corporal means'.[53] But this must be wrong, at least if it is taken to mean that a Hobbesian government can treat its subjects in just the same way as slaves without forfeiting its authority over them. The corporal liberty that Hobbes claims is granted to the servant, but not to the slave, must be a liberty that will not be taken away arbitrarily, without due process of law. Otherwise, the subject would have to continue to consider the conqueror an enemy, and to make use of the first opportunity to kill or overpower him. In making a promise of submission in exchange for corporal liberty, the vanquished gives up the natural right to try to kill or overpower the conqueror. Hobbes holds that we cannot enter into a valid contract without receiving a sufficiently valuable return for the rights that we transfer or lay down.[54] And it is hard to see how this condition could be fulfilled if the conqueror tried to reserve to himself the right to kill or imprison his new subject on completely arbitrary grounds. If obedience did not assure protection against a renewed attack on the part of the conqueror, the subject's chances of self-preservation couldn't possibly benefit from giving up the right to make war against the conqueror.[55] Hence, even a

51 *Ibid.*, 141. 52 *Ibid.*

53 Pettit, 'Liberty and Leviathan', 145.

54 Hobbes, *Leviathan*, 93.

55 It might be objected that Hobbes denies that the relationship between sovereign and subject can be contractual. However, Hobbes explicitly claims that a commonwealth by acquisition is based on a covenant between the conqueror and the conquered. Hobbes, *Leviathan*, 141: 'And this Dominion is then acquired to the Victor, when the Vanquished, to avoid the present stroke of death, covenanteth either in expresse words, or by sufficient signes of the Will, that so long as his life, and the liberty of his body is allowed him, the

conqueror must be willing to offer governance by law to those he intends to make his subjects.[56]

I conclude that Pettit is wrong to attribute to Hobbes the view that it does not matter whether our liberty is restricted by a physical obstacle or by a sanction-backed law. Hobbes was perfectly aware that physical obstruction and lawmaking can't be equivalent means of social control, since he acknowledges that it will sometimes be impossible for a ruler to achieve through the latter what he can achieve through the former.[57] Lawmaking, or the attempt to provide behavioural guidance through the issuance of authoritative rules, can be successful only if people are treated in accordance with rule-of-law standards, and are thus given a reason to prefer voluntary compliance with a sovereign's directives to the state of nature and to war against the sovereign. Hobbes's awareness of this point explains why he is very careful to distinguish, in *Leviathan* at least, between subjects and slaves, and why he holds that to treat a subject like a slave, by unlawfully detaining or assaulting the subject, is an act of hostility that severs the bond of civic subjection.[58] Hobbes, in sum, held that it cannot be reasonable for people to give up their natural freedom of non-obligation to a power altogether arbitrary.

Hobbes on the liberty of a subject

Hobbes defines the liberty of the subject as the freedom of subjects 'of doing what their own reason shall suggest, for the most profitable of

Victor shall have the use thereof, at his pleasure.' Whether this introduces inconsistency into Hobbes's theory of sovereignty is an issue that I cannot settle here.

[56] In *De Cive* Hobbes describes servants and subjects as different kinds of slaves, as Pettit points out. But he draws essentially the same distinction between subjection and physical slavery we find in *Leviathan*: 'The obligation, therefore, of a slave to a Master does not arise simply because he spared his life but because he does not keep him bound or in prison. For an obligation arises from agreement, and there is no agreement without trust … Hence in addition to the benefit of sparing his life there is also the trust by which the Master leaves him in physical liberty, so that he could not only run away but could even take the life of the Master who saved his, if it were not for the obligation and bonds of agreement between them' (Thomas Hobbes, *On the Citizen*, edited by Richard Tuck and Michael Silverthorne (Cambridge University Press, 1997), 103). Hobbes claims a little later on that a 'Master therefore has no less right and dominion over the unbound slave than over the bound' (*ibid.*, 104). But in this passage Hobbes is clearly concerned to argue that the sovereign is entitled to interfere with property-rights without the subject's consent, not to deny that he is bound to rule-of-law standards.

[57] See Hobbes, *Leviathan*, 98.

[58] See *ibid.*, 93, 214–219.

themselves' in 'all kinds of actions, by the laws praetermitted'.[59] It might seem at first glance that the liberty of a subject must be either a freedom of non-obstruction, a residue of the natural freedom of non-obligation, or some combination of both. But this view is false and it is therefore wrong to claim that freedom as non-obstruction and freedom as non-commitment are the only two freedoms recognized by Hobbes.

I already explained why the liberty of a subject cannot be understood as a residue of the natural freedom of non-obligation. The liberty of the subject is equally irreducible to the freedom of non-obstruction, since the latter is normally more encompassing than the former. In civil society, we do, after all, have the liberty of non-obstruction to commit crimes,[60] though it is likely that we will be punished for criminal acts. For me to have the liberty of a subject to φ it is not sufficient, hence, that I enjoy the liberty of non-obstruction to φ. It is not necessary either, since another person might unrightfully block me from φ-ing though I have the liberty of a subject to φ.

What it means for me to have the liberty of a subject to φ is that the state is committed to using its force to protect my opportunity to φ without facing an impediment. In a well-functioning state I am unlikely to see actions that fall within my liberty as a subject frustrated by the obstruction of others. Others who might want to obstruct actions that I am legally entitled to perform are liable to punishment if they obstruct me and are thus likely to be deterred from interfering with my actions (as well as from threatening to interfere). As a result, I can reliably expect that actions I am legally entitled to perform will not face external obstruction. Moreover, since the sovereign and his representatives will apply punishments only consequent upon prior breach of known laws, by complying with the law I am in a position to avoid collision with the state's coercive power.

Are Pettit's two theses applicable to the liberty of a subject? It is of course true that the liberty of a subject will only be restricted through actual exercises of legislative power. And we may grant as well that a loss of a certain amount of the liberty of a subject is always in itself bad for the persons concerned. But it does not follow that our interest in the liberty of a subject provides us with no reason to prefer non-arbitrary to arbitrary governance. The liberty of a subject can exist only in the context of a system of legal governance, which, as we have seen, implies that the exercise of political power is non-arbitrary in important respects. Hobbes makes it clear that any attempt on the part of the government to obstruct

[59] *Ibid.*, 147. [60] See *ibid.*, 146–147.

me from doing something that I have the liberty of a subject to do, or any attempt to sanction me for having done something that it was in my liberty of a subject to do, is an act of hostility that severs the bond of subjection between citizen and sovereign.[61] My liberty of a subject can only be conditioned and modified through public and prospective legislation and impartial adjudication.

The liberty of a subject, moreover, sheds an interesting light on another of Pettit's claims about Hobbes's understanding of freedom. Pettit argues that Hobbes does not recognize the idea of freedom as non-coercion (i.e. the idea of a freedom from threats of coercion that stop me from forming a will to do what I wish to do).[62] It is true that Hobbes holds that a mere threat of coercion never takes away the freedom of non-obstruction. It is also true that, for Hobbes, a threat of coercion doesn't take away freedom of non-obligation, as only a contract can abrogate that freedom. But since Hobbes acknowledges a third form of liberty over and above natural non-obligation and physical non-obstruction, these observations do not imply that he fails to recognize freedom of non-coercion or that he doesn't hold it to be valuable. The liberty of a subject, after all, clearly is a freedom of non-coercion.

On the condition that the state is doing its job well, I can expect not to be subject to threats of coercion issuing from other private individuals. Of course, the liberty of a subject is not a complete freedom from coercion, as the state will continue to use threats of coercion to deter me from performing acts it has declared to be illegal. But as we have seen, natural non-obligation can only be alienated to, and civil non-obligation can only be provided by and conditioned by, a sovereign power that governs in accordance with the rule of law and that we have sufficient reason to support apart from its threats of coercion. Hobbes is therefore in a position to claim that we do not lack any freedom from coercion that we ought to possess.

Conclusion: the neo-republican critique of Hobbes

Let me ward off a possible misunderstanding of the argument I have presented. I am not denying that there are important differences between the rule-of-law based understanding of non-arbitrariness I have attributed to

[61] See *ibid.*, 214–219.

[62] See Pettit, 'Liberty and Leviathan', 146–148; see also Skinner, 'Hobbes on the Proper Signification of Liberty', 232–237.

Hobbes and the neo-republican conception of non-domination. Hobbes's conception of the rule of law does not promise to create a polity that will fully realize the ideal of non-domination as Pettit understands it.[63] The rule of law will not give me assurance that my will is never going to be bent to laws that I judge to violate the public interest, it does not require that legislative decisions be taken democratically, and it does not imply that every public decision must be endlessly contestable. All I have argued is that Hobbes wasn't unconcerned with the problem of arbitrary power. But of course, his solution may strike the republican as too thin and undemanding to be very interesting.

Whether this would be an appropriate republican response is a question I cannot definitively answer here. However, it does seem to me that neo-republicans tend not to take Hobbes's views seriously enough as a possible alternative to their own conception of non-arbitrariness.

Neo-republicans assume that Hobbes started from the aim to defend constitutional indifferentism. They take it that this is tantamount to the aim of defending arbitrary government, and then go on to argue that Hobbes's conception of liberty must have been a mere rationalization of this prior commitment.[64] This rationalization, to be successful, or so the story goes, had to define away the idea of freedom as non-domination, which forced Hobbes to invent out of whole cloth a novel conception of liberty, one that is clearly less attractive than the republican ideal of freedom.[65] Neo-republicans portray Hobbes as having been immensely successful in his endeavour to make people forget the ideal of freedom as non-domination.[66] But they never quite explain why Hobbes's redefinition of liberty should have been so influential, given that it is allegedly little more than a feeble rationalization of a prior commitment to authoritarianism.

The reason why this narrative does not add up is that the dispute between Hobbes and republicans is not about whether we should take an interest in non-arbitrary rule. It concerns two competing conceptions of non-arbitrariness, one relatively thin and formal, the other thicker and more substantive. A charitable reader of *Leviathan* will not find it difficult to reconstruct the reasons that led Hobbes to opt for the thin alternative. Hobbes feared that the pursuit of a thick and demanding ideal of

[63] See Pettit, *Republicanism*, 55–56.
[64] See Skinner, *Hobbes and Republican Liberty*, 138–177.
[65] See Pettit, 'Liberty and Leviathan', 146; Skinner, *Hobbes and Republican Liberty*, 151.
[66] See Skinner, *Liberty Before Liberalism*; Pettit, *Republicanism*, 17–50.

non-domination that requires endless contestability would turn out to be incompatible with the existence of well-functioning political institutions capable of securing public order and social co-ordination. If that concern with institutional coherence is still relevant today, and it might well be, we should conclude that to have recovered the ideal of non-domination is not the same as to have successfully defended its most demanding version. Hobbes may well have been right that the scope of a feasible notion of non-domination is rather limited. And if that is the case, the neo-republican attempt to build a complete normative political theory on the notion of non-domination is likely to turn out to be ill-motivated.[67]

[67] See for a fuller development of this argument Vinx, 'Constitutional Indifferentism and Republican Freedom'.

9

Hobbes on equity

DENNIS KLIMCHUK

Hobbes uses 'equity' in a wide variety of ways, and claims a broad range of effects on its behalf. Probably there is no one concept to which each use answers. But there is, I will argue, one principal idea running through the roles played by equity in what we might call Hobbes's legal theory: his account, that is, of the nature of law and of the institutional structures required to realize the rule of law. The core of this principal idea is expressed in a law of nature Hobbes sometimes calls 'equity'. I will begin, in the first section of this chapter, by unpacking in some detail what this law of nature requires. I will then turn to consider, in the second through fourth sections, the other roles played by equity in Hobbes's account of law. Conformity with equity, we will see, serves as a criterion of legality in the common law (the second role) and as a principle of statutory interpretation (the third role). Finally, the obligation to see equity done is given institutional expression in the foundation of the jurisdiction of Chancery.

Equity as a law of nature (or its observance)

In its most basic use by Hobbes, 'equity' variously names a law of nature (see e.g. L 15.40), its observance (see e.g. L 15.24) or the virtue

Thanks to Arash Abizadeh, Michael Cufarro, Evan Fox-Decent, Kinch Hoekstra and Susanne Sreedhar for very helpful comments on earlier drafts of this chapter. This chapter makes the following references to Hobbes's works. 'EL' to Thomas Hobbes, *The Elements of Law Natural and Politic*, edited by J.C.A. Gaskin (Oxford University Press, 1994); 'DC' to Thomas Hobbes, *De Cive* in Bernard Gert (ed.), *Man and Citizen* (Indianapolis: Hacket, 1991); 'L' to Thomas Hobbes, *Leviathan*, edited by Edwin Curley (Indianapolis: Hacket, 1994); 'D' to Thomas Hobbes, *Dialogue between a Philosopher and a Student of the Common Laws of England*, edited by Joseph Cropsey (University of Chicago Press, 1971); 'B' to Thomas Hobbes, *Behemoth*, edited by Ferdinand Tönnies (University of Chicago Press, 1990). Citations to EL, DC and L are to chapters and paragraph, to D to the original pagination, and to B to the contemporary edition pagination.

exhibited in observing it (see e.g. L 15.40).[1] Hobbes's characterization of this law changed over the course of his major works in political philosophy. This section begins by tracing this development. The story will require us to keep track of what in his later works Hobbes distinguishes as three distinct laws of nature. I will refer to each by the number Hobbes assigns to it in his final enumeration of the laws of nature, in *Leviathan*.

The Elements of Law *account*

The law of nature whose observance Hobbes calls 'equity' in *The Elements of Law* is justificatorily anchored to a law of nature that aims to undo the effects of a pernicious view shared by 'common men' and Aristotle, namely that 'one man's blood [is] better than another's' (EL 17.1). Hobbes thinks this view is false, because it gets the facts of the matter wrong and because judgements of worth are purely subjective outside of a shared convention. But his main point is that no one will think herself to be naturally subordinate to another. Either way it is a law of nature '[t]hat every man acknowledge [an]other for his equal' (EL 17.1; see DC 3.13 and L 15.21 for slightly different formulations). This is the ninth law of nature in the *Leviathan*.

The justification for the ninth law of nature is common among the three works, but best put in *Leviathan*:

> If nature therefore have made men equal, that equality is to be acknowledged; or if nature have made men unequal, yet because men that think themselves equal will not enter into conditions of peace but upon equal terms, such equality must be admitted. (L 15.21)

On the first disjunct, the law is justified on the facts, so to speak: we must acknowledge that others are our equals just because they are. On the second it is justified on grounds of a duty to which we are antecedently subject: acknowledging others to be equals is a condition of their entering into an agreement which is the means by which we form a set of institutions necessary for realizing peace, the realization of which we are directed to seek by the first law of nature.

[1] Elsewhere Hobbes uses 'equity' to name a *percept* of the law of nature (L 30.15), and sometimes *the* law of nature (L 27.17, 24) – though Hobbes seems careful to say '*common* equity' in the latter cases – and it is, he tells us, the Law of Reason (D 26). I'll not try to account for these variations here, and stick to the first and most common of the uses, as the name of one law of nature among many or what is exhibited in its observance.

Next Hobbes reminds us that a necessary condition for securing peace is giving up some of the right of nature. This is what the second law of nature requires – in the *Elements* formulation, 'that every man divest himself of the right he hath to all things by nature' (EL 15.2). It is no less necessary, Hobbes continues, that each person *retains* the rights to some things: 'to his own body (for example) the right of defending, whereof he could not transfer; to the use of fire, water, free air, and place to live in, and to all things necessary for life' (EL 17.2). This list sets a minimum, one whose scope we can set out in advance of any particular actual agreement. But the list of our retained rights might well turn out to be more generous, depending on the terms of the agreement we reach. The law of nature, Hobbes tells us, requires that we divest ourselves only of those rights 'which cannot be retained without the loss of peace' (EL 17.2). Another law of nature governs how we negotiate this: 'Whatsoever right any man requireth to retain, he allow every man to retain the same' (EL 17.2). '[H]e that doth not do so', Hobbes continues, 'alloweth not the equality mentioned in the former section' (EL 17.2) – that is, the equality whose observation is required by the ninth law of nature. Part of what it means to acknowledge another for an equal is to retain no more rights than one allows her to; one cannot be said to do the former if one refuses to do the latter.

So far so good. But then things get complicated. Hobbes continues:

> For there is no acknowledgement of the equality of worth, without attribution of the equality of benefit and respect. And this allowance of *aequalia aequalibus*,[2] is the same thing with the allowing of *proportionialia proportionalibus*.[3] For when a man alloweth to every man alike, the allowance he maketh will be in the same proportion, in which are the numbers of men to whom they are made. And this is it men[4] mean by distributive justice, and is properly termed EQUITY. (EL 17.2)[5]

Here Hobbes is describing what taking equality seriously requires of someone in a position to attribute or distribute benefits and respect. *This*, he says, is what is called equity. Note, however, that the law, 'Whatsoever right any man requireth to retain, he allow every other man to retain the

[2] 'Equal things to equals' in the translation of the same phrase in the first English edition of *De Cive* (1651).

[3] 'Proportionate things to proportionals.'

[4] Beginning with Aristotle. See *Nicomachean Ethics* 5.2–3.

[5] On the link Hobbes draws between equity and distributive justice see Johan Olsthoorn, 'Hobbes's Account of Distributive Justice as Equity' *British Journal for the History of Philosophy* (forthcoming).

same' is not addressed to a distributor. Instead it is addressed to a party negotiating her take in a distribution. Hobbes returns to this first perspective in the conclusion of EL 17.2. Immediately following the passage in the block quotation above Hobbes tells us that the breach of this law is called in Greek *pleonexia*: 'encroaching' in Hobbes's translation, often rendered as 'grasping'.[6] Iniquity, on this account, consists in taking more than one's due. But this is puzzling: a distributor cannot in this sense be iniquitous.

De Cive *and* Leviathan

Hobbes undoes this knot (though not without leaving some loose threads) in *De Cive* and *Leviathan* by distinguishing between two distinct laws of nature collected in the *Elements* account. The tenth law of nature (again on the *Leviathan* enumeration) requires 'that at the entrance into conditions of peace, no man require to reserve to himself any right which he is not content should be reserved to every one of the rest' (L 15.22; italics removed). As in *Elements*, in both *De Cive* and *Leviathan*, those who violate this law are called grasping. They take more than their share. However in *De Cive* Hobbes, confusingly, still associates this law with ascribing equal things to equals and giving things proportional to proportionals (DC 3.14).[7]

The eleventh law of nature holds that 'if a man be trusted to judge between man and man … that he deal equally between them' (L 15.23; italics removed; see DC 3.15). I will call the principle whose observance the eleventh law enjoins the *principle of equal dealing*. It is in observing the eleventh law that one is said to do equity in both the *De Cive* and *Leviathan* accounts and in the latter it is this law that Hobbes characterizes as akin to distributive justice (L 15.15, 15.24). Its distinction from the tenth law is brought into relief by the fact that its violation has a different name: not *pleonexia*, grasping, but rather *prosopolepsia* or 'acception of persons' – that is, favouritism, or, in a sense used by Hobbes and others in his time, 'respect of persons'.[8]

In both *De Cive* and *Leviathan* the tenth law of nature is justified as it was in *Elements* (in which, recall, Hobbes characterizes its observance

[6] See, for example, Urmson's revision of Ross's translation of *Nicomachean Ethics* 5.1 in Jonathan Barnes (ed.), *The Complete Works of Aristotle*, vol. II (Princeton University Press, 1984).

[7] I say 'confusingly' because grasping is a vice exhibited by someone who is party to the distribution of a good rather than someone in charge of the distributing.

[8] In 1649, for example, the Digger Gerrard Winstanley argued that a system of private property in which the earth is kept in the hand of a few who buy and sell it amongst themselves dishonours the creator, who made the earth a common treasury for all, by implying

as the doing of equity): it is required by the principle that we must each acknowledge one another as our equals. But once distinguished from the tenth law, the eleventh law (the law that requires us to respect the principle of equal dealing, the observance of which, again, Hobbes calls 'equity' in *De Cive* and *Leviathan*) no longer inherits this justification. In *De Cive* he argues that the favouring judge 'reproaches him whom he thus undervalues' (DC 3.15), contrary to the law of nature forbidding reproach which prescribes 'that no man, either by deeds or words, countenance or laughter, do declare himself to hate or scorn another' (DC 3.12). Now, the line between reproaching another and failing to treat her as an equal is very fine. Hobbes says, after all, that the favouring judge *undervalues* the party he reproaches. So reproaching is a way to treat someone as less than the equal of another. Perhaps, then, the *De Cive* account enriches rather than departs from the *Elements* justification of the arbitrator's obligation to treat parties as equals.

The sharper line is between both and *Leviathan*. There, Hobbes justifies the eleventh law by a direct appeal to peace: partial judges deter men from using arbitrators and so send them back into the state of war (L 15.23). Is there anything to be found in this change? Perhaps not. Hobbes seems to have regarded peace as more fragile as the years went on, and perhaps that is all the contrast between the justifications of the eleventh law in *Leviathan* and in his earlier works reflects. But there is, I think, something exactly right about the view that the tenth and eleventh laws, though obviously deeply related, are justified on different grounds. This is because they concern different relationships: that between parties to a distribution (or, more generally, an agreement) and that between an arbitrator or judge and the parties to the dispute she has been charged to resolve. The former can interact on terms of equality in a way that the latter cannot. What an arbitrator can do is prevent a party from treating another as an unequal.

What the eleventh law of nature and the principle of equal dealing require

The eleventh law of nature, again, requires 'if a man be trusted to judge between man and man … that he deal equally between them'. This can be

that he is a 'respecter of persons'. Winstanley, 'The True Levellers' Standard Advanced' in Christopher Hill (ed.), *Winstanley: 'The Law of Freedom' and Other Writings* (Cambridge University Press, 1983), 78.

understood in more or less robust terms. It means, at least, what is often characterized as a kind of formal equality before the law. So Hobbes tells us that equity requires:

> that justice be equally administered to all degrees of people, that is, that as well the rich and mighty as poor and obscure persons may be righted of the injuries done them, so as the great may have no greater hope of impunity when they do violence, dishonour, or any injury to the meanest sort, than when one of these does the like to one of them. (L 30.15)

Similarly at the level of form and procedure, equity also entails the law of nature that no one can be a judge in her own case. She is likely to prefer her own case but even if not, equity requires that she allow the other party to judge as well and so the controversy between them is in principle insoluble (L 15.31). 'For the same reason', Hobbes continues – though the reason he has in mind seems to be that war will continue – it is a law of nature that no one may be an arbitrator who will benefit from the victory of either party (L 15.32). Finally, though he does not draw the link explicitly, I think we can see the law of nature that all witnesses relevant to a case be heard and that they be treated impartially (L 15.33) as a corollary of the eleventh law of nature.

The principle of equal dealing, however, does not only require that a judge treat parties as equals in these formal and procedural terms. It also requires that we respect something like a modest substantive equal right to the world and its resources.[9] This is expressed in two laws of nature Hobbes explicitly claims follow from the eleventh law. The first holds that 'such things as cannot be divided be enjoyed in common, if it can be; and if the quantity of the thing permit, without stint; otherwise proportionably to the number of them that have a right' (L 15.25; italics removed) and the second that among those things that can neither be divided nor held in common that 'the entire right (or else, making the use alternate, the first possession) be determined by lot' (L 15.26; italics removed), either arbitrary lot or the natural lot of primogeniture (L 15.27).

Who are the addressees of these two laws? It depends, I think, on whether the law of property is statutory or common law in a given jurisdiction: if the former, then with these laws equity constrains the legislator,[10] if the

[9] Here Hobbes follows (or at least echoes) Grotius who argues that in determining the scope of private property rights we must assume that the intention of those who first established property rights was to recede from natural equity, and so from common property, as little as possible. Hugo Grotius, *The Rights of War and Peace* [1625] 2.2.6.1.

[10] As Hobbes elsewhere says it does. For example, in *De Cive* he argues that equity prefers taxing people on what they spend rather than on the value of what they own (DC

latter, judges. That over-simplifies a bit, because equity constrains judges' interpretation of statutes as well. But its effect in each case is different. I'll start with the common law and then turn to statutory law. In each case I will ask how far we can understand what equity requires of judges to be an instance of the obligation imposed by the injunction to observe the principle of fair dealing: in short how far we can understand these roles of equity as derived from the eleventh law of nature.

Conformity with equity as a criterion of legality

Legality and interpretation

There are, Hobbes holds, three conditions that must be satisfied for laws to be obligatory. First, they must issue from the sovereign. Second, they must be 'sufficiently published'. Finally, because 'it is not the letter, but the intendment, or meaning (that is to say, the authentic interpretation of the law, which is the sense of the legislator) in which the nature of the law consisteth' (L 26.20), the laws must be given an authentic interpretation. Because '[i]t is not Wisdom, but Authority that makes a Law' (D 4), and because the sovereign in the source of law, 'it [is] also Reason he should be sole Supream Judge' (D 28), through the judges he appoints: 'For else, by the craft of an interpreter the law may be made to bear a sense contrary to that of the sovereign, by which means the interpreter becomes the legislator' (L 26.20).[11]

Now, '[a]ll laws, written and unwritten, have need of interpretation' (L 26.21). By unwritten laws, Hobbes means laws of nature. It is not clear to me which of a judge's responsibilities count for Hobbes as interpreting the laws of nature. He gives one example. In it a judge interprets a law of nature when she brings common law into conformity with it. Here, we will see, conformity with equity imposes a criterion of legality. In the

8.11). For a helpful discussion of Hobbes's argument on this point see William Mathie, 'Justice and Equity: An Inquiry into the Meaning and Role of Equity in the Hobbesian Account of Justice and Politics', in Craig Walton and P.J. Johnson (eds.), *Hobbes's 'Science of Natural Justice'* (Dordrecht: Martinus Nijhoff, 1987), 260–1.

[11] Earlier in the same chapter Hobbes claims that a subordinate judge 'ought to have regard to the reason which moved the sovereign to make such law, that his sentence may be according thereunto; which is then his sovereign's sentence; otherwise it is his own, and an unjust one' (L 26.11). It's not clear to me that Hobbes is entitled to claim the interpretation is *unjust*, in his sense, except perhaps if we were to say that in substituting his own judgment the subordinate judge is in breach of an oath he had taken or agreement into which he entered.

third section of this chapter we will see that it plays a different role in the interpretation of statutes.

Stare decisis *and the authentic interpretation of the common law*

Hobbes sometimes refers to the interpretation of unwritten law as 'a judgment of equity' and illustrates what this means in a passage aimed against *stare decisis* (though not named as such). '[B]ecause there is no judge, subordinate nor sovereign, but may err in a judgment of equity', Hobbes argues, 'if afterward, in another like case he find it more consonant to equity to give a contrary sentence, he is obliged to do it' (L 26.24). No one's error becomes law to her or to other judges, because such laws as judgments are authority for are mutable, while the laws of nature are not. Thus 'all the sentences of precedent judges that have ever been cannot all together make a law contrary to natural equity' (L 26.24).

Hobbes illustrates this claim with an imagined case that involves the operation of a common law doctrine that he argues cannot be an interpretation of a law of nature, and so cannot properly speaking be made law by any judgment that upholds it:

> Put the case now that a man is accused of a capital crime, and seeing the power and malice of some enemy, and the frequent corruption and partiality of judges, runneth away for fear of the event, and afterwards is taken, and brought to a legal trial, and maketh it sufficiently appear he was not guilty of the crime, and being therefore acquitted, is nevertheless condemned to lose his goods. (L 26.24)

Hobbes clarifies that this isn't a case in which a penalty is imposed by statute on innocent persons who flee before trial. We are to understand the forfeiture imposed on the accused here, then, as part of the penalty that would have been imposed had he been convicted. Liability to forfeiture was for hundreds of years a defining element of felonies. We know that Hobbes had a felony in mind because all and only felonies were in his time capital offences.[12]

Imposing the penalty on the acquitted accused offends equity twice over. First, it punishes the innocent, which equity forbids (L 21.7, 28.22).[13]

[12] See K.J. Kesselring, 'Felony Forfeiture in England, c.1170–1870' (2009) 30 *Journal of Legal History* 201.

[13] Critics of felony forfeiture contemporary to Hobbes argued that even in cases of convicted felons forfeiture punished the innocent, by depriving the felon's family and heirs of her or his estate. Kesselring, 'Felony Forfeiture', 217.

It might seem that 'equity' is being used here in a more substantively robust sense than is captured in the eleventh law of nature – which, again, provides that 'if a man be trusted to judge between man and man … that he deal equally between them'. Certainly a principle more substantive than, say, that forbidding one to be a judge in one's own case is needed to catch the punishment of the innocent. But on Hobbes's account the eleventh law of nature is at least substantive enough. It catches the punishment of the innocent because in punishing an innocent person a law fails to uphold an equal distribution of justice (L 28.22).

Now this might seem to make out the charge that something more substantive than the principle of equal dealing is being brought to bear here. This is because one can only make the case that in punishing an innocent person a judge distributes justice unequally only if one finds in here Aristotle's view that a distribution is equal in the sense relevant to distributive justice when each gets her due. The problem is that one's due is in turn set by a substantive principle which allows the formal structure of distributive justice – according to which persons are treated justly if they receive benefits and bear burdens in proportion to their merit, specified by an independent principle – to apply in a particular domain.

But two things can be said in Hobbes's defence here, or rather in defence of the claim I am making on his behalf, that one can get the prohibition on punishing the innocent from the eleventh law of nature. The first is that even if a substantive principle must be relied upon to get the derivation – something that links punishment to wrongdoing – nonetheless the wrong in punishing the innocent does consist in imposing a benefit out of proportion to its bearer's desert. The second is that the punishment of the innocent marks a kind of limit condition in the circumstances: even if it is not merely true by definition that 'punishment' applies to wrongdoings it requires only the thinnest principle to find harming those who have not done wrong to be outside of its scope.

So, Hobbes says, '[h]ere you see *an innocent man judicially acquitted, notwithstanding his innocency* (when no written law forbad him to fly) after his acquittal, *upon a presumption of law*, condemned to lose all the goods he hath' (L 26.24; emphasis in the original). Hobbes points out in this description of the impugned judgment, I would argue, a second feature of the imposition of forfeiture in such a case that offends the principle of equal dealing. Part of Hobbes's criticism is that the only way the law can justify the imposition of forfeiture is by taking the accused's flight as non-rebuttable proof of his guilt. (Recall that in the case we are imagining there is no independent statutory prohibition of flight for which forfeiture is provided as punishment.) A judge who takes a legal presumption to be immune to rebuttal by evidence to the contrary – indeed by a judicial finding of innocence – displays prejudice against the accused party in refusing to hear evidence relevant to determining her guilt or innocence. In so doing, she violates the principle of equal dealing even interpreted modestly to impose only principles of procedure.

'This [the impugned law] therefore', Hobbes concludes, '*is no law of England*' (L 26.24; emphasis added in part). Because the impugned forfeiture law cannot be rendered an interpretation of the law of nature, that is, because it is inconsistent with the eleventh law of nature,[14] it is, in fact, no law at all. So here, we see, conformity with equity is a condition of legality.

Two objections might be raised to this interpretation. The first[15] is that perhaps by claiming that the impugned law is no law of England Hobbes is just reiterating the general anti-*stare decisis* point of L 28.24: it is no law because judgments do not in themselves bind judges hearing later cases. Two considerations count against this interpretation. The first, and more decisive, is that Hobbes twice says that the interpretation of the judge hearing a particular case is law (his language) to the parties (L 26.23 and 26.24). By saying it is no law of England owing to its inconsistency with the eleventh law of nature Hobbes, as I read him, is denying that the forfeiture rule can be law even to the parties of a case. The second is that in discussing the disputed forfeiture rule Hobbes claims that it could not be made law by successive judges holding it to be so '[f]or he that judged it first, judged unjustly, and no injustice can be a pattern of judgment to succeeding judges'. This arguably implies that while not *binding* on future judges, a judgment consonant with equity may be, or serve to establish, a pattern of judgment on which they may draw. In other words it seems that for Hobbes while a judgment may not be, or may not establish, law in the sense of constituting or justifying a rule to which citizens are henceforth bound as they would be under the principle of *stare decisis*, it nonetheless may guide judgment in future cases. By saying it is no law of England

[14] Later Hobbes argues that the punishment of the innocent is also inconsistent with the law of nature that forbids persons in their revenges to look to anything other but some future good and the law of nature that forbids ingratitude 'for seeing all sovereign power, is originally given by the consent of every one of the subjects, to the end they should as long as they are obedient, be protected thereby; the punishment of the innocent, is a rendering of evil for good' (L 28.22).

[15] Which was raised to me by Kinch Hoekstra. My response draws in part on a very helpful comment by Michael Cuffaro.

owing to its inconsistency with the eleventh law of nature Hobbes might then be understood to further claim it cannot (or ought not) serve as or serve to establish a pattern of judgment in the future.

The second objection to my interpretation of this passage[16] raises a concern about its conclusion. The conclusion that the disputed forfeiture rule is no law of England is arguably at odds with Hobbes's claim that 'long use [can] obtaineth the authority of law' not owing to the length of use in itself but rather because we can infer from his silence the sovereign's consent to the rule (L 26.7). So perhaps the forfeiture rule *was*, or at least could have been, a law of England. Hobbes, however, goes on to say that 'if the sovereign shall have a question of right grounded, not upon his present will but upon the laws formerly made ... the question shall be judged by equity' (L 26.7).[17] I think we can put these claims together this way: we may infer consent from the sovereign's silence only when doing so is consistent with equity. (This hints at an important point about how we are to think about the sovereign that I take up at the beginning of the next section.)

But now what if the sovereign explicitly endorses the forfeiture rule? What if a statute is passed? It will depend in part on what it forbids. Nothing in Hobbes's argument here impugns a law forbidding, under threat of penalty, persons accused in some official way of committing a crime from fleeing the jurisdiction. What the eleventh law of nature forbids is the imposition of the penalty on the grounds that the accused was guilty of a crime that he in fact did not commit. But what if instead the sovereign upheld through legislation the presumption in law on which the disputed common law rule rests? This is trickier, and brings us to the next sense of equity in Hobbes's legal theory.

Conformity with equity as a principle of statutory interpretation

The interpretation of written law

Hobbes holds, again, that 'it is not the letter, but the intendment, or meaning (that is to say, the authentic interpretation of the law, which is the sense

16 Which was raised to me by Evan Fox-Decent.

17 Similarly, in the *Dialogue* the Philosopher says to the Student 'if [a] Custom be unreasonable, you must with all other Lawyers confess that it is no Law, but ought to be abolished; and if the Custom be reasonable, it is not the Custom, but the Equity that makes it Law' (D 80). This unpacks but in one sense complicates the more briefly expressed claim in *Leviathan*: here Hobbes seems to say that an inequitable custom is both not a law and ought to be abolished.

of the legislator) in which the nature of the law consisteth' (L 26.20). From this, one might be led to think that what the law is in a given instance is an empirical question, one solved by collecting evidence of the intentions of the particular statute's author. And this is, indeed, part of the story. Hobbes says, for example, that judges' interpretations of statutes ought to be guided in part by whatever insight into the legislator's intentions can be discerned from the text of the statute's preamble (D 7). But the question what a legislator's intentions were is in part objective. And here is where equity comes in:

> Now the intention of the legislator is always supposed to be equity; for it were a great contumely for a judge to think otherwise of the sovereign. He ought, therefore, if the words of the law do not fully authorize a reasonable sentence, to supply it with the law of nature; if the case be difficult, to respite judgment till he have received more ample authority. (L 26.26)

Let's unpack this crucial passage. There are three key ideas here. Firstly, if it is *always* supposed that the legislator's intention is equity then we need to think of 'the legislator' as, in Hobbes's terms, an artificial person. The legislator names an office occupied by a particular natural person (or group of natural persons) whose actions are actions in the capacity of the holder of that office only when and to the extent that they are in conformity with the principles that set its mandate. Constitutive of the office of the legislator is that her intentions are in conformity with equity.

Secondly, a judge acts on this supposition by 'supplying' a law whose strict reading does not fully authorize a reasonable sentence with 'the law of nature'. Two questions arise: what does it mean to 'supply' a statute with the law of nature? And to what, exactly, does 'the law of nature' refer? We can see the answers in the examples Hobbes gives.

'For example', he writes first, 'a written law ordaineth that he which is thrust out of his house by force shall be restored by force; it happens that a man by negligence leaves his house empty, and returning is kept out by force, in which case there is no special law ordained' (L 26.26). On a strict reading of the law, the plaintiff is out of luck. However, Hobbes argues, '[i]t is evident, that this case is contained in the same law; for else there is no remedy for him at all, which is to be supposed against the intention of the legislator' (L 26.26). As, again, the intention of the legislator must be supposed to be equity, we can reasonably infer that Hobbes means to claim that it would be against equity if the plaintiff in this case were left without remedy. How so? One answer is just that it would be unfair. But I think we can see the reasoning Hobbes describes tersely here as relying on the eleventh law of nature and the principle of equal dealing. Let me explain.

'[T]he incommodity that follows the bare words of a written law', Hobbes says, 'may lead him [the judge] to the intention of the law, whereby to interpret the same the better' (L 26.26). The intention of a particular law is the end for the sake of which it was written, for example, providing a remedy for a particular sort of wrong. By saying that the intention of the legislator is equity Hobbes isn't saying that equity or its realization is the legislator's goal, but rather that one must understand the legislator to have undertaken to act in conformity with the requirements of equity. In the example under discussion, the judge reasonably concludes that it is inessential to the availability of the remedy the law provides that the plaintiff has been thrust out of his house by force. What matters is that he is by force prevented from entering his house when he chooses. It would violate the principle of equal dealing to treat the plaintiff who 'by negligence leaves his house empty, and returning is kept out by force' differently from a plaintiff in the position described by the statute.

In Hobbes's second example 'the word of the law commandeth to judge according to the evidence; a man is accused falsely of a fact which the judge himself saw done by another, and not by him that is accused' (L 26.26). So the judge is in a bind: he must either follow the letter and condemn an innocent person, or give a sentence contrary to the evidence (strictly and technically understood). The solution, Hobbes says, is that he 'procure of the sovereign that another be made judge', so he can serve as an exculpatory witness.

Here the law at issue is one that applies to the judge, requiring him to judge according to the evidence. On Hobbes's telling it would plainly be contrary to the intention of the legislator to convict in this case. We need not formulate exactly what the ends of the rule requiring judges to judge according to evidence are to conclude that they cannot be served by a judge condemning a party he knows to be innocent when an alterative is available.[18] We can, arguably, see the principle of equal dealing play two roles in the reasoning Hobbes recommends here. First, it condemns punishing the innocent, and so forces the dilemma raised by the strict interpretation of the statute. Second, it points the way to the solution by requiring (I argued above) that all witnesses relevant to a case be heard.

[18] We can presume the rule serves to sort the guilty from the innocent, but arguably the legislator sought to realize other goods as well, such as allowing each party to a dispute to be heard and ensuring that the courts are seen to do justice.

So, to answer the questions raised above: the law of nature, in at least these examples, is the eleventh law of nature and the judge 'supplies' the law with it by interpreting the written law in a way that renders that law in conformity with what the eleventh law of nature requires.

Finally, Hobbes says that 'if the case be difficult, to respite judgment till he [the judge] have received more ample authority'. This is a limit in the case of the interpretation of the statute. Thus, conformity with equity can serve as a criterion of legality for a common law doctrine, but not for a statute. While, in Hobbes's language, the incommodity that follows the bare words of a written law can lead a judge to interpret that law in terms of the end for which the law was written and thus interpret it better (his word), 'no incommodity can warrant a sentence against the law', because it is beyond the judge's authority to issue such a sentence. So conformity with equity can serve only as a principle of statutory interpretation, that holds that statutes ought to be interpreted so as to bring them as far in conformity with equity – and so, I've argued, with the eleventh law of nature – as possible.

Or so Hobbes appears to argue here. Two considerations, however, complicate things. The first is that Hobbes seems therefore to be saying that judges might sometimes be forced into insulting the sovereign by implying that he acted contrary to equity. The second is that Hobbes seems elsewhere to imply that equity imposes a limit on what a sovereign may be understood to do through legislation. What he says is that:

> by the law of equity … a man that has the sovereign power, cannot, if he would give away the right of anything which is necessary for him to retain for the good government of his subjects, unless he do it in express words, saying, that he will have the sovereign power no longer. For the giving away that, which by consequence only, draws the sovereignty along with it, is not (I think) a giving away of the sovereignty; but an error, such as works nothing but an invalidity in the grant itself. (B 118)

This implies that any grant of an inalienable right of sovereignty to another by the sovereign – including (presumably) any made through legislation – is invalid by the law of equity. So while conformity with equity is a not a general condition of the legality of statutory law, inconformity at this limit – the limit marked by the essential and inalienable rights of sovereignty – may be.[19]

[19] Hobbes argues that grants to divest essential rights of sovereignty are void in L 18.17, though there does not also claim that such grants are in violation of equity. See David

Recall, however, that Hobbes's instruction to judges is only to postpone judgment in cases in which the language of a statute cannot be brought into conformity with equity, not to vindicate the iniquity with their judgments. But what if the sovereign, in turn, insists on the iniquity? This puts us, I think, on the horns of a deep dilemma. On the one hand, the answer to the question is: then, to that extent, this is not properly speaking an act of sovereignty[20] and can therefore be ignored. The reply is: but that judgment rests on supposing that one has interpreted the laws of nature correctly – and only the sovereign may make that claim. We have come up against one of the most difficult puzzles in Hobbes's political philosophy, namely whether sense can be made of his claims that the sovereign is both bound by the laws of nature and final authority on their interpretation. We can, I suggest, understand Hobbes as working out his answer through his account of the institutional structure of the judiciary and of sovereignty more generally, which I will consider in the fourth section.

What Hobbes is (strictly speaking) not saying

I'll close this section with a brief postscript. On Aristotle's account, equity corrects for the imprecision of laws, often by asking what the legislator would say in a particular case for which a law is silent or its strict interpretation yields an injustice.[21] Aristotle's view made its way into English law indirectly, by way of St. German's *Dialogues Between a Doctor of Divinity and a Student in the Laws of England* (1523).[22] Possibly owing to St. German's influence, the approach to statutory interpretation by which the judge fills in or departs from the strict letter of a law in light of that law's objective came to be known as equitable construction. In his annotation to *Eyston* v. *Studd* (1574) in the second volume of his Reports, Edmond Plowden wrote:

> it is not the words of the law, but the internal sense of it that makes the law. And it often happens that when you know the letter, you know not the sense, for sometimes the sense is more confined and contracted than the letter, and sometimes it is more large and extensive. And equity, which in

Dyzenhaus's contribution to this volume (Chapter 10) for a very interesting analysis of this passage.

20 Not, at least, in cases in which the iniquity is grave.

21 See *Nichomachean Ethics* 5.10.

22 In fact, doubly indirectly. St. German got his Aristotle by way of Jean Gerson. See Paul Vinogradoff, 'Reason and Conscience in Sixteenth-Century Jurisprudence' (1908) 24 *Law Quarterly Review* 373, 374–5.

> Latin is called *equitas*, enlarges or diminishes the letter according to its discretion.[23]

Equity does this, Plowden held, guided by the end we ought to suppose the legislator had in mind.[24]

While this describes just what Hobbes recommends in the examples above – particularly the first, concerning the dispossessed homeowner – in fact Hobbes does not use 'equity' to describe a method of or approach to statutory interpretation. He leaves the method or approach unnamed. What it names for him is a substantive principle conformity with which must, on his account, guide the sort of purposive interpretation Plowden described. Now, in the *Dialogue* Hobbes *does* associate equity with the interpretation of law more generally, but there, as we'll see, the claim is in service of another idea, the final of the four roles of equity I claim to find in Hobbes's legal theory.

Equity as the basis of the adjudicative jurisdiction of Chancery

The question

For some time before Hobbes wrote,[25] Chancery was associated with equity, and its jurisdiction to hear cases was cast in terms of its right to uphold equity against the rigour of the common law. There is a complex and important political story here, because the Chancellor's jurisdiction in this matter derived from the King's claim to the right to hear any subject's appeal for justice in cases in which she alleged to have been subject to unfair or hard treatment by the courts. So at issue, in part, was whether and in what way the King's authority is subject to law. It is easy to see how this political side of the debate engaged Hobbes. But in the *Dialogue* he treats it narrowly (for the most part), as a question about the administration of justice.

The question that needs to be answered is why there ought to be a separate court of equity. Chancery's answer came in *The Earl of Oxford's Case*.[26] There Lord Ellesmere, drawing on St. German, argued that Chancery came in to prevent injustices that arose through the strict application of

[23] 2 Plowden 465, 75 ER 695.

[24] Plowden's formulation is echoed in Coke's description of equitable construction in the *Commentary on Littleton* 21.24.b and by Matthew Hale in *A New Abridgment of the Law* vol. IV (Dublin: Luke White, 1783), 649, on which the court drew in the celebrated case of *Riggs* v. *Palmer* 115 N.Y. 506 (1889).

[25] At least by 1468. See Gary Watt, *Equity Stirring* (Oxford: Hart, 2009), 49 n10.

[26] 1 Chan. Rep. 1, 21 ER 485 (1615).

law, where that application was in a sense perfectly correct but gave rise to injustice. A nice example is of a debtor who has paid her debt but not received (or perhaps lost) her receipt. The creditor would succeed in a suit to compel a second payment. In finding for the plaintiff, Lord Ellesmere held, a court of common law would be correct about the law. But it would be contrary to conscience for the plaintiff to press his claim. Chancery would intervene to prevent him from doing so.

Arguably this only goes so far. Even if sound in all its details it is not clear Lord Ellesmere's argument shows that justice required the jurisdictional status quo. For Hobbes the puzzle is deepened by his insistence, in the *Dialogue*, that the common law seeks to do equity and that every court is in a sense bound to do equity. So why for Hobbes must there be a separate court of equity?

Hobbes's answer

There are two answers in *Dialogue*, one explicit and one not quite explicit. The explicit answer is given by the Philosopher in response to the question posed by the Student:

> *La.* Seeing all Judges in all Courts ought to Judge according to Equity, which is the Law of Reason,[27] a distinct Court of Equity seemeth to me to be unnecessary, and but a Burthen to the People, since Common-Law, and Equity are the same Law. (D 32)

The Philosopher answers:

> Ph. It were so indeed [i]f Judges could not err, but since they may err, and that the King is not Bound to any other Law but that of Equity, it belongs to him alone to give Remedy to then that by the Ignorance, or Corruption of a Judge shall suffer dammage. (D 32)

So Chancery, on this account, is in effect a court of appeal, with jurisdiction to hear errors owing to the ignorance or corruption of judges. This jurisdiction arises owing to the fact that the King (through the Chancellor) is bound only by Equity.

Two main questions are raised by the Philosopher's answer. Firstly, what does Hobbes mean by 'Equity' here? Two things point to its having a broad meaning. First, a few lines earlier the Philosopher held that Iniquity is a transgression of the Law of Reason – that is, of the laws

[27] By this point the Philosopher has ceded, indeed defended, both of these claims.

of nature. That interpretation is implied, secondly, by the claim that the King is bound to no other law than Equity. It had all along been Hobbes's view that while the sovereign necessarily cannot be subject to positive law, he is subject to the laws of nature, and he had earlier expressed this by saying that the sovereign may commit iniquity but not injustice (L 18.6). But note that the grounds of appeal the Philosopher names here can both be captured, more narrowly, by the principle of equal dealing. The judge's ignorance matters to the appellant, presumably, because she has been given less than her due, in violation of the principle that she be dealt with as an equal of the defendant. And corruption, we can assume, gives rise to partiality, forbidden, I argued above, as a corollary of the eleventh law of nature.

Secondly, how does the fact that the king is subject only to 'Equity' grant him, through Chancery, this appellate jurisdiction? It is not clear that it does. There is arguably a non sequitur here. The argument seems to show only that the only sorts of appeal Chancery could hear are those based on the laws of nature, not that only Chancery could hear such appeals. The laws of nature bind courts of common law no less than courts of equity. We can save the argument, however, if we think appellants' interests are best served by courts bound to uphold *only* the laws of nature: courts, that is, not constrained by the legislation and so not limited by the letter of the law in the qualified way we saw in the last section. This, however, does not reach cases based in common law. Here we might invoke on Hobbes's behalf his claim – and this would reach all appeals, regardless of the source of the law from which they commenced – that judges in courts of equity should be persons especially studied in equity, 'Doctors in Cases of Conscience' such as Bishops (D 84).

In sum, the first argument is that, we might say (using 'justice' in a non-technical non-Hobbesian sense), justice is served by having an appellant court charged with upholding equity – in particular the principle of equal dealing – against particular sorts of errors judges are apt to commit. We can reconstruct a second argument on Hobbes's behalf that rests, to begin, on identifying particular sorts of wrongs persons may commit. The idea emerges in a passage in which the Student and the Philosopher are discussing statutory interpretation. The Philosopher is defending the idea we saw earlier, from *Leviathan*, that the meaning of a statute is not always captured by what he here calls the 'Grammatical Construction' of it – which I take to be the same as what he called its 'bare meaning' in *Leviathan*. Here he goes (perhaps) a bit farther and argues that the letter of the law may be contrary to the legislator's meaning. The student asks:

La. In what Cases can the true Construction of the Letter be contrary to the meaning of the Lawmaker?

Though taken in isolation it might be understood differently – owing to the adjective 'true' – in the context I believe we should take 'the true Construction of the Letter' to refer to an interpretation of the provision in question limited to its express language. The Philosopher answers:

Ph. Very many, whereof Sir *Edw. Coke* nameth 3, Fraud, Accident, and Breach of Confidence; but there be many more; for there by a very great many reasonable Exceptions almost to every General Rule, which the makers of the Rule could not foresee; and very many words in every Statute, especially long ones, that are, as to *Grammar*, of Ambiguous signification, and yet to then that know well, to what end the Statute was made, perspicuous enough. (D 83)

The list Hobbes takes from Coke enumerates matters 'to be judged in court of conscience', that is, in a court of equity, rather than enumerating cases in which the letter of the law may be contrary to the legislator's intention.[28] But in implicitly lining these categories up Hobbes is just echoing the idea first articulated by St. German that Aristotle's idea that equity requires correcting errors arising from the imprecision of general rules tracks the traditional jurisdiction of Chancery as a court that prevents parties from standing on their positive law rights contrary to conscience. Neither St. German nor Lord Ellesmere in *The Earl of Oxford's Case* explain this link, but there is a plausible way to draw it. One thing an imprecise rule does is allow someone – a 'stickler' in Aristotle's words – to exploit their rights: their strict rights, that it, or their rights according to the letter of the law.[29] What Chancery does is prevent that by preventing her from exercising her right in cases in which this is true.

Now, why does this need a separate court? Lord Ellesmere's answer, again, was that the common law courts in fact got the law right. They did just as they were supposed to. What Chancery does is prevent the

[28] See Joseph Cropsey's annotation to D, 98 n 32. For a helpful explanation of what sorts of wrongs Coke's list named see Mike Macnair, 'Equity and Conscience' (2007) 27 *Oxford Journal of Legal Studies* 659, 677.

[29] As Henry Smith suggests in 'An Economic Analysis of Law versus Equity' (unpublished). See www.law.yale.edu/documents/pdf/LEO/HSmith_LawVersusEquity7.pdf at 4 n10.

exercise of those rights when it is contrary to conscience to do so. It asks a question, that is, not asked of courts of common law. The jurisdictional contrast reflects a conceptual one.

That answer, however, is not available to Hobbes. That is because he is committed to the idea that the law, properly understood, cannot be in error – or, rather, that we cannot step outside the best interpretation of the law and ask whether it is in error. That is because the only standard on which laws can be judged is equity and the legislator's intention, again, must be presumed to be equity. So Hobbes couldn't say with Lord Ellesmere that in cases calling for equity common law judges got the law right; that, to recall the example above, they would have been correct in enforcing the payment of the debt the second time over. Nor then could he accept Coke's definition of Equity, which he recounts as: 'Equity is a certain perfect Reason that Interpreteth, and Amendeth the Law Written.' Instead, Hobbes says (and in so saying departs, he tells us, 'not much' from Coke) that 'Equity Interprets the Law; and amends Judgments given upon the same Law.' However 'no one can mend a Law but he that can make it' so it falls to the sovereign to set things right. And this he does through the office of the Chancellor.

One might respond that judges are, on Hobbes's account, agents of the sovereign: so why can't they bear this responsibility? The answer, at least in the *Dialogue*, is that agency isn't the same as identity. Let me explain. In the *Dialogue*, we see this exchange:

Ph. [S]ince … the King is sole Legislator, I think it also Reason he should be sole Supream Judge.

La. There is no doubt of that; for otherwise there would be no Congruity of Judgments with the Laws. (D 28)

It is on any account a principle of the rule of law that judgments be congruous with positive law. Thus, contrary to the long-received (though more recent) view that the ideal of the rule of law requires the separation of powers, on Hobbes's view were the King not also supreme judge the rule of law could not be upheld. For Hobbes the ideal of judicial fidelity to law is expressed in the institutional claim that judges and legislators are agents of the same artificial person. Let's call the claim that were the King not supreme judge the rule of law principle that judgments be congruous with positive law could not be upheld the *principle of the unity of sovereignty*. Hobbes's endorsement of this principle seems to undo the argument that a body distinct from the common law judiciary is necessary to uphold equity.

The answer to the puzzle, I think, is found in what the student of laws says next (to which the philosopher responds ''Tis true' (D 29)). It is, the student argues, evidence for the conformity of English legal practice with the principle of the unity of sovereignty that common law judges hold office by authority of letters of patent. It is, in other words, sufficient to respect the principle of the unity of sovereignty that judges hold office by the authority of the king. It is consistent with this institutional interpretation of the principle to assign to a separate body the role of an appellant court charged with ensuring that common law judges do not permit defendants to exploit the strict letter of the law and to understand this court to thereby be delivering an authentic interpretation of the law.

One final point. I claimed above that the particular sorts of judicial errors from which aggrieved parties could, on Hobbes's account, appeal to Chancery for relief could be understood as breaches of the eleventh law of nature. I'd like to suggest now that the same is true of the traditional categories of wrongs on which basis parties would appeal to Chancery that Hobbes's Philosopher alluded to in the list of cases in which the true meaning of a statute could be contrary to its letter. These are, again, categories in which defendants exploit the strict letter of the law. They are Aristotle's sticklers. My suggestions is that sticklers – like the creditor in our running example – can be understood to use the law, inappropriately, as an instrument to realize their ends, while at the same time insisting that others be subject to the law. They treat others as unequal to themselves, and so undertake to act in violation of the ninth law of nature. In denying them the right to do so, a judge upholds the principle of equal dealing.

Conclusion

There is, then, a unifying idea underlying the four roles equity plays in Hobbes's legal theory. At the core of this idea is a conception of equality before the law expressed in the eleventh law of nature that equity, in its first role, requires judges to uphold. This obligation is discharged by imposing on common law the criterion of legality and adopting the principle of statutory interpretation that comprise the second and third roles of equity. And, finally, its proper institutional expression, Hobbes argues, requires establishing a distinct court of equity, and so in its fourth role equity serves as the basis of the adjudicative jurisdiction of Chancery. In making the case for these claims I hope to have shown as well that attending to Hobbes's treatment of equity enriches our understanding of his account of the nature of law and of the institutional structures required to realize the rule of law, though here I have only made preliminary sketches of these broader implications.

10

Hobbes on the authority of law

DAVID DYZENHAUS

Hobbes wrote and finished *Leviathan*[1] during a time of great political turmoil, which included the civil war. He thus wrote during a time of the deepest disagreements imaginable about fundamental political and religious matters, disagreements that were so intense that people were ready and did fight to the death over them. Society was ripped apart in the ways that inspired Hobbes to write one of the most famous chapters in the history of political philosophy, chapter 13 of *Leviathan*, where he describes the state of nature.

The orthodox view of Hobbes is that he was, as contemporaries termed his followers, a 'Hobbist': someone who argued that since one is better off in any stable society than in the state of nature, it is rational to understand that one has consented to the rule of the de facto sovereign of that society. Further, stability is achievable only if sovereign authority is concentrated in the hands of one natural individual, or one body of natural individuals, who

This chapter started as one about the Engagement Controversy and Hobbes on authority for a symposium organized by Thomas Poole (LSE). Comments on that chapter, especially from Jeffrey Collins, Dennis Klimchuk, Lars Vinx, and an anonymous reviewer for Cambridge University Press led me to contemplate radical revisions. Further comments on a related paper given to the Berkeley Jurisprudence workshop helped me to see the appropriate way to proceed, and here I thank in particular Andrew Brighten, Richard Flathman and Kinch Hoekstra. In addition, for illuminating comments on successive drafts of that much revised paper, I thank Gurpreet Rattan, Luciano Venezia and all the participants in: a Workshop on Hobbes and the Law at the University of Western Ontario, especially Dennis Klimchuk, its organizer, and Lars Vinx, who provided the formal commentary on my paper; Massimo La Torre's legal philosophy seminar at the Università di Catanzaro; a seminar in the Faculty of Law, University of Copenhagen; the graduate student Proseminar in the Toronto Philosophy Department in the Fall of 2011; and the undergraduate student 'Socrates' Seminar in the same Department in the Spring of 2012. Finally, I gave the paper as a plenary lecture at the Internationalen Vereinigung für Rechts- und Sozialphilosophie in Frankfurt and I thank the organizers for the opportunity and those who participated in the discussion after the lecture.

[1] Thomas Hobbes, *Leviathan*, edited by Richard Tuck (Cambridge University Press, 1997).

then issues commands that people should understand they are obliged to obey no matter the content of the commands, since they must understand that the sovereign's commands are always just; indeed they are the subjects' own commands since they authorized the sovereign to rule them. (If they don't understand their obligation, they should in any case be motivated by the sanctions attached to disobedience to the law, that is, obedience is guaranteed by the public sword.) Finally, the sovereign is himself legally unlimited and answerable only to God for any wrongdoing against the people; in fact, from the people's perspective, the sovereign can do no wrong.

A Hobbist then seems to propose a highly authoritarian solution to the problem of deep political disagreement, something compounded by the fact that Hobbes made it clear that he thought that an absolute monarchy was the best form of government; democracy is dangerous just because it invites deliberation in public about what should be done and thus invites conflict.

This orthodox view of Hobbes echoes in the view taken of his legal theory, including his account of legal authority. Hobbes is commonly regarded as an early legal positivist, in that he considers law to be the commands of a legally unlimited sovereign. Just as commonly, he is regarded as holding not only that the law that the sovereign makes is always by definition just, but also that all of those who are subject to his law must understand that they have consented to be bound by it. They must adopt this understanding because it serves their interest in securing the kind of peace and security that only a legally unlimited, all-powerful sovereign can deliver. They trade, as Hobbes tells us at the end of *Leviathan*, their obedience for the sovereign's protection.[2]

The combination of a command theory of law with the claim that those subject to the commands must understand that their de facto sovereign is legitimate seems highly authoritarian to a late twentieth or twenty-first century sensibility, and so the absence of Hobbes from legal philosophical debate might seem hardly a matter for regret. Since most legal philosophers are profoundly uninterested in the history of political and legal thought, it might seem, in addition, that study of Hobbes's legal theory can be safely left to those of an antiquarian persuasion.

Some features of Hobbes's position should, however, make one a little cautious here. First, Hobbes's authoritarian reputation is inconsistent

[2] *Leviathan*, 491. Thus Norberto Bobbio says that we should think of Hobbes as an 'ideological positivist', a philosopher whose positivist theory of law is constructed to serve certain political values; Norberto Bobbio, 'Sur Le Positivisme Juridique' in Bobbio, *Essais de Théorie Du Droit*, translated by Michel Guéret (Paris: Buylant, 1998), 23, 27–29.

with the aim that Hobbes himself stated for *Leviathan*: to show how one could pass 'unwounded' between those 'who contend, on one side for too great Liberty, and on the other side for too much Authority'.[3] We need, he suggests, to avoid both the position of those who think that when authority clashes with their view of right there is no authority and the position of those who think that the commands of the powerful are always right or authoritative.

Second, Hobbes does not fit comfortably into the category of 'early legal positivist', one who holds a command theory of law. He does not define law as H.L.A. Hart's predecessors in the positivist tradition were to do, as the commands of a legally unlimited sovereign to which sanctions attach. Rather, he says that law is the command not 'of any man to any man: but only of him, whose Command is addressed to one formerly obliged to obey him'.[4] In other words, for Hobbes coercion is not part of his definition of law whereas obligation based on prior consent is. He thus puts forward a very different position from the two figures who are rightly considered to be Hart's predecessors, Jeremy Bentham and John Austin, who reject any idea that there is a prior agreement or contract on which consent can be based, and so focus exclusively on the coercive power of the sovereign to explain obedience to law.

Of course, that Hobbes regards de facto sovereignty as legitimate will only serve to bolster Hobbes's reputation for authoritarianism. But, as I will now argue, the other reasons that make it difficult to squeeze Hobbes into the category of early legal positivist explain why his reputation for authoritarianism is not well deserved. I will argue, that is, that unlike both the command theorists and contemporary legal positivists, Hobbes advances a theory of legal authority in which the 'laws of nature' are given a prominent role in the determination of the content of the law.[5] That role helps to clarify both what Hobbes meant when he asserted that

[3] See Hobbes's dedication to Francis Godolphin – *Leviathan*, 3.

[4] *Ibid.*, 183.

[5] Hobbes's account of the operation of these laws is hardly ever analysed, rather a reason is found for bypassing them that fits with the orthodox interpretation. For example, Bobbio argues that the 'true function' of Hobbes's extensive account of the laws of nature 'and the only one that cannot be eliminated, is to provide the most absolute ground to the norm according to which there is no other valid law than positive law'; Bobbio, *Thomas Hobbes and the Natural Law Tradition*, translated by Daniela Gobetti (Chicago University Press, 1993), 'Natural Law and Civil Law in the Political Philosophy of Thomas Hobbes', 114, 148. More recently, S.A. Lloyd, *Morality in the Philosophy of Thomas Hobbes: Cases in the Law of Nature* (Cambridge University Press, 2009) argues that the laws of nature are 'self-effacing'. They play a role in grounding obedience but once civil society has been established, they go missing in action. This way of understanding Hobbes is represented

the sovereign is legally unlimited and why he thought that his theory of authority could help us to pass unwounded between those 'who contend, on one side for too great Liberty, and on the other side for too much Authority'. We can then appreciate why Hobbes could claim, on the one hand, that law is the commands of a legally unlimited and legitimate sovereign and, on the other, that he was not putting forward an authoritarian account of law.

In a nutshell, my argument is that Hobbes's laws of nature reveal the commitments of political morality that are involved in a society in which political power inheres in a particular kind of 'artificial' person: a state that is legally constituted and that thus exercises its power through law.[6]

The limits of legal authority

There is yet another reason for doubting Hobbes's authoritarianism, though it creates a puzzle for Hobbes scholars. Despite Hobbes's general argument that there is no such thing as an unjust law or command, he also argues that subjects are not obliged to obey certain commands that they could not have consented to in their agreement to constitute the sovereign. His argument is that no individual can be taken to consent to an act that threatens the very survival that consenting to sovereign rule is meant to secure. It might seem to follow easily from this argument that, as Hobbes suggests, subjects are entitled to resist acts of punishment, and to disobey commands to kill or hurt themselves, or that put them in danger.[7] However, in *Leviathan* Hobbes generalizes the right of resistance to the extent that he was accused of creating a 'rebel's catechism', since he says that the subject may disobey the sovereign in any matter where 'the end for which the Soveraignty was ordained' is frustrated by the sovereign's commands.[8]

Moreover, Hobbes gives subjects a right to resist commands that bring dishonour on them,[9] and here the issue seems to be more the inhumanity of the command than its threat to the survival of the individual. One

extensively in this volume, most strongly by Ross Harrison in Chapter 3, but also to a large extent in Chapters 2, 4 and 5 contributed by Martin Loughlin, Michael Lobban and Thomas Poole.

6 My argument is primarily methodological or about the philosophical structure of Hobbes's position. Moreover, it is primarily about that position as it is elaborated in *Leviathan*, though I will refer to other works. I leave to another occasion the task of showing how Hobbes's views on such matters changed and developed across his entire corpus.

7 *Leviathan*, 98, 150–152.

8 *Ibid.*, 151. 9 *Ibid.*

particular example in this regard bothers him in particular, for he discussed it in *De Cive* (1642) and returned to it in *Behemoth or the Long Parliament* (1679),[10] a reflection on the civil war some 17 years after *Leviathan.*

In *De Cive*, Hobbes says that a son commanded to kill his father would not be obliged by the command because he would 'rather die, than live infamous, and hated of all the world'.[11] Hobbes also says others could do the job in place of the son and generalizes the point by saying: 'There are many other cases, in which, since the Commands are shamefull to be done by some, and not by others, Obedience may, by Right, be perform'd by these, and refus'd by those; and this, without breach of that absolute Right which was given to the Chief Ruler.'[12]

One might well conclude that Hobbes is saying here that there is no way in which the sovereign's power is threatened because someone else can easily be found to kill the father.[13] Thus Susanne Sreedhar says that these are cases in which obedience cannot be 'systematically expected' because the 'threat of punishment is likely to be ineffective'; in addition, they are cases that the 'sovereign can systematically permit'.[14] And she plausibly supposes that this example shows that 'Hobbes's sovereign is absolute (and absolutely authorized) in that he can command with impunity … But unlike many absolutists Hobbes does not think that absolute sovereignty requires absolute obedience'.[15]

In order to solve the puzzle Hobbes creates of the subject being entitled to consider himself not bound in this and other situations, Sreedhar relies on the idea in contemporary legal positivist accounts of legal authority that an authoritative decision announces to those subject to the decision a reason that excludes reliance by those subject to it on the reasons that were in dispute before the authority decided. It thus excludes reliance on reasons within a certain scope.[16] Sreedhar argues that for Hobbes there is a determinate set of reasons that are non-excludable – reasons that preclude killing oneself, bringing dishonour

[10] Thomas Hobbes, *Behemoth or the Long Parliament*, edited by Ferdinand Tönnies (London: Frank Cass, 1969).

[11] Thomas Hobbes, *De Cive (On the Citizen)*, edited by Richard Tuck (Cambridge University Press, 1998), 6.13.

[12] *Ibid.*

[13] See Susanne Sreedhar, *Hobbes on Resistance: Defying the Leviathan* (Cambridge University Press, 2010), 125.

[14] *Ibid.*, 130. [15] *Ibid.*, 129.

[16] See especially, Joseph Raz, 'Authority, Law, and Morality' in Raz, *Ethics in the Public Domain: Essays in the Morality of Law and Politics* (Oxford University Press, 1994), 194.

on oneself, etc. Hobbes has to concede that there is such a set because the premise of his whole argument for subjection to the sovereign is ensuring self-preservation. And he can make that concession without undermining the argument because the concession does not threaten the absolute nature of sovereignty.[17]

Sreedhar's positivist solution does have a plausible basis in Hobbes's theory of authority. Consider that early in *Leviathan* Hobbes provides an advance synopsis of his whole political argument when he explains the rationality of consent to arbitration in cases of disagreement:

> But no one mans Reason, nor the Reason of any one number of men, makes the certaintie; no more than an account is therefore well cast up, because a great many men have unanimously approved it. And therfore, as when there is a controversy in an account, the parties must by their own accord, set up for right Reason, the Reason of some Arbitrator, or Judge, to whose sentence they will both stand, or their controversie must either come to blowes, or be undecided, for want of a right Reason constituted by Nature; so it is also in all debates of what kind soever; And when men that think themselves wiser than all others, clamor and demand right Reason for judge; yet seek no more, but that things should be determined, by no other mens reason but their own, it is as intolerable in the society of men, as it is in play after trump is turned, to use for trump on every occasion, that suite whereof they have most in their hand.[18]

Here Hobbes says that when two parties disagree and need a resolution of their disagreement, they should appoint an arbitrator whose decision they undertake in advance to obey. That requires that they take the decision as the correct resolution, as right reason, and thus that they may not dispute the decision on the basis of the reasons about which they disagreed in the first place. And just this account of the rationality of consent to arbitration is adopted and elaborated in contemporary legal positivism.[19]

But Sreedhar's positivist solution to the puzzle that arises because Hobbes seems to place limits on what he considered to be otherwise unlimited authority does not work as well when Hobbes returns to this

[17] Sreedhar, *Hobbes on Resistance*, 108–122. I am grateful to Luciano Veneziana for letting me read a draft version of his illuminating doctoral thesis, 'Political Authority and Political Obligation in Hobbes's *Leviathan*', which also argues that Hobbes's theory of authority is best explained in legal positivist, i.e. Razian, terms.

[18] *Leviathan*, 32–33.

[19] Compare it to Raz's discussion of the rationality of consent to arbitration, 'Authority, Law and Morality', 196.

example in *Behemoth*, a book in the form of a dialogue where B is the pupil and A his master:

> B: Must tyrants also be obeyed in everything actively? Or is there nothing wherein a lawful King's command may be disobeyed? What if he should command me with my own hands to execute my father, in case he should be condemned to die by the law?
> A: This is a case that need not be put. We have never read nor heard of any King so inhuman as to command it. If any did, we are to consider whether that command were one of his laws. For by disobeying Kings, we mean the disobeying of his laws, those his laws that were made before they were applied to any particular person; for the King, though as a father of children, and a master of domestic servants command many things which bind those children and servants yet he commands the people in general never but by a precedent law, and as a politic, not a natural person. And if such a command as you speak of were contrived into a general law (which never was, nor never will be), you were bound to obey it, unless you depart the kingdom after the publication of the law, and before the condemnation of your father.[20]

The passage is intriguing, first, because while A does not mention explicitly the distinction between a tyrant and a lawful king on which B relies in his question, neither does A explicitly reject it, whereas Hobbes in *Leviathan* and other earlier works was adamant that such a distinction is both politically pernicious and conceptually confused.[21] It is intriguing, second, because A's remarks about why the case 'need not be put', especially when these are read in the light of the legal theory elaborated in *Leviathan*, reveal an account of law's authority that is very different from the positivistic accounts usually attributed to Hobbes.

In this passage, Hobbes expresses doubt that any sovereign would enact the law proposed in the question to him. This doubt is evidence of his optimism that sovereigns will not produce pathologies – situations that undermine legal subjects' basis for obedience or continuing consent to sovereign rule. But Hobbes nevertheless thinks it is important openly to confront the pathology. His first point is that we have to be careful about what counts as a law. There is a difference between personal authority – the commands of a father to his children or to his servants – and political authority – the commands of the same individual who happens to be king when he wishes to fulfil his role as sovereign, as the artificial person who

[20] Hobbes, *Behemoth*, 51.

[21] For discussion of Hobbes's changing views on this distinction, see Kinch Hoekstra, 'Tyrannus Rex vs. Leviathan' (2001) 82 *Pacific Philosophical Quarterly* 420.

has ultimate legal authority in the legal order. In the latter case, his commands have to be issued as laws, with the result that no command has any effect until it is in proper form.

Hobbes's second point is that proper form requires not only that the law precede any official act, but also that it be couched in general terms, and only then applied to particular circumstances.[22] A law that commanded *me* to execute *my* father if he were found guilty of a particular offence would not count as a law. Hobbes does, however, suggest that the sovereign could 'contrive' to put such a command into general form. Such a law would have to set out a crime punishable by the death penalty and stipulate that if the convicted criminal happened to have a son of a certain age in the country, the son must take on the office of executioner. This would be a cumbersome and curious law, cumbersome because of the conditional clauses piled on top of each other, curious because it would be a puzzle to legal subjects why the sovereign was going to such trouble to single out for special, inhuman treatment criminals who happened to have sons of a certain age.

However, such flaws do not preclude enactment and once the law is enacted, I am bound to obey, Hobbes says, unless I get out of the country before the condemnation of my father. So whilst it would be difficult to wrestle legal form into the right kind of shape to deliver a result that Hobbes clearly regards as inhuman, he admits that it could be done.

Notice that while Hobbes is bothered by the sheer inhumanity or immorality of the law, his analysis in *Behemoth* does not focus on that fact. As I will argue in the next section, his earlier texts, in particular *Leviathan*, make it clear that the basis for the resistance of certain kinds of inhumanity is the laws of nature. These laws, derivable from the right of nature, play a role in the legal order of a civil society since they are a kind of constitutional morality intrinsic to legal order.[23] In particular,

[22] Hobbes's overall commitment to the generality of law is not undermined by passages such as that in *Leviathan*, 183, where Hobbes gives his definition of civil law: 'In which definition, there is nothing that is not at first sight evident. For every man seeth, that some Lawes are addressed to all the Subjects in generall; some to particular Provinces; some to particular Vocations; and some to particular Men.' For every legal theory that is committed to the generality of law acknowledges the necessity of particular directives, for example, the command of a police officer directed at an individual, but requires that such directives be based in general authorizing laws. (See Joseph Raz, 'The Rule of Law and Its Virtue' in Raz, *The Authority of Law: Essays on Law and Morality* (Oxford: Clarendon Press, 1983), 215.)

[23] As Michael Oakeshott put it, for Hobbes the laws of nature make up the content of *ius*: 'But they should not be seen as independent principles which, if followed by legislators,

Hobbes's account of authority differs in regard to an aspect of the one usually attributed to him – that an authoritative command's success depends on it having a factually (i.e. not morally) determinable content.

The discipline of legality

In the orthodox understanding of Hobbes as an early legal positivist, law is a transmission mechanism for judgments made by the sovereign to those subject to the sovereign's authority. It serves, that is, to transmit the factual content of the sovereign's judgments to his subjects. In contemporary legal positivism, the idea of exclusionary reason, as well as the rest of the conceptual apparatus that goes with it, elaborates the claim that an authoritative decision's success in providing an exclusionary reason depends on it having such a determinate content. 'Determinate' in this context means factually determinable, that is, determinable without having to rely on moral considerations and arguments.[24] It is this claim that provides the essential continuity between early and contemporary legal positivism.[25]

But there is a gap between the claim that subjects must accept that they cannot challenge an authoritative decision by reopening the conflict of reasons that the decision is supposed to settle and the claim that the content of such a decision has to be determinable in this sense. And I will now show that Hobbes denies that an authoritative decision's success depends on its having such a content. The reasons for that denial explain why he thought it would be difficult for the sovereign to 'contrive' to make the command he discussed in *Behemoth* into law. His argument, or so I shall claim, is that there are certain kinds of inhumanity that legal form resists, as we can see when we set the sovereign's command to the son to kill his father in the context of Hobbes's theory of legality – the theory about the commitments inherent in the idea that a king 'commands the people

would endow their laws with a quality of "justice"; they are no more than an analytic break down of the intrinsic character of law … the *jus* inherent in genuine law which distinguishes it from a command addressed to an assignable agent or a managerial instruction concerned with the promotion of interests.' Oakeshott, 'The Rule of Law' in Oakeshott, *On History and Other Essays* (Indianapolis: Liberty Fund, 1999), 173. For my own attempts to elaborate this idea, see David Dyzenhaus, 'Hobbes's Constitutional Theory' in Ian Shapiro (ed.), *Leviathan* (New Haven: Yale University Press, 2010), 453 and 'How Hobbes met the "Hobbes Challenge"' (2009) 72 *Modern Law Review* 488.

[24] See Raz, 'Authority, Law, and Morality', 203.

[25] I set out the justification for this view in *Hard Cases in Wicked Legal Systems: Pathologies of Legality* (Oxford University Press, 2nd edn, 2010), chapters 8 and 9.

in general never but by a precedent law, and as a politic, not a natural person'.

First, in order to take advantage of the gap between publication of the law and the condemnation of my father, I would have to be fairly sure that he would be convicted despite the fact that he would have to be tried and found guilty by a judge. For only after such a finding had been made, could the judge issue the particular command that I execute my father. This factor complicates matters because Hobbes has a rich understanding of the judicial role.

Hobbes argues that in arbitration in the state of nature, and in a dispute before a judge in civil society, the parties must on pain of irrationality accept the decision as representing right reason, and hence that they are not permitted to return to the original conflict of reasons between them to contest the judgment. They must take, in other words, the decision as settling the dispute. Hence, the orthodox interpretation of Hobbes is that it matters more in a conflict that the conflict is resolved or settled by a definitive decision than how it is resolved. The 'principle of settlement' seems then what makes it altogether rational to submit to arbitration, and thus by parity of reasoning to the decisions of an all-powerful political sovereign, whatever the content of the decision of the arbitrator or the decisions of the sovereign.[26]

If this interpretation captured the whole of Hobbes's argument, his solution to the problem of the state of nature would be wholly procedural. Further, his conception of an arbitrator in the state of nature and of the arbitrator's equivalent in civil society, the sovereign and his subordinate judges, would amount to no more than the person with authority to decide a dispute, however that person wanted to decide it. Indeed, there would be no need for Law 16 of the laws of nature, which makes it a duty on conflicting parties to submit to arbitration by a third party if they find themselves in conflict.[27] It would be far more efficient for the conflicting parties simply to agree to the result of a coin toss.

But as Hobbes makes clear, there is much more to arbitration than the principle of settlement. Once the conflicting parties' consent constitutes an arbitrator, that person is not simply a natural individual. Rather, he is an artificial person in that he takes on a role in which at least four of the other laws of nature are implicated. Law 11 is the law of equity, that '*if a man be trusted to judge between man and man*, it is a precept of the Law of

[26] See Jeremy Waldron, 'The Concept and the Rule of Law' (2008) 43 *Georgia Law Review* 1.
[27] *Leviathan*, 108–109.

Nature, *that he deal Equally between them*'.[28] And because, says Hobbes, 'every man is presumed to do all things in order to his own benefit, no man is a fit arbitrator in his own cause', which gives us Law 17.[29] For the same reason, Law 18 holds that no man is to be judge who '*has in him a natural cause of partiality*'.[30] Law 19 is that in controversies of fact, the judge must give credit to the witnesses.[31]

These last four laws are both procedural and substantive in that they affect, without determining, the content of any decision by an arbitrator who is faithful to the moral discipline of his role. Moreover, when the parties submit a dispute to an arbitrator, they do so not only in the expectation that he will give a decision which provides a definitive resolution to the dispute, and so permit them to avoid fighting it out by whatever means they choose. They also submit in the expectation that the decision will accord with the laws of nature that set out the moral discipline of the arbitrator's role.

The authority of the arbitrator comes, then, not only from the consent of the parties to abide by his decision, but also from the kind of decision that they are entitled to expect. A complaint by one of the parties that the decision is flawed because the arbitrator failed to act in accordance with these constraints of role is different in kind from the complaint that Hobbes rules out – that the party simply does not like the way the arbitrator settled the dispute over right reason.[32]

[28] *Ibid.*, 108, his emphasis. [29] *Ibid.*, 109.

[30] *Ibid.*, his emphasis. [31] *Ibid.*

[32] Raz almost gets to the point of seeing this in 'Authority, Law, and Morality', 197, when he says that the arbitrator's word is not an 'absolute reason which has to be obeyed come what may. It can be challenged and justifiably disobeyed in certain circumstances. If for, example, the arbitrator was bribed, was drunk while considering the case, or of new evidence unexpectedly turns up, each party may ignore the decision'. Raz does not, however, seem to see that to ignore the decision is to treat it as no longer authoritative, that is, as a decision outside of the authority of the arbitrator, whether one considers him to be a de facto authority or a legitimate one. The complete list of such non-excluded reasons that permit one to say – 'You failed to exercise authority even though you are capable of exercising authority' – will put in doubt Raz's claim that a de facto authority is identified by 'non-moral' attributes; 202. Moreover, if some of the non-excludable reasons for challenge are observed by the arbitrator, e.g. fairly considering all the evidence, or deciding in accordance with equity, that both makes a difference to the content of the decision and, at least in the case of equity, makes a difference on a moral ground. Thus Raz generally fails to appreciate that the fact that parties may not say after the decision that they will ignore it because they still think their original view of the balance of reasons is correct does not entail the thesis that the law has to have a factually determinable content; for it might be the case that the judge is under a duty to use moral tests to determine the content of the law, tests that do not resurrect the reasons at play in the original dispute.

When the arbitrator is a judge in civil society, he is subject to more than the natural law discipline of role. He is also under a duty to decide in accordance with the positive law enacted by the ultimate judge, the sovereign. But that he is still subject to the laws of nature has the result that for Hobbes the specific authority of law comes not only from the fact that law provides an institutionally conclusive way of settling a dispute because it provides determinate conclusions about the obligations of legal subjects. Such authority also comes from the fact that conclusions about what the law requires will be based on sound reasons, reasons that include the laws of nature.[33] In play here is not the principle of settlement, but a principle of justification.

Of course, Hobbes does see differences between the situation of the arbitrator in the state of nature and the judge in a civil society. He tells us that legal order of civil society has to be staffed by subordinate judges because all laws require interpretation,[34] and that a good judge is one who, in interpreting the written law, relies on his understanding of the unwritten law, the laws of nature.[35] Moreover, one should not think that there is anything illegitimate in judges interpreting the positive law through the lens of the laws of nature, because it would be a great insult if subordinate judges were to attribute to the ultimate judge, the sovereign, an intention to flout the laws of nature.[36]

In my view, a lot turns on the fact that Hobbes regards subordinate judges as under a duty to the sovereign to interpret his positive law as if it complied with the laws of their nature. This duty flows not to a natural individual, even if the sovereign happens to be one natural individual. As the quote from *Behemoth* makes clear, from the judicial perspective the sovereign is the body that makes the written laws that judges must interpret. That is, the sovereign is a legally constituted sovereign: the person or body that has the authority to make laws provided that it complies with the public criteria recognized in that society for certifying that a law is valid. For example, in a simple society in which sovereignty resides in one natural individual, subjects know that the sovereign has commanded X, when X appears on the notice board in the town square. That there are such public criteria is a precondition of law's efficacy, on any conception

[33] I adapt here the illuminating argument in Kenneth Winston, 'Introduction', to Winston (ed.), *The Principles of Social Order: Selected Essays of Lon L. Fuller* (Oxford: Hart Publishing, 2001), 36–37.

[34] *Leviathan*, 190–191.

[35] *Ibid.*, 95–96. [36] *Ibid.*, 194.

of law. They are not, that is, themselves laws of nature; rather, they are requirements of effective public communication.[37]

I will call the requirement that enacted law meet such criteria in order to count as law the 'validity proviso'.[38] Those who think that Hobbes regarded the sovereign as legally unlimited in the sense of being utterly unconstrained rely especially on the passage in which Hobbes says that the sovereign is 'not Subject to the Civill Lawes':

> For having power to make, and repeale Lawes, he may when he pleaseth, free himselfe from that subjection, by repealing those Lawes that trouble him, and making of new; and consequently he was free before. For he is free, that can be free when he will: Nor is it possible for any person to be bound to himselfe; because he that can bind, can release; and therefore he that is bound to himselfe only, is not bound.[39]

But they fail to see that for an artificial person to be free 'when he will' he has to *will* publicly, that is, to express himself in a way that is publicly accessible and recognizable to his subjects as an expression of will. The better interpretation is that Hobbes did not mean by 'legally unlimited' that the sovereign could make law without complying with public criteria for law-making. Rather, he had in mind a legal order in which the sovereign may at will change any law, including the public criteria for valid legal change, as long as he complies with those criteria when he enacts the new law.

They also fail to notice that Hobbes, in coming back to this point in a discussion of the claim that that the sovereign must have final authority in order to avoid an infinite regress of interpretations, repeats his constant

[37] The public criteria need not be written or enacted. They might exist simply as a matter of practice. See H.L.A. Hart, *The Concept of Law* (Oxford: Clarendon Press, 1961), chapter 6. Note that the criteria, whilst not themselves laws of nature, are responsive to the conception of the rational agent presupposed by the laws of nature, as I suggest below, the self of a free and equal individual. That there be such criteria is thus a requirement of natural law.

[38] This proposition commits me to the view that all acts of sovereignty must comply with the law to be recognizable as acts of sovereignty. That view is at odds with many important passages in Hobbes, for example, the way he tells the story of David and Uriah (*Leviathan*, 148). But that way is totally inconsistent with his account of the sovereign as an artificial person, as I argue in 'How Hobbes met the "Hobbes Challenge"'. Hobbes also says that the subject may contest the sovereign's act when the sovereign relies on a law as the warrant for the act but not when the sovereign acts by 'vertue of his Power'; *Leviathan*, 153. But if subjects have to be able to identify what counts as a sovereign act by reference to publicly recognizable criteria, before an act of power can count as a sovereign act it must be attributable to the sovereign as an artificial person.

[39] *Ibid.*, 184. Compare the similar passage at 224.

claim that the sovereign is subject to the laws of nature.[40] And that subjection brings into play a second proviso, the 'legality proviso': the laws the sovereign makes have to be interpreted, and so must be interpretable, in light of the laws of nature.[41]

If Hobbes is indeed committed to the legality proviso, two important conclusions follow. First, the sovereign's subjection to the laws of nature is not only, as Hobbes sometimes says, a matter between the sovereign and God, with no effect for the relationship between the sovereign and his subjects.[42] For the legality proviso tells us that it is not sufficient for an enacted law to comply with the public criteria. The content of the enacted law must also be interpretable by judges in light of the laws of nature. These interpretations condition the content of the laws as they apply to particular subjects, and thus affect the relationship between the subject and the sovereign on the basis of the laws of nature, the set of which Hobbes calls 'the true and onely Morall Philosophy'.[43] Thus, the sovereign as ultimate judge is constrained by the laws of nature, not because he owes duties to his subjects, and despite the fact that Hobbes rejects arguments for the separation of powers. Rather, the constraints come about because of the duty the judges owe to the sovereign to interpret his enacted law in the light of their understanding of the laws of nature. Of course, the sovereign as first and ultimate judge can either preclude or override such interpretations. However, that does not make the constraints cease to be such; it simply makes them overridable by very explicit words, and, as I will argue below, an overridable constraint can be of great moral significance.

40 In the passage, *ibid.*, 224

41 The validity proviso tells us that Hobbes was well aware of the existence of something like H.L.A. Hart's 'rule of recognition' (Hart, *The Concept of Law*, 92), the ultimate rule of legal order that provides criteria for certifying the validity of particular laws; see *Leviathan*, 189. Hart and legal positivists after him have taken for granted Hart's claim that the rule of recognition corrected the mistake of his positivist predecessors Bentham and Austin in supposing that the sovereign is legally unlimited, a supposition that Hobbes is allegedly even more famous for making. But Hart did not perhaps have the best understanding of his tradition on this score. The better interpretation is that Hobbes, Bentham and Austin did not mean by 'legally unlimited' that the sovereign could make law without complying with public criteria for law-making. Rather, they had in mind a legal order in which the sovereign may at will change any law, including the public criteria for valid legal change, as long as he complies with those criteria when he enacts the new law. The legality proviso was, however, expressly rejected by Bentham and Austin after Hobbes. Legal positivists today are still struggling with the question of how to cope with it.

42 For example, *Leviathan*, 148.

43 *Ibid.*, 110.

Second, Hobbes is not a legal positivist at least in so far as he does not subscribe to the claim that creates the continuity between early and contemporary legal positivists – that the content of the law has to be determinable by factual tests since for him the content of the law is often in part determinable only by an interpretative exercise that relies on the laws of nature.

At this point my argument has to contend with the point about the sovereign's ability to override subordinate judges. Those who hold the orthodox view of Hobbes emphasize that for him if a law makes sense, and is validly promulgated, that is enough. A lot turns, however, on whether my argument is contending with the strict positivist claim that is part and parcel of the orthodox interpretation of Hobbes, or with a moderate position.[44] On the strict positivist position, an authoritative decision has to have a factually determinable content, in which case the legality proviso plays no role at all in the interpretation of the law. This position has to ignore or explain away large parts of Hobbes's text.

The moderate position, in contrast, takes these chunks of text into account, but maintains that the legality proviso is operative only to the point that it comes into conflict with the content of law that is valid in terms of the validity proviso. At that point, the validity proviso trumps the legality proviso, so that, for example, if the sovereign commands that all mediators should be killed on sight, that command must be taken by subordinate judges as the correct interpretation of Law 15 of the laws of nature that all those who mediate peace should be granted safe passage.[45] Similarly, if the sovereign commands that judges should act partially, or should not take account of the evidence, or against equity, they must treat the content of these commands as correct statements of the laws of nature. In addition, those subject to the laws interpreted in this manner must accept the laws as interpreted in accordance with right reason.

The moderate position thus leads to a peculiar conclusion. The sovereign may outright contradict one of the laws of nature thus showing that there are no limits at all on interpretation. But, as I will now explain, whilst the conclusion has to be rejected, it does latch onto something important.

[44] For those who have been involved in or have observed the internecine debates within legal positivism in the last 30 years, the strict position corresponds roughly to that put forward by 'exclusive' legal positivists and the moderate position to that put forward by 'inclusive' legal positivists.

[45] *Leviathan*, 108–109. For the argument that this is how we should understand Hobbes using just this example, see Mark Murphy, 'Was Hobbes a Legal Positivist?' (1995) 105 *Ethics* 846.

The sovereign may explicitly override a law of nature in that he issues a valid command that contradicts one of the laws of nature and subordinate judges find that they do not have the resources to invalidate the command. However, at the point when judges can no longer fulfil their duty to the sovereign to interpret his commands in light of the laws of nature, the sovereign oversteps the limits of his authority vis-à-vis his subjects. Put differently, the moderate position wrongly equates something the sovereign does have – an unlimited power to override the laws of nature – with something he lacks – an unlimited authority to interpret them.

The public conscience of the law

We saw that Hobbes's treatment of the son commanded to kill his father in *Behemoth* focuses more on the legally problematic aspects of the law than on its sheer inhumanity. That is, Hobbes focuses on the difficulties attendant on getting to the point where it is true that, legally speaking, it is the case that you must execute your father. But we need to recall that he does not rule out the possibility that the point can be reached.

My excursus into Hobbes's understanding of the role of a judge shows that the statement that the son is under a legal duty to kill his father would have to follow not only the successful enactment of the general law, but also a full trial. That entails that from law's own perspective the judge would have to take into account any argument that sought to show that a law of nature required him to interpret the law in a particular way, perhaps one that goes against what might have seemed at first the self-evident meaning of the law. For Hobbes's remark that judges insult the sovereign if they fail to interpret his law in light of the laws of nature makes it clear that judges must take the meaning of any particular law to be the one that complies best with the laws of nature, even when another interpretation would seem the more obvious one outside of the interpretive context provided by natural law.

There are two laws of nature that might give the judge pause in interpreting the command to the son. First, Hobbes elaborates Law 11, the law of equity, as forbidding '*Acception of Persons*'.[46] The law thus seems to rule out the kinds of statutes that the common lawyers fitted into the category of Bills of Attainder, that is, laws that depart from generality in singling out particular individuals for penalties and punishments; and the law in

[46] *Leviathan*, 108. For an extensive discussion of the significance of equity in Hobbes's political and legal philosophy, see Dennis Klimchuk, Chapter 9, this volume.

the example singles out fathers and sons in a way intended to expose both to grave dishonour.[47]

Second, Law 7 forbids the infliction of punishment 'with any other designe, than for correction of the offender, or direction of others'.[48] Hobbes must suppose that the death penalty may be inflicted when this would help to direct others by deterring them from certain crimes, even though it cannot 'correct' the offender.[49] Thus, a judge might conclude, but the conclusion will be strained, that my knowing that my own son will have to execute me should I be found guilty of committing a particular crime could be regarded as a plausible interpretation of this law of nature because the very inhumanity of the law might have a great deterrent effect.

But while the judge might think he can makes sense of his role in ordering that I execute my father, can he make sense of the claim that I am under a duty to do as he commands? Recall that in *De Cive*, Hobbes supposes there is no duty at all. In contrast, in the passage from *Behemoth* he says that that I will be 'bound' unless I escape the country before my father's actual condemnation.

Hobbes's vacillations create the kinds of puzzles that Sreedhar invokes the idea of exclusionary reason and a legal positivist account of authority to solve, for example, that I am entitled to resist the sovereign's punishments. An attempt to consent not to resist is void because the punishment undermines the end of self-preservation for which I transferred to the sovereign my right to judge how best to preserve myself. In *Leviathan*, Hobbes calls this the 'true liberty' of the subject, and says that the words of the covenant that give the sovereign a complete authorization to govern cannot 'by themselves' bind a man 'either to kill himselfe, or any other man' or to 'execute any dangerous or dishonourable Office'.[50]

But set in the context of Hobbes's discussion of the interaction of civil and natural law in *Leviathan* a different aspect of the command's

[47] Compare on this point Thomas Poole's and Evan Fox-Decent's contributions to this volume (Chapters 5 and 7), especially Fox-Decent's discussion of the passage in *Behemoth*, 118, 'And I think that even by the law of equity …'; the passage is reproduced in full in note 67 below.

[48] *Leviathan*, 106.

[49] Though Mario A. Cattaneo suggests that the logical conclusion of Hobbes's argument is that the death penalty should be outlawed because of its deep irrationality; 'Hobbes's Theory of Punishment' in K.C. Brown (ed.), *Hobbes Studies* (Oxford: Basil Blackwell, 1965), 275. And see the illuminating discussion by Alice Ristroph of Hobbes on criminal law in this volume (Chapter 6).

[50] *Leviathan*, 151.

problematic nature emerges. The command's inhumanity is legally problematic because it undermines the basis for law's claim to authority over me. This basis is not reducible, as is commonly supposed, to my interest in security – a trade of protection for obedience – though even on those terms one might argue that the law undermines security. For Hobbes is clear that a civil society is not merely one in which there is centralized power. What makes it civil is in large part that the power is exercised through law. To clamour for freedom from the law, he argues, is absurd because that it is to demand a return to the state of nature.[51] This argument is rightly taken to be an attempt to debunk the claim that people may legitimately rise up against their leaders in the name of liberty.[52] But it is not only that. It is also an argument about the quality of civic liberty, a kind of liberty we can have only when a system of civil law is in place.[53]

The basis for the law's claim to authority is that it serves our interest in civic liberty.[54] This is the liberty of one who enjoys the security of a stable order of laws, made by a lawgiver whose authority rests on the fact that his subjects have authorized him so to act, and who has no interest in making law other than the provision of such security. In addition, the legal subject knows that in cases where the law seems unreasonable because it does not accord with the laws of nature derivable from that interest, he may ask a judge for an authoritative interpretation of the law, which the judge will strive to ensure complies with the laws of nature.[55]

Now while Hobbes does say that the laws of nature are derivable from the interest we all share in self-preservation, it is clear from many of the laws that the preservation of *self* is not for him a bare knuckles kind of existence. Indeed, he tells us at the end of chapter 13 of *Leviathan* that we are 'drawn to agreement' in order to secure 'commodious living',[56] an idea that he elaborates at the beginning of chapter 30, 'Of the Office of the Sovereign Representative'.[57] So his understanding of the laws of nature is that they serve the interest in self-preservation. But because his

[51] *Ibid.*, 147.

[52] See, for example, Quentin Skinner, *Liberty Before Liberalism* (Cambridge University Press, 1998) and *Hobbes and Republican Liberty* (Cambridge University Press, 2008) and Philip Pettit, 'Liberty and Leviathan' (2005) 4 *Politics, Philosophy, & Economics* 131.

[53] For a more elaborate account of Hobbes on liberty that has a great deal of sympathy with my own, see Lars Vinx, Chapter 8, this volume.

[54] Hobbes calls this the '*Liberty* of *Subjects*'; *Leviathan*, 147, his emphasis.

[55] The third way in which the quality of the space of civic liberty differs from mere negative liberty is that individuals are enabled both to create juridical relations for themselves and, more generally, to act as just men; *ibid.*, 103–104.

[56] *Ibid.*, 90. [57] *Ibid.*, 231.

conception of the self that has to be preserved is the self of free and equal individuals, it is no surprise that the laws of nature are both liberty- and equality-serving.

Similarly, for Hobbes the paradigmatic way for this authorization of the sovereign to come about is through sovereignty by institution, an agreement between free and equal individuals in the state of nature.[58] Once the sovereign is instituted, the equality of the state of nature is preserved in a law we have already encountered, the law of equity that requires that those who are 'trusted to judge between man and man' deal equally between them,[59] and in Law 10, the law against arrogance, that 'at the entrance into conditions of Peace, no man require to himselfe any Right, which he is not content should be reserved to every one of the rest'.[60] Law 10, says Hobbes, secures for men the liberty to do those things without which 'a man cannot live, or not live well' and it thus amounts to an 'acknowledgment of naturall equalitie'.[61] In addition, liberty is preserved both through the institution of civic liberty and through the residual right to question whether 'the End for which the Soveraignty was ordained' is frustrated.

Now, both liberty (other than the residual true liberty of the subject) and equality are transformed in the transition from the state of nature to civil society through the way in which the conditions for both are determined through enacted law. But, as we have seen, just because it is the task of sovereignty to decide how to effect that transformation, subordinate judges are under a duty to try to ensure that the enacted law lives up to the principles it seeks to effect. Indeed, while it is crucial for Hobbes that when subordinate judges perform this task they do so in an impartial fashion, that is, that they make an independent judgment about what the law (both enacted and natural) requires, they should not be seen as checking sovereignty. Rather they are completing the sovereign act of law-making as part of the artificial person of sovereignty. Judges are, as Hobbes tells us in 'The Introduction' the 'artificall *Joynts*' of the 'Artificiall *Soul*' of sovereignty.[62]

Liberty and equality are thus built into the laws of nature, since one cannot make sense of the project of erecting the 'firme and lasting edifice'[63] of a civil society – one in which subjects enjoy civic liberty – in

[58] I will not here go into why I think that sovereignty by institution, in contrast to the alternative method of acquiring sovereignty described by Hobbes – sovereignty by acquisition – is paradigmatic.

[59] *Leviathan*, 108, emphasis removed.

[60] *Ibid.*, 107, emphasis removed.

[61] *Ibid.* [62] *Ibid.*, 9. [63] *Ibid.*, 221.

the absence of a legal order, which is to say an order of positive law that complies with the principles of natural law. The principles are structural in nature since they are the principles with which there has to be conformity in order to have a society in which the exercise of power through law has a plausible claim to the obedience of the individuals subject to the law, such that they may be said to have authorized it. Hence, the task of ensuring that the positive law is interpreted in the light of these principles is inseparable from an inquiry about how the law serves both liberty and equality, and so also inseparable from an inquiry into the kind of moral relationship that law secures.

Of course, Hobbes's sovereign is the supreme judge and can enact any law that he likes, including laws that undermine the relationship between sovereign and subject. But, as I have already indicated, the sovereign's freedom from the law is not a freedom for the artificial person and its agents to act outside of the law.[64] Rather, it is a freedom to enact new laws that override old laws, including the public criteria for what counts as a valid law. In addition, it is within this account of freedom to legislate that the validity proviso applies, that is, it applies only to statutes and to the authority delegated to public officials by statutes. It is thus a necessary condition for an important class of legal statements to be true. But it is not a necessary condition for the truth of other legal statements. It is, as we have seen, not true about judgments about what the law requires that depend on the subordinate judge arriving at a conclusion about what is warranted by the best interpretation of the laws of nature.[65]

It is also not the case that meeting the validity proviso is a sufficient condition for the validity of a statute. Hobbes remarks in *Leviathan* that there are certain essential rights of sovereignty that the sovereign cannot grant away however explicit the grant, including the right to make law and the right of 'Judicature'. The latter is the right:

> of hearing and deciding all controversies, which may arise concerning Law, either Civill, or Naturall, or concerning Fact. For without the decision of Controversies, there is no protection of one Subject, against the injuries of another; the Lawes concerning *Meum* and *Tuum* are in vaine; and to every man remaineth, from the naturall and necessary appetite of his own conservation, the right of protecting himselfe by his private

[64] Contrast Thomas Poole, Chapter 5, this volume.

[65] In this regard, Hobbes differs from the common law tradition in general and from Ronald Dworkin's 'interpretive' account of how judges should reason, mainly because he is opposed to any doctrine of precedent; *Leviathan*, 101–102.

> strength, which is the condition of Warre; and contrary to the end for which every Common-wealth is instituted.[66]

Such a grant, Hobbes says, is 'void',[67] and he must mean void even if it is the case that the grant is explicit and contained in a command that fully complies with the validity proviso.

So here we have an example where subordinate judges would not only be entitled to disregard a perfectly valid command, but also under a duty so to do. If they did not, as Hobbes tell us in the quotation, the end of Commonwealth – the preservation of civic peace and security – is subverted. Moreover, if the grant is void, it could not be immunized from a judicial declaration to that effect by the sovereign including in it a provision that prohibited subordinate judges from exercising such a review power, the equivalent of the legislative provision called either a privative or ouster clause in the twentieth century.

But recall that for Hobbes it is not order as such – the mere absence of conflict – that is in issue when it comes to Judicature. Rather, it is the kind of order that makes possible a certain kind of interaction between subjects, one that requires a stable system of law that makes it possible for individual subjects to live together as equal members of the civic community. This point establishes one end – the 'duty end' – of what we can think of as a continuum of legality where judges are under a duty to strike down a law, even though that law complies with the validity proviso, and even though they are not given any explicit authority by any other kind of enacted law to do so.

The other end – the 'aspiration end' – is established by Hobbes's claim in chapter 30 of *Leviathan* that the sovereign must make 'Good Lawes'. Hobbes does not mean by 'good' 'just' since his view is that all the sovereign's laws are by definition just. Rather, a good law is that which is '*Needfull*, for the *Good of the People*, and withall *Perspicuous*'.[68] He goes on to say that the use of laws is 'not to bind the People from all Voluntary actions; but to direct and keep them in such a motion, as not to hurt themselves by their own impetuous desires, rashnesse, or indiscretion;

[66] *Ibid.*, 125.

[67] *Ibid.*, 127. Compare *Behemoth*, 118: 'And I think that even by the law of equity, which is the unalterable law of nature, a man that has the sovereign power cannot, if he would, give away the right of anything which is necessary for him to retain for the good government of his subjects, unless he do it in express words, saying that he will have the sovereign power no longer. For giving away that, which by consequence only, draws the sovereignty along with it, is not (I think) a giving away of the sovereignty; but an error, such as works nothing but an invalidity in the grant itself.'

[68] *Leviathan*, 239.

as Hedges are set, not to stop Travellers, but to keep them in the way'.[69] Further, while one might think that the true end of a law is the benefit of the sovereign this is not the case, for 'the good of the Soveraign and People, cannot be separated'.[70] Finally, perspicuity consists not so much in the words of the law, but in a 'Declaration of the Causes, and Motives, for which it was made'.[71] And it seems clear that for Hobbes law should have all of these features in order that it might be 'the publique Conscience, by which [the subject] ... hath already undertaken to be guided'.[72]

As one moves away from the duty end, matters become complex because when a statute is not clearly void but seems to undermine one or other law of nature, the judge is under a duty to try to find an interpretation of the statute that will make it less problematic from the perspective of legality. The duty end of the continuum of legality is the end at which the lawmaker has to conform in very particular ways with legality in order for its acts to be recognized as legislative acts. Correspondingly, when the lawmaker fails so to conform, judges are under a duty to declare that the act fails to be law. As one moves away from this end, answers to the question of what legality requires will not be so clear; nevertheless, the judges remain under a duty: the duty to interpret the law so as to make it as consistent as possible with the aspirations of legality, thus ensuring that law lives up to its internal commitments to serving the equality and liberty of the subject.

There is, in short, a judicial duty to enforce strictly the requirements of legality at the duty end. But as one moves away from that end, there is also a judicial duty to make the law live up to the aspirations of legality, one that is derived from the legislative duty to comply with these aspirations.[73]

It follows that any of the following examples would be legally speaking problematic from Hobbes's perspective on law: a statute that flatly contradicted the content of one of the laws of nature; a statute that precluded judges from relying on a particular law of nature in interpreting the law;

[69] *Ibid.*, 239–240. [70] *Ibid.*, 240.

[71] *Ibid.* [72] *Ibid.*, 223.

[73] Kinch Hoekstra notes in his manuscript, 'Thomas Hobbes and the Creation of Order', that 'valid' in Hobbes's day meant strong as well as valid in the sense of 'not void'. Hence, when Hobbes means to use valid at important points in the former sense, he must intend that validity comes in degrees of strength. On this view, a statute can be more or less valid depending on its ability to meet the legality proviso. For a relevant argument in a very different context, see David Dyzenhaus, 'The Juristic Force of Injustice' in Dyzenhaus and Mayo Moran (eds.), *Calling Power to Account: Law, Reparations, and the Chinese Head Tax Case* (University of Toronto Press, 2005), 256.

or, even more radically, a statute that prohibited judges from ever relying on the laws of nature. Judges are required in all of these cases to try to do something to preserve the laws of nature, even if Hobbes would not say that the judges are under a duty to declare the statute void. And that suffices to show that Hobbes has a rich and complex legal account of law's authority, one in which the complexities are generated from within. They are so generated because the principle of justification is always in play, a principle which requires attention to the laws of nature as well as enacted laws, and which thus requires judges to show that laws that meet the validity proviso also meet the legality proviso.

Put differently, the issue is not about whether judges are entitled to exercise the kind of review power that, say, judges in the United States of America have (or have arrogated) under the Bill of Rights. Rather, Hobbes helps us to understand that the kinds of conflicts such review might resolve will arise in any legal order, because they are conflicts internal to the exercise of legal authority. Moreover, addressing such conflicts is part of the judicial role even when judges are confined to interpretation of the law and a legislative body has authority to overrule them by enacting an altogether explicit statute. The result will be that at times judges will find themselves on points of the continuum towards the aspiration end and unable to decide a conflict between the two provisos in favour of the legality proviso.

The difference between these two forms of judicial review in this context is only about whether there is a judicial remedy available in the limit case – when the validity proviso clashes with the legality proviso in such a way that the individual's interests in liberty and equality are threatened. Sreedhar's positivist argument is one way of responding to the limit case through a claim about non-excludable reasons, in essence inalienable rights against the sovereign.[74]

My account is different. The authority of the sovereign is not a matter of his being able to decide as he pleases with each individual subject obliged to obey him unless the decision has a negative impact on the non-excludable reasons of that individual. Rather, the limit case reveals the fundamental norms of the moral community of which all legal subjects are members and that make it possible for the artificial person of the sovereign to have and to exercise authority, by which I mean *de jure* or legitimate authority.[75]

[74] See Yves Charles Zarka, 'The Political Subject' in Tom Sorell and Luc Foisneau (eds.), *Leviathan After 350 Years* (Oxford: Clarendon Press, 2004), 167.

[75] See Stephen Darwall, *The Second-Person Standpoint: Morality, Respect, and Accountability* (Cambridge, MA: Harvard University Press, 2006), 12, n. 25. See also Darwall, 'Authority

In the limit case, the subject is entitled to disobey because the sovereign has put into doubt the subject's membership of the moral community that is a precondition for the subject to recognize the sovereign as an authority. In other words, while the subject might understand perfectly well that he is threatened with harm by the person or people who happen to have most of the power in the event of non-compliance with a directive, the directive is no longer intelligible to him as authoritative, as the command of one to whom he was formerly obliged.

As we have seen, not only is it the case that the laws of nature condition the content of the law, but they do so through their relationship to the reasons for obedience. The way in which the laws of nature interact in civil society with enacted law makes the content of enacted law in part dependent on its compliance with the laws of nature. Before one gets to the limit case in Hobbes's civil society, judges will have the opportunity to try to interpret the law in such a way as to make it conform to the moral commitments of the political community, expressed in the laws of nature. Hence, because the laws of nature protect our interest in liberty and equality in a way that makes it rational for us in the first place to authorize the sovereign, the content of the enacted law will reflect those interests until the sovereign chooses explicitly to undermine those interests, in which case he ceases to act as sovereign, even if no judge has the legal resource to make a declaration to this effect.

In other words, the content of the civil law has to reflect subjects' interests in a way that is intelligible or 'perspicuous' to the legal subject. When intelligibility in this sense is not achievable, it will also be the case that the validity and the legality provisos are in conflict, which brings into question the most fundamental, moral presuppositions of the well-functioning political community that Hobbes calls a civil society. Hobbes's account of a civil society as one in which the legally constituted sovereign governs his subjects according to law thus goes a long way to showing how one might pass 'unwounded' between those 'who contend, on one side for too great Liberty, and on the other side for too much Authority'.

and Reasons: Exclusionary and Second Personal' (2010) 120 *Ethics* 257 and 'Authority and Second Personal Reasons for Acting' in David Sobel and Steven Wall (eds.), *Reasons for Action* (Cambridge University Press, 2009), 135. While I cannot go into this issue here, Hobbes, or so it seems to me, supplies the account of public, political authority that Darwall needs in order to elaborate his second-personal account of moral authority.

11

Hobbes and the civil law

The use of Roman law in Hobbes's civil science

DANIEL LEE

Two concepts of 'civil law'

In Chapter XXVI of *Leviathan*, titled 'Of Civill Lawes', Hobbes carefully distinguished between two distinct meanings of the term, 'civil law' – i.e. between (1) a general sense and (2) a particular sense. Hobbes understood the general sense of 'civil law' to mean the 'Lawes of a Common-wealth', *simpliciter*.[1] It was, as he proposed, the concept – not the content – of law, 'what is Law as *Plato, Aristotle, Cicero* and divers others have done, without taking upon them the profession of the study of the Law'.[2] It was law as understood from the lay perspective of the outsider, from that of the philosopher of law, rather than that of the practitioner of law.

This general sense of 'civil law', however, was to be distinguished from a more particular sense, as understood conventionally by early modern jurists. To them, 'civil law' carried a very specific meaning, signifying not the 'Law of a Common-wealth' in general, but the particular legal system of a specific commonwealth – i.e. the Roman Empire. This particular understanding of 'civil law' was a point of conventional

This chapter makes the following references to Hobbes's works: *De Cive* to Thomas Hobbes, *Elementa Philosophica de Cive* (Amsterdam, 1647); *Dialogue* to Thomas Hobbes, *A Dialogue between a Philosopher and a Student of the Common Laws of England*, edited by Joseph Cropsey (University of Chicago Press, 1991); Dig. English to *The Digest of Justinian*, 4 vols., translated by Alan Watson (Philadelphia: University of Pennsylvania, 1985); Dig. Latin to *Corpus Iuris Civilis: Iustiniani Digesta*, edited by Theodor Mommsen and Paul Krueger (Berlin, 1954); *Elements of Law* to Thomas Hobbes, *Elements of Law Natural and Politic*, edited by J.C.A. Gaskin (Oxford University Press, 1994); Latin *Leviathan* to Thomas Hobbes, *Leviathan, sive de Materia, Forma, et Potestate Civitatis Ecclesiasticae et Civilis* (Amsterdam, 1670); *Leviathan* to Thomas Hobbes, *Leviathan*, edited by Richard Tuck (Cambridge University Press, 1991); *On the Citizen* to Thomas Hobbes, *On the Citizen*, edited by Richard Tuck and Michael Silverthorne (Cambridge University Press, 1998).

[1] *Leviathan* 183. [2] *Leviathan* 183.

wisdom, widely accepted by the 'Civilians' – practitioners or professors of Roman law, so called because they studied the Justinianic codebooks compiled in the later Roman Empire, the *Corpus Iuris Civilis*. As Hobbes observed:

> The antient Law of Rome was called their *Civil Law* ... And those countries, which having been under the Roman Empire, and governed by that Law, retaine still such part thereof as they think fit and call that part the Civill Law, to distinguish it from the rest of their own Civill Lawes.[3]

He alluded to the distinction earlier in the *Leviathan*, in Chapter XVIII, where again, he differentiated the general sense of 'civil law' as 'Lawes of each Common-wealth' and the particular sense of 'the antient Civill Lawes of the City of Rome; which being the head of a great part of the World, her Lawes at that time were in these parts the Civill Law'.[4]

In carefully distinguishing between these two senses of civil law, Hobbes's purpose was to treat the notion of civil law, as such, in the general sense and in isolation from Roman law. In so doing, he stressed that civil law in the particular sense (i.e. Roman law) was not necessarily civil law in the general sense (i.e. the valid law of a commonwealth), because one sense was not fully reducible in meaning to the other.

The point might seem obvious. But so entrenched was the Romanist-inflected understanding of 'civil law' in early modern legal discourse, that it was necessary to disambiguate explicitly the two divergent meanings connected to the term before proceeding to treat the law, as Hobbes desired, as a subject proper for philosophical inquiry, and not exclusively in the domain of juridical expertise. But even though Hobbes sought to treat the philosophy of law in isolation from Roman law, he nevertheless found the Roman law a valuable classical source in explicating his political doctrines about the state, or commonwealth.

This chapter is an attempt to study Hobbes's use of Roman law in his political thought. Although Hobbes was not formally educated in law – whether English or Roman – he had developed a formidable command of law from his many years of practical experience as a private secretary to the Cavendish household, as I discuss below. By investigating this background and the broader historical context of early

[3] *Leviathan* 183.

[4] *Leviathan* 125. Latin *Leviathan* 89: *Vocantur autem Regulae illae Leges Civiles, sive Civitatis illius Leges cujus Civibus praescribuntur, quamquam nomen illud Lex Civilis restringatur hodie ad significandum Leges Romanas antiquas, quia Civitatis Romanae propter Imperium Romanum late expansum nos etiam olim pars suimus.*

modern jurisprudence, I show how, despite Hobbes's disavowal of Roman 'civil law' in his general philosophy of law, Roman law nevertheless functioned as a rich fund of concepts in framing central aspects of his civil science. I will begin, first, by exploring some historical background concerning the uses of Roman law in early modern Europe, particularly in legal education and legal reform. As I show, Roman law had a considerable intellectual impact in early Stuart England through the work of English Civilians who studied and taught Roman law in the English universities and practised Roman law in courts of specially-defined jurisdictions. With this background, I proceed then to look at how Hobbes might have absorbed this background of Roman law by looking at two particular areas of his political thought where Civilian doctrines came out most clearly – in his theory of representation and his doctrine of sovereignty.

Roman law in legal education

Why did Hobbes bracket aside Roman law from his notion of 'civil law?' One general reason was to remove the apparent ambiguity embedded in the meaning of the term 'civil law'. Hobbes's requirement to strive for consistency in the use of words was axiomatic in his civil science and, thus, applied to his theory of law.[5] But Hobbes was more specifically concerned to dethrone Roman law from its traditional privileged status in European legal thought. By decoupling Roman law from 'civil law', Hobbes suggested that Roman law, by itself, could not command authority, independent of the assent of the legislative sovereign.

This suggestion certainly would not have endeared Hobbes to some Civilians because the Roman law of the *Corpus Iuris Civilis*, for a very long time, enjoyed a privileged status in European legal history. Since the High Middle Ages, when the Justinianic codebooks were first recovered and glossed in the Italian universities, it became common for jurists to treat the Roman law as *jus commune*, that is, as a universally valid and rational system of learned law, applicable across jurisdictional and national boundaries.[6] Medieval jurists even hailed the Roman codebooks as 'written reason' [*ratio scripta*]. As Peter Stein put it, jurists treated Roman law as

[5] Philip Pettit, *Made with Words: Hobbes on Language, Mind, and Politics* (Princeton University Press, 2008).

[6] Manlio Bellomo, *Common Legal Past of Europe, 1000–1800*, translated by Lydia Cochrane (Washington, DC: Catholic University Press, 1995); James Whitman, *The Legacy of Roman Law in the German Romantic Era* (Princeton University Press, 1990), ch. 1.

a kind of eclectic 'legal supermarket' which supplied doctrines, concepts and remedies readily applicable to diverse legal contexts.[7]

For Hobbes, however, the jurists' intellectual dependence upon Roman law was potentially antagonistic to his basic doctrine concerning the jural supremacy of the sovereign authority within a commonwealth because the interpretive activity of the jurists would effectively neutralize and supplant the sovereign's legislative role. If, as the Civilians claimed, a rule of Roman law was thought to be valid and part of the legal order, whether or not a ruling sovereign formally declared it to be so, it would undermine the juridical function of sovereignty. The sovereign would turn out not really to be sovereign after all, but rather the jurist or judge. Nor could the Hobbesian argument of 'tacit command' apply here because, at least in the Civilian tradition, princes who 'outsourced' juridical functions to professional learned jurisconsults were regarded as having effectively abdicated away their residual right to derogate or fully abrogate a settled legal rule. Roman law, it seemed, was valid, independent of the ruler's assent.

Hobbes's definition of law directly attacked the supposed independence of the jurist: 'Law in generall, is not Counsell, but Command … but only of him whose Command is addressed to one formerly obliged to obey him … *Persona Civitatis*'.[8] Thus, a rule of civil law – whether Roman law, Common Law, or otherwise – can be deemed valid and in force, only insofar as the sovereign, as the sole legislating authority, permits it to be valid, and not because of other extraneous reasons, such as the rule's inner rationality or long customary usage. No jurist, therefore, can by the mere exercise of reason declare what is and is not law, unless he is officially granted leave to do so – or 'authorized' – by the lawmaking sovereign authority, whether by express commission or by tacit command.

For Hobbes, this was a sufficient explanation for why, after over eight centuries of Roman legal history, the Emperor Justinian must rightly be regarded the true author of the Roman law. Even though the Roman codebooks were filled with the learned written opinions of the classical jurisconsults, such as Ulpian and Gaius, or the *responsa prudentium*, it was Justinian who ultimately permitted and authorized those opinions to have the effective force of law. Thus, it was not, as Hobbes writes in his *Dialogue*, 'the Lawyers of Rome that made the Imperial Law in Justinian's time, but Justinian himself'.[9] The same principle, he thought, must apply even to Civilians of his time in the seventeenth century. No lawyer or

[7] Peter Stein, *Roman Law in European History* (Cambridge University Press, 1999), 2.

[8] *Leviathan* 183. [9] *Dialogue* 59.

judge, by himself, can say with any authority what law counts as valid or invalid; that is the sole prerogative of the sovereign.

To be sure, Hobbes was certainly not alone in his critical treatment of the Roman law. In the sixteenth century, for example, French legal humanists such as Guillaume Budé and Jacques Cujas, who revolutionized the study of Roman law, stressed the notion that Roman law should not necessarily be regarded as an authoritative source of law in early modern France but merely a cultural artefact, even a legal relic, of an ancient civilization that once ruled Gaul.[10] While the legal humanists' position was partly motivated by academic concerns to 'historicize' the treatment of the Roman codebooks, the more pressing political concern was to argue that Roman law was not legally binding in any way on the French Crown, which, they argued, was regulated by its own distinct native customs, such as the Salic Law and the local provincial customs that humanist jurists, such as Charles Dumoulin, began to document and register.[11]

Among the more notable, yet politically radical, of the legal humanists was the Huguenot jurist, François Hotman, perhaps most famous for his Monarchomach treatise, *Francogallia*, exploring the legality of public resistance. In his anti-Romanist polemic, the *Anti-Tribonian* (1567, published in 1603), he declared the Roman law to be an alien, even tyrannical, system of law, originating from an ancient slaveholding culture and threatening to compromise France's juridical independence.[12] But perhaps most noteworthy among the French critics of Roman law was the young Jean Bodin who, though trained as a Civilian in the humanist law faculty of Toulouse, nevertheless ridiculed in his *Methodus* 'the absurdity of attempting to establish principles of universal jurisprudence from the Roman decrees', and later dismissed Justinian, in his *Six Livres de la République*, as 'a blockish and unlearned prince'.[13]

[10] Julian Franklin, *Jean Bodin and the Sixteenth Century Revolution in the Methodology of Law and History* (New York: Columbia University Press, 1963).

[11] Donald Kelley, *Foundations of Modern Historical Scholarship* (New York: Columbia University Press, 1970); Donald Kelley, '*De Origine Feudorum*: The Beginnings of an Historical Problem' (1964) 39 *Speculum* 207; Ralph Giesey, *Juristic Basis of Dynastic Right to the French Throne* (Philadelphia: American Philosophical Society, 1961).

[12] Donald Kelley, *The Human Measure: Social Thought in the Western Legal Tradition* (Cambridge, MA: Harvard University Press, 1990), 201–202.

[13] Jean Bodin, *Method for the Easy Comprehension of History* [*Methodus ad facilem historiarum cognitionem*], translated by Beatrice Reynolds (New York: Columbia University Press, 1945), 2; Jean Bodin, *Six Bookes of a Commonweale* [1606], translated by Richard Knolles, edited by Kenneth McRae (Cambridge, MA: Harvard University Press, 1962), 17 [1.3].

Even Germany, which significantly allowed the formal Reception of Roman law in 1495 by the Imperial decree of the Emperor Maximilian I establishing the *Reichskammergericht*, nevertheless accepted the underlying principle stressed by Hobbes concerning legal validity. Roman law was valid in Germany, not because of its inner rationality or de facto use, but only because the Emperor decreed that it should formally be recognized as the law of the Empire.

But while jurists may have been divided on the technical question whether the *Corpus Iuris Civilis* was a source of valid law, there was wide agreement that Roman law could nevertheless be independently valuable as an analytical tool, especially as a pedagogical tool for legal education in the universities.[14] Thus, even if critics were technically right to say that Roman law had little or no force in the early modern world, it was still possible to treat the Roman codebooks as models for proper legal reasoning.

An analogy might be drawn here between the humanist treatment of Roman law and the humanist study of 'dead' classical languages in the Renaissance, as a way to extract and recover principles and rules of grammar and rhetoric. As Quentin Skinner has observed, the humanist curriculum of the Renaissance universities centered on Latin and Greek texts, which humanists treated as 'an indispensable propaedeutic to the grasp of the liberal sciences'.[15] Roman law, it seemed, functioned in a very similar way for the student of law, as a 'propaedeutic' for the study of legal and civil science.

Viewed in this way, Roman law proved to be of enormous practical utility, so much so, that even the most anti-Romanist jurists such as Hotman could nevertheless admit, without contradiction, the practical value of studying Roman law.[16] As Donald Kelley observes, even though the Renaissance civilians 'did not ... accept the authority of Roman law,

[14] Ian Maclean, *Interpretation and Meaning: The Case of Law* (Cambridge University Press, 1992), especially on pedagogical uses of the penultimate rubric of the *Digest*, *De verborum significatione* [Dig. 50.16]. On uses of Roman law in legal education, see James Brundage, *The Medieval Origins of the Legal Profession: Canonists, Civilians, and Courts* (University of Chicago Press, 2008); Gerald Strauss, *Law, Resistance, and the State: The Opposition to Roman Law in Reformation Germany* (Princeton University Press, 1986), ch. 6.

[15] Quentin Skinner, *Reason and Rhetoric in the Philosophy of Hobbes* (Cambridge University Press, 1996), 22.

[16] Hotman, for example, strongly believed that Roman law had no validity in early modern France, and yet his Monarchomach treatise, *Francogallia*, contains numerous references and doctrines derived from Roman law. See Daniel Lee, 'Private Law Models for Public Law Concepts' (2008) 70 *Review of Politics* 370.

especially in its modern Italian form', they nevertheless accepted that 'that pristine law was to be respected not for its authority, which was wholly obsolete, but for its rationality and for its historical illumination'.[17] And indeed, in recognition of this practical value, derived from its 'virtues of clarity and uniformity', the Justinianic codebooks continued as core texts for the legal curriculum of the Renaissance universities, functioning as models of legal reasoning to be imitated by the lawyer-in-training.[18]

While the broad influence of Roman law in Continental Europe is well known, it is often forgotten that Roman law made a considerable intellectual and social impact even in England, where the legal profession centered not on Roman law, but chiefly on the Common Law. Beginning in the sixteenth century, Roman law began to attract sustained intellectual interest from among the so-called 'English Civilians'. This was, in large part, due to the endowment in 1546 by Henry VIII, of the two Regius Professorships in Civil Law at Oxford and Cambridge, which permitted Roman law to be taught as an approved area of study and examination in the English universities,[19] as a counterweight to the juridical autonomy and power exercised by the Common Lawyers, but also as training for lawyers to practice in jurisdictions which more directly applied rules derived from Roman law, such as in ecclesiastical, equity and admiralty courts, and especially in areas of international law.[20] As the 'belief that the study of civil law helped to cultivate the art of statesmanship' prevailed in England, the Stuart Monarchy recruited Civilians in various areas of service to the Crown, as consultants to the Privy Council, as Masters in Chancery, and as Diplomats.[21]

[17] Donald Kelley, 'Civil Science in the Renaissance: Jurisprudence in the French Manner' (1981) 2 *History of European Ideas* 265.

[18] Strauss, *Law, Resistance and the State*, 85.

[19] The seventeenth-century University Statutes of Oxford, enacted during the Chancellorship of Archbishop Laud, detail the examination procedure for candidates for the degree of Doctor of Civil Law, which include *sex solemnes lectiones* on titles from the *Code* and the *Digest*. John Griffiths, *Statutes of the University of Oxford Codified in the Year 1636* (Oxford: Clarendon Press, 1888), 115–116 [*Pro Inceptore in Iure Civili*].

[20] Brian Levack, *The Civil Lawyers in England 1603–1641: A Political Study* (Oxford: Clarendon Press, 1973), ch. 4; Benedict Kingsbury and Benjamin Straumann (eds.), *The Roman Foundations of the Law of Nations: Alberico Gentili and the Justice of Empire* (Oxford University Press, 2010); Ken MacMillan, *Sovereignty and Possession in the English New World: The Legal Foundations of Empire, 1576–1640* (Cambridge University Press, 2006) discusses the Crown's uses of Roman law possessory interdicts and real actions to assert territorial control over the New World.

[21] Levack, *Civil Lawyers in England*, 25.

As on the Continent, the English universities treated the classical Roman lawbooks 'almost entirely theoretical[ly] and did not train the students in court procedures and techniques'.[22] Indeed, during the years of Hobbes's studies at Magdalen Hall, Oxford, the Italian-born jurist, Alberico Gentili, in his official capacity as Regius Professor in Oxford, delivered regular lectures in the Schools of the University of Oxford on Justinian's *Institutes*, *Code*, and the *Digest* – what has been described as the 'hard core of the [civil-law] curriculum'.[23] And like the Continental universities, the English universities strongly advised their civil-law students to study the medieval and Renaissance commentators on Roman law.[24] It was advice taken to heart by Hobbes's own tutor at Magdalen Hall, Sir James Hussey. Indeed, Hussey, who originally recommended the young Hobbes for service to the Cavendish family, was himself a Civilian, who was admitted in 1601, upon completion of the civil-law curriculum, to the degree of Doctor of Civil Law.[25]

Roman law and legal reform

In addition to its intellectual impact in the Renaissance universities, Roman law functioned as a state-building tool and drove the contentious early modern politics of legal reform and modernization. Jurists actively attempted to modernize and rationalize what they viewed to be primitive – oftentimes, unwritten – customs by codifying legal rules and defining them, often in the terms of the *Corpus Iuris Civilis*. In short, jurists attempted to modernize the law by 'Romanizing' the law.

22 Levack, *Civil Lawyers in England*, 16.

23 Levack, *Civil Lawyers in England*, 17; Mark Curtis, *Oxford and Cambridge in Transition, 1558–1642* (Oxford: Clarendon Press, 1959), 155.

24 William Fulbecke, *A Direction or Preparative to the Study of the Lawe* (London, 1600), fol. 26: 'Of the auncient writers I thinke these are most convenient to be read, Bartolus [of Sassoferrato], Baldus [de Ubaldis], Paulus de Castro, Philippus Decius, [Andrea] Alciatus, [Ulrich] Zasius. Of the latter writers [Guillaume] Budaeus, [François] Duarenus, [Jacques] Cuiacius, [François] Hotomannus, [Hugues] Donellus, and amonge these, yea above these, him whom I lately named Albericus Gentilis, who by his great industrie hath quickened the dead bodie of the Civil Law written by the auncient Civilians, and hath in his learned labours expressed the iudgement of a great state-man: the soundnes of a deepe philosopher, and the skill of a cunning Civilian: Learning in him hath shewed all her force.'

25 Levack, *Civil Lawyers in England*, 241. Hussey would eventually leave Oxford to enter Doctors' Commons in London and practice in a variety of ecclesiastical and admiralty courts.

Roman law thus served as a model to drive early modern European efforts at legal reform, to 'rationalize' existing legal customs by bringing them into conformity with the system formalized in the *Corpus Iuris Civilis*. This was especially the case in the various legal reform movements in Europe, such as in Germany, whereby Roman law was introduced to reform various municipal codes and the Imperial law to make it cohere with the form and substance of the Justinianic system – or, as Melchior Kling put it, to put the law 'in its right order' [*in eine richtige ordnung gebracht*].[26] These included Romanist reforms in criminal procedure influenced by the use of the inquisitorial method, as reflected in the *Constitutio Criminalis Bambergensis* of 1507 and *the Constitutio Criminalis Carolina* introduced over the Imperial seal of the Emperor Charles V in 1532 which did much to standardize criminal procedure throughout the German lands.[27] At the local level and in principalities, the introduction of Roman law often resulted in the wholesale revision of local custom by professional jurists, such as in the Romanist *Neu Landrecht* of Württemberg devised by the Tübingen jurist, Johann Sichard and the codification of the laws of Freiberg by Ulrich Zasius. In Saxony which, for centuries, was governed according to principles recorded in the medieval German lawbook, the *Sachsenspiegel*, the Prince-Elector August I would order the Doctors of Leipzig and Wittenberg to revise – indeed, to 'Romanize' – the local laws so as to systematize them into a rational order, resulting in the *Constitutio* of 1572.

In the case of England, the effort to 'Romanize' the law meant especially that English Common Law should be 'Romanized', so that it would cohere more closely with the Justinianic system. Perhaps one of the most well-known, if 'only partially successful', efforts to 'Romanize' English law in this way was carried out by John Cowell, Master of Trinity Hall and Regius Professor of Civil Law in Cambridge.[28] A devoted scholar of Roman law, Cowell was perhaps best known for authoring the first law-dictionary in England, *The Interpreter*, originally published in 1607. *The Interpreter* is novel as a legal text in English. But it is especially noteworthy in its attempt to align and assimilate English legal terms with what Cowell thought to be its Roman law equivalent. Thus, for example, his entry on 'Prerogative' – a politically charged term in Stuart

[26] Strauss, *Law, Resistance, and the State*, 96. See also Franz Wieacker, *A History of Private Law in Europe: With Particular Reference to Germany*, translated by Tony Weir (Oxford: Clarendon Press, 1995).

[27] Strauss, *Law, Resistance, and the State*, 123. Michael R. Weisser, *Crime and Punishment in Early Modern Europe* (Atlantic Highlands: Humanities Press, 1979).

[28] Levack, *Civil Lawyers in England*, 138.

constitutional thought – suggests a corresponding term in Justinian's *Code*:

> This word (*Praerogatiua*) is vsed by the Ciuilians in the same sense [citation follows here to an imperial rescript, Cod. 10.41] ... [as] that absolute heighth of power that the Ciuilians call *maiestatem, vel potestatem, vel ius imperii*.[29]

Cowell's analysis was controversial to both Royalists and Parliamentarians, but for different reasons. Whereas Parliamentarians feared that Cowell opened the way for absolutist doctrines in Continental legal theory to transform English law, Crown lawyers of James I complained, in an official reprimand, that 'to define [the prerogative] is to limit' it.[30] Other Civilians, such as Alberico Gentili and Richard Zouch, similarly attempted to reform and recast English legal ideas in a Romanist mould – particularly by treating the King of England as a latter-day Roman *princeps* with broad legislative authority. This practice, indeed, was one of the chief reasons why royalists tended to favour Roman law and why Roman law was often regarded to be hostile to constitutionalism.[31]

But perhaps one of the more notable English admirers of Roman law was the philosopher and later Lord Chancellor of England, Sir Francis Bacon. Bacon is of special interest, not only because of his intellectual affinity and personal association with Hobbes, who served as Bacon's private secretary, but also because Bacon's legal writings, critical of the perceived defects in English Common Law, pointed to Roman law as the ideal model to guide the project of legal reform. What Bacon expressed and idealized was not a version of English Common Law, but a 'Romanized' system, such that English Common Law and statute law 'were to be separately reduced and recompiled just as in "the plan followed by Trebonianus ... in the Digest and Code"'.[32] Bacon even suggested specific Roman texts, such as Justinian's *Institutes* and the last two rubrics of the *Digest, De Verborum Significatione* [Dig. 50.16] and *De Diversis Regulis Iuris Antiqui* [Dig. 50.17], to guide such reform.[33] As Bacon served as a model for Hobbes's Philosopher of law in

29 John Cowell, 'Prerogative of the King' in Cowell, *The Interpreter, or, Booke Containing the Signification of Words* (Cambridge, 1607).

30 Levack, *Civil Lawyers in England*, 98.

31 This conventional wisdom was challenged by legal historians such as Charles Howard McIlwain.

32 Bacon's *Maxims of Law*, cited in Markku Peltonen, 'Introduction', *Cambridge Companion to Bacon* (Cambridge University Press, 1996), 22.

33 The significance and impact of these two rubrics in early modern jurisprudence are discussed in Maclean, *Interpretation and Meaning in the Renaissance* and Peter Stein, *Regulae Iuris: From Juristic Rules to Legal Maxims* (Edinburgh University Press, 1966).

his *Dialogue*, it is to be expected that the values of Roman law would flow into Hobbes's own legal thought, which I must now explore directly.

Roman law in Hobbes's political thought

Hobbes, of course, was not a lawyer and received no formal professional training as a lawyer. That did not mean, however, that Hobbes had no access to legal learning or that Hobbes found no use for legal sources in developing his civil philosophy. As Noel Malcolm and Quentin Skinner have stressed, the young Hobbes very likely acquired close practical familiarity with the law in dealing, as private secretary, with the legal and financial affairs of the Cavendish household and, for the period from 1619 to 1623, also as secretary to Francis Bacon, while he was Lord Chancellor.[34] Indeed, during his years of service to the Cavendish household, Hobbes would have had 'daily contact with business matters', managing 'contracts and bills of sale' related to his patron's businesses.[35] So it is not surprising that Hobbes would have developed a considerable knowledge of law, 'even in its technical aspects'.[36]

Indeed, for a young secretary such as Hobbes in a position of service, reliable access to 'mirrors', nutshells or handbooks of law would have been immeasurably beneficial in carrying out his duties. Fortunately for Hobbes, the Cavendishes possessed a splendid private library at their Chatsworth estate, to which Hobbes had regular access. Indeed, Hobbes had compiled, by his own hand, a catalogue of the Chatsworth library at around 1630.[37] Most remarkable about Hobbes's inventory, however, was its extensive legal collections. While the Chatsworth collection, not surprisingly, carried standard sources in English law, such as casebooks, statute-books, law dictionaries and commentaries,[38] it also held, more

[34] Noel Malcolm, 'Hobbes, Sandys, and the Virginia Company' in Malcolm, *Aspects of Hobbes* (Oxford: Clarendon Press, 2002), 54–55; Quentin Skinner, *Reason and Rhetoric in the Philosophy of Hobbes* (Cambridge University Press, 1996), 221–227.

[35] Grover Robinson, 'The Legal Origins of Thomas Hobbes's Doctrine of Contract' (1980) 18 *Journal of the History of Philosophy* 178.

[36] Robinson, 'Legal Origins', 179.

[37] I am deeply grateful to Kinch Hoekstra for sharing the details of the manuscript source (MS E.1.A) of the catalogue contained in the Hobbes Papers at the Chatsworth Library. See also Robinson, 'Legal Origins', 178–179, although he focuses only on Christopher St. German's *Doctor and Student*, while neglecting to mention the extensive Civilian sources in the collection.

[38] Inter alia, Hobbes's inventory lists *Exposition of termes of ye Law*, *Plowden's Reports* and *Statutes at Large*. Especially noteworthy are Coke's *Reports* and Littleton's *Tenures*, which are cited in *Leviathan* 102, and Christopher St. German's *Doctor and Student*.

importantly, standard sources in Roman civil law. Given that Hobbes had compiled this catalogue personally, he would have known 'exactly what was available in the library', of both English and Roman legal sources.[39] The collection included the full *Corpus Juris Civilis*, as well as Civilian commentaries on the law, such as Gentili and Grotius.[40] It also carried, more important, law dictionaries that explained central concepts and doctrines in Roman law, such as the *Institutiones Iuris Anglicani ad Methodum et Seriem Institutionum Imperialum Compositae et Digestae* of John Cowell (author of *The Interpreter*) and the *Lexicon Iuridicum* of the German jurist, Johann Kahl [Calvinus].[41]

Unfortunately, it is impossible to say with any certainty just how much exposure to these texts of Roman law (or even English law) Hobbes may have actually had. But it is possible to propose some conjectures, given the access he had and, more significantly, his 'tendency to understand and to state political questions as legal questions', by the direct use of the legal sources available to him.[42] Grover Robinson has, for example, suggested that Hobbes's doctrine of contract originated from his reading of Christopher St. German's *Doctor and Student*, a well-known sixteenth-century text that would function as a model for Hobbes's own *Dialogue*.

But what commentators on Hobbes have generally neglected to observe is Hobbes's careful, though often unacknowledged, use of Roman law and Civilian commentaries in his political writings, not only as a source of legal concepts and doctrines, but also as a fund of legal metaphors to illustrate ideas central to his political theory, such as representation. We know, first of all, that Hobbes must have consulted the classical law of Justinian's *Institutes*, because he cites it directly in Chapter XXVI of *Leviathan*, identifying the canonical sources of Roman law:[43]

> Edicts, Constitutions, and Epistles of the Prince [Inst. 1.2.6, *Edicta, Constitutiones, et Epistolae Principum*]
> Decrees of the whole people of Rome [Inst. 1.2.4, *Decreta Populi Romani*]

[39] Robinson, 'Legal Origins', 179.

[40] The catalogue lists, in particular, *Corpus Juris Civilis, Justiniani Institutiones*, as well as Gentili's *De Legationibus* and Grotius's *De Jure Belli ac Pacis*.

[41] Cowell's *Institutiones* was first published in 1605, two years before the appearance of *The Interpreter.*

[42] Robinson, 'Legal Origins', 179.

[43] *Leviathan* 196–197 [Ch. 26]. The square brackets indicate the corresponding text in the Latin *Leviathan* 135, as well as the likely source of the passage in the *Institutes* under the rubric, *De Iure Naturali, Gentium et Civili.* He uses this Civilian vocabulary at various points in his earlier writings, such as in *De Cive*, which also treats of *Edicta et decreta Principum* at *De Cive* 237 [XIV, para. 13] and *Responsa Prudentium*, at *De Cive* XIV, para. 15.

Decrees of the Common People [Inst. 1.2.4, *Decreta Plebis Romanae*]
Orders of the Senate [Inst. 1.2.5, *Senatusconsulta*]
Edicts of the Praetors [Inst. 1.2.7, *Edicta Praetorum*]
Responsa Prudentum [Inst. 1.2.8]
Unwritten Customs [Inst. 1.2.9, *Consuetudines*].

We can also say with some confidence that Hobbes used Roman law because of his appropriation of the distinctive legal vocabulary of the *Corpus Iuris Civilis*. For example, in Chapter II of *De Cive* and Chapter XIV of *Leviathan*, which almost read as if they were textbooks on the law of obligations, he described obligation as a 'bond', which is just how Civilians classically described it in the law of obligations, as a *iuris vinculum*.[44] In both the *De Cive* and the Latin *Leviathan*, Hobbes translated 'contract' and 'covenant' by the Romanist terms, *contractus* and *pactum*, respectively, thus following the convention assigned by English Civilians.[45] In connection with his discussion of 'contract', he explained the difference between 'transferring of Right to the Thing [*Jus transferre*]' and 'transferring, or tradition, that is, delivery, of the Thing it selfe [*Rem transferre, sive tradere*]', in the same juridical terms governing commercial transactions in Roman law.[46] In particular, the phrase 'Right to the Thing', was an attempt to translate the Civilian phrase, *jus ad rem*, an assertion of property right. The description of mere delivery as a *traditio* also originated in the law of property, which similarly allowed that a thing may be delivered [*traditur*] without full right of ownership also being transferred in the transaction,[47] as in the example of a Roman contract that Hobbes supplied, the contract of buying-and-selling, or

[44] Inst. 3.13.pr.

[45] For example, in *The Interpreter*, the Cambridge Regius Professor of Civil Law, John Cowell, writes, 'Contract (*Contractibus*) is a covenant or agreement with a lawful consideration or cause. [Here follows a citation to *De verborum significatione*, Dig. 50.16.19]'. Contract [*contractus*], however, is to be distinguished from 'Covenant' [*pactum*], which Cowell defines as 'the consent of two or more in one self thing' and 'in the Civil Law is perpetual'.

[46] *Leviathan* 94; Latin *Leviathan* 68.

[47] Dig. 41.1.31 (Paul) *Nunquam nuda traditio transfert dominium*. Under the *jus honorarium*, the recipient's possession of the delivered good would be protected by the *Actio Publiciana* which would give the recipient protection against the donor by pleading the Civilian defence, *exceptio rei venditae et traditae*. This remedy required the use of a legal fiction which allowed the recipient to litigate his *exceptio*, as if his possession had already 'ripened' into a full right of ownership. But this did not derogate from the donor's legal right of ownership which technically continued even after property changed hands by delivery. On the *Actio Publiciana*, see the discussion under the title, Dig. 6.2.1, Dig. 6.2.7.6 and Dig. 6.2.13.

Emptio-Venditio, one of four major consensual contracts in the Roman law of obligations.[48]

Roman law in Hobbes's doctrine of representation

Hobbes's appeal to Roman law was even more transparent in his discussion of principal-agency relationships in juridical terms, as expressed in his famous Chapter XVI on representation in *Leviathan*, 'Of persons, authors, and things personated' [*De Personis et Authoribus*]. As Hobbes wrote, an agent (or 'Actor') – such as 'a Representer, or Representative, a Lieutenant, a Vicar, an Attorney, a Deputy, a Procurator ... and the like' – appointed to speak and act on behalf of a principal (or 'Author'), was certainly to be regarded a person, but a special kind of person – that is, an 'artificial' person [*persona repraesentativa*], one 'representing the words and actions of an other', not of his own.[49] Such an 'Actor' or agent who 'acteth another' was said to carry or 'beare his Person' [*Personam alicujus gerere aut sustinere diceretur*].[50] As Monica Brito Vieira has observed, the description of such relationships in terms of 'Actors' and 'Authors' followed a 'distinctively legal understanding of the actor ... in Roman law'.[51]

What was, however, most remarkable about Hobbes's presentation of principal-agency relationships (or 'Authors' and 'Actors') in *Leviathan* was the turn to classical law which Hobbes evidently felt compelled to make in crafting his doctrine of representation. Perhaps the most important clue we have for this is Hobbes's comment in Chapter XVI describing the position of a principal or 'Author' as an 'Owner' – that is, as one who 'owneth his words and actions'.[52] In this exposition, it is clear that what he had in mind was the specifically juridical Roman-law notion of ownership since he introduced the Romanist terms, *Dominus* and 'Dominion' [*dominium*] to refer respectively to 'Owner' and 'Ownership'.[53]

48 Latin *Leviathan* 68. 49 Latin *Leviathan* 79.

50 Latin *Leviathan* 80.

51 Monica Brito Vieira, *Elements of Representation in Hobbes* (Leiden: Brill, 2009) 149. Vieira cites Dig. 26.8.3, which treats the *tutor* as *auctor*. I would also cite Dig. 3.3.74, which speaks of the *actor civitatis*. A comparison is also drawn to Monarchomch treatises such as the *Vindiciae Contra Tyrannos* (1579) 59 [Quaestio II] which treat the people as *author* and the princely ruler as *actor* who acts by *populi authoritate*.

52 *Leviathan* 112.

53 Hobbes draws an analogy between 'Dominion' [*dominium*] as the 'right of possession' [*jus habendi*] and 'Authority' [*authoritas*] as 'the right of doing any act' [*jus agenda*].

This was a strategic move of monumental importance on Hobbes's part, as commentators have noted, since it allowed him to develop more fully a concept of attributive action – that is, it allows Hobbes to say that the actions of a representative 'Actor' belong not to the 'Actor', but belong instead to the 'Author' who commissioned or 'authorized' the performance of such an act on his behalf.[54] In addition, the introduction of the juridical language of *dominium* permitted him to appropriate a vast fund of ready-made Civilian models and doctrines to illustrate how such 'personation' might work.

In this respect, the use of *dominus* in fixing agency-relations was especially critical and deliberate. This was because, for the Roman jurisconsults, the word *dominus* functioned as a generic term in private law to mean both 'owner' (over private property) as well as 'principal' (as in a principal-agent relationship).[55] Indeed, the codebooks juxtaposed the *dominus*, as a property-owning principal, against all sorts of agents or legal persons, such as usufructs, slaves, guardians, administrators, bona fide possessors and procurators.[56] What united this seemingly disparate and otherwise unrelated group of agents was the singularly unique fact that they, unlike their *dominus*, all lacked full *dominium* over the property [*res*] they are permitted to use, or over the matter [*negotia*] they are appointed to oversee. For example, a 'usufruct' [*usus fructus*] – defined as having a 'right to use and enjoy the things of another' – was described in the *Digest* not as *dominium* but as resembling a mere 'fraction' of *dominium* [*pars dominii*].[57] Thus, in all these pairings, the *dominus* was always seen to be in the juridically superior position, because whatever legal right the agent possessed or exercised was fully derived from the permissive grant of the principal [*mandatu domini*].[58]

This Civilian background helped frame Hobbes's understanding of simple agency-relationships shared by Author and Actor. It explained,

[54] Hannah Pitkin, *Concept of Representation* (Berkeley: University of California Press, 1972); Quentin Skinner, 'Hobbes and the Purely Artificial Personality of the State' in Skinner, *Visions of Politics*, Vol. III (Cambridge University Press, 2002); David Runciman, 'What Kind of a Person is Hobbes' State? A Reply to Skinner' (2000) 8 *Journal of Political Philosophy* 268; Ben Holland, 'Sovereignty as *Dominium*: Reconstructing the Constructivist Roman-Law Thesis' (2010) 54 *International Studies Quarterly* 465.

[55] Indeed, the versatility of *dominium* is picked up by Hobbes who uses it in his discussion of lordship and slavery, as well as his discussion of sovereignty, as a possible cognate for *potestas summa* or *summum imperium*, at *De Cive* 88 [V, para. 11].

[56] Peter Garnsey, *Thinking about Property: From Antiquity to the Age of Revolution* (Cambridge University Press, 2007), ch. 7, especially 184–190 and 195–203.

[57] Dig. 7.1.13.pr; 7.1.13.4. [58] Dig. 3.3.63.

for example, why the agent could not licitly perform certain legal acts – especially acts potentially detrimental to the interests of his *dominus*, such as the alienation of property without explicit mandate, which Modestinus explicitly prohibits.[59] Since, as Paul notes in the *Digest*, 'the status of a principal [*domini condicio*] should not … be made worse through his agent [*per procuratorem*]',[60] the agent is not properly empowered or 'authorized' to decide on matters reserved exclusively to the *dominus*.

The Civilian background also provided the reason undergirding ethical principles governing agency relationships. For example, Hobbes explains in *Leviathan* that, 'When the Actor maketh a Covenant by Authority, he bindeth thereby the Author, no lesse than if he had made it himself; and no lesse subjecteth him to all the consequences of the same'.[61] The principle expressed here had its roots in Romanist sources. In his *Institutiones Juris*, for example, Cowell observes that, 'An obligation is acquired unto us by procurators [*Acquiritur nobis obligatio per procuratores*] … provided they covenant and bargain in our names [*nomine nostro*]'.[62]

Just as the use of the Roman-law framework enabled Hobbes to discuss the status of agents or 'Actors' tied in agency relationships, it also enabled Hobbes to investigate the status of principals or 'Authors'. In particular, he was concerned with more complex agency-relationships, such as those cases where the principal is incapacitated from acting on its own. What was unusual in these cases was that such principals 'cannot be Authors, nor therefore give Authority to their Actors', because they, like inanimate objects, lacked the ability to speak or act independently.[63] Instead, they must by a legal fiction be treated as if they authorized their agent to act on their behalf.

Like Hobbes, Roman lawyers were most concerned with these sorts of special cases, where a *dominus* was unable, for reasons of incapacity, to exercise his *dominium*. One of the key areas of Roman law that explored such urgent cases was the law of guardianship, whereby a legal guardian [*tutor*] represented a legally incapacitated *dominus* – that is, one 'who on account of his age, is unable to protect himself' and, thus, required the 'force and power' [*vis ac potestas*] of an intermediary.[64] Here, while the underage or mentally incompetent ward was technically regarded a *dominus*, as the

[59] Dig. 3.5, *De negotis gestis*, or 'unauthorized actions'.

[60] Dig. 3.3.49. Cf. Dig. 7.1.13.4.

[61] *Leviathan* 112.

[62] John Cowell, *Institutiones Iuris Anglicani ad Methodum et Seriem Institutionum Imperialium Compositae et Digestae* (Cambridge, 1605), 195 [Book III, Title 29].

[63] *Leviathan* 113. [64] Dig. 26.1.1.pr.

passive beneficiary and author of the guardian's actions, it was the guardian that conferred a jural personality on the ward and enabled the ward, by legal fiction, to be an author to authorize the performance of acts, such as entering contracts, or buying and selling property. The Roman jurist, Iulianus, even treated legal guardians, such as *tutores* and *curatores*, in the terms of 'bearing' the personality of a legally-incapacitated *dominus*, such as a minor. He wrote specifically that the guardian 'bears the person of the *dominus* [*curator ... personam domini sustinet*]'[65] and is even 'held to be in the place of a *dominus* [*domini loco habetur*]', such that the actions of the guardian are always taken to be those of the ward.[66] It was precisely this Civilian idea that Hobbes must have had in mind when he wrote that, 'Children, Fooles, and Mad-men that have no use of Reason, may be Personated by Guardians or Curators [*per Tutorem*]'.[67]

Hobbes made use of the Roman law again in the final paragraph of Chapter XVI (and of Part I of *Leviathan*), which concluded his analysis of principals by specifying two species of 'Authors' – (1) those 'simply so called ... that owneth the Action of another simply' [*simpliciter*], and another category, 'Authors conditionall' (2) those 'that owneth an Action, or Covenant of another conditionally' [*conditionaliter*].[68] Noting that such 'Authors conditionall' were ordinarily called pledges, or 'Suretyes', Hobbes returned, as before, to the Roman law to appropriate Civilian models such as *fidejussores*, *sponsores*, *praedes* and *vades* illustrating conditional authorship. And again, Hobbes followed the conventional translation assigned by English Civilians, linking surety to the Roman *fidejussor*.[69] What is especially interesting is that these 'sureties' are risk-limiting devices to guarantee, or pledge, the performance of an obligation which the original principal cannot perform, perhaps an indication of how he understood the functioning of shared civil obligations among subjects in a well-ordered commonwealth.[70]

[65] Dig. 47.2.56.4 (Iulianus): *Sed et circa curatorem furiosi eadem dicenda sunt, qui adeo personam domini sustinet, ut etiam tradendo rem furiosi alienare existimetur.*

[66] Dig. 41.4.7.3 (Iulianus): *Nam tutor in re pupilli tunc domini loco habetur, cum tutelam administrat, non cum pupillam spoliat.*

[67] *Leviathan* 113. Latin *Leviathan* 81: *Infantis, et ejus qui mentis compos non est, Persona geri potest per Tutorem.*

[68] *Leviathan* 115; Latin *Leviathan* 82. Cf. *De Homine* XV, para. 3.

[69] Cowell, *Institutiones Iuris*, 164–165 [Book III, Title 21, *De Fideiussoribus*].

[70] Vieira, *Elements of Representation*, 149, note 6, suggests that the conditional creditor–debtor relationship was a reference to Monarchomach theories articulating a joint-obligation of the prince and the people to God, such that, where the prince fails to perform his obligation, the people must act as a surety for the prince's non-performance.

Taken together, Hobbes's analysis of agency-relationships in Roman law completed the preliminary conceptual work necessary for establishing his understanding of sovereignty, when he declared that, 'A Multitude of men, are made *One* Person, when they are by one man, or one Person, Represented ... It is the Representer that beareth the Person'.[71] That 'Representer' was, of course, what he called the 'Soveraigne', the one that bore the personality of a commonwealth. Hobbes's doctrine was unusual because, if we are to follow his understanding of Roman law, the sovereign turns out not to be a *dominus*, but merely an agent or Actor for a *dominus* – indeed, he insists on calling the sovereign a 'Soveraign Representative'. Instead, the sovereign is – like a procurator, usufruct or administrator – an agent lacking full *dominium* in the affairs or properties [*res*] of his principal.[72] In structure, Hobbes, perhaps unintentionally, followed the interpretation of Roman law crafted by medieval and early modern political theorists, such as the French Monarchomachs, who similarly regarded a ruling king to be like a guardian overseeing the kingdom, as if it were his underage *dominus*.[73] But whereas the Monarchomachs stressed the jural superiority of the kingdom over the king because it retained *dominium* (and thus could enter legal actions such as *restitutio in integrum* or *actio tutelae* against the ruler), Hobbes was not prepared to allow a kingdom to act independently of its sovereign king, even if they are held to be the original 'authors' or *domini* of the sovereign's actions.

Roman law in Hobbes's doctrine of sovereignty

It is, however, in Hobbes's doctrine of sovereignty where his intellectual debt to Roman law is most apparent. Indeed, there are important elements of Hobbes's core doctrine of sovereignty that bear a strikingly close

[71] *Leviathan* 114.

[72] Still, this does not stop Hobbes from calling the sovereign a *dominus*, as in *De Cive* VI, para. 18, *supremus civitatis dominus*, in part because he understands that *dominium* carries multiple meanings, as in in *De Cive* VIII, para. 1, where he discusses three different types of *dominium*.

[73] A similar argument is deployed by Canonists in the office-theory of the Church, which holds that a bishop, as an officer of the Church, is not a *dominus* in his benefice, but merely its usufruct or curator. See Peter Riesenberg, *Inalienability of Sovereignty in Medieval Political Thought* (New York: Columbia University Press, 1955); Janet Coleman, '*Dominium* in Thirteenth and Fourteenth-Century Political Thought and Its Seventeenth-Century Heirs: John of Paris and Locke' (1985) 33 *Political Studies* 73 and Coleman, 'Medieval Discussions of Property: *Ratio* and *Dominium* according to John of Paris and Marsilius of Padua' (1983) 4 *History of Political Thought* 209. I discuss the Monarchomach argument from the law of guardianship in Lee, 'Private Law Models and

resemblance to ideas originating in the *Corpus Iuris*. Building on his prior analysis on personation, Hobbes famously described the 'Soveraigne' in the same jural terms of personality expressed earlier, as in the famous passage of the *Leviathan*: 'He that carryeth this Person [of the Common-Wealth] is called *SOVERAIGNE*, and said to have *Soveraigne Power*', because it represented the personality of the commonwealth as a thing, like an incapacitated ward, which has no natural voice but only by the fiction or artifice of representation.[74] In the corresponding passage of *De Cive*, Hobbes declared that the union of men forming a commonwealth [*civitas*] or civil society [*societas civilis*] was properly to be called a 'civil person' [*persona civilis*], similar in structure to the corporate personality of a 'company of merchants' [*sodalitates mercatorum*] who 'unite as one person for the purpose of transacting certain business'.[75]

Hobbes's description of sovereignty as an absolute 'Power unlimited' and above the law also had roots in the Roman tradition, in Ulpian's famous declaration in the *Digest* that 'the Emperor is loosened from the laws' [*princeps legibus solutus est*].[76] Indeed, it was perhaps for this reason that Hobbes observed, 'To most men this sovereignty and absolute power seems so harsh that they hate the very name of it'.[77]

Perhaps most interesting was Hobbes's adoption of the Roman jurists' justification for the legislative powers of the Emperor, the so-called *lex regia*. In the *Digest* and the *Institutes*, the law asserts, 'What pleases the prince has the force of law' [*Quod principi placuit, legis habet vigorem*].[78] The reason for this, according to the Roman codebooks, is to be traced to the primitive popular origins of princely sovereignty: 'By a royal law [*lege regia*] which was passed concerning his sovereignty [*imperio*], the people [*populus*] conferred upon him all their own sovereignty and power [*suum imperium et potestatem*]'.[79] Hobbes took this

Public Law Concepts', 392 See also the dissertation of Robert Freegard, 'Roman Law and Resistance Right' (University of Iowa, 1971).

[74] *Leviathan* 121 [Ch. 17]. Latin *Leviathan* 86 renders the passage: *Is autem qui Civitatis Personam gerit, Summam habere dicitur Potestatem.*

[75] *On the Citizen* 73 [5, paras. 9–10]; *De Cive* 88. Dig. 3.4.1.1 similarly compares *corpus collegii* and *societatis* with the rights of a *res publica* to have 'a common treasury [*res communes*], and an attorney or syndic [*actorem sive syndicum*] through whom, as in a state [*tamquam in republica*], what should be transacted and done in common is transacted and done'.

[76] *Leviathan* 155; *De Cive* VI, para. 14; Dig. 1.3.31.

[77] *On the Citizen* 87 [Ch. 6, para. 17]

[78] Dig. 1.4.1, Inst. 1.2.6.

[79] Dig. 1.4.1: *utpote cum lege regia, quae de imperio eius lata est, populus ei et in eum omne suum imperium et potestatem conferat.* Note that the corresponding *locus* in the *Institutes*

civil law argument from Roman law and superimposed it on the case of the English commonwealth to explain why the King of England, like the Roman *princeps*, can make legally valid proclamations and decrees. Hobbes's answer was just the same as the Roman answer – i.e. 'because the power of the people was in him' [*qui Summam habuere in Civitate Romana Potestatem*].[80]

But perhaps the most compelling indication of Hobbes's intellectual debt to the tradition of Roman law and the political thought of the Civilian jurisconsults is to be found in his framing of the doctrine of sovereignty in the juridical terms of right [*jus*], and specifically in the Roman language of property [*jus in re*]. As Hobbes asserted in his major political writings, sovereignty was properly to be conceptualized as an indivisible bundle of rights, belonging exclusively to the sovereign. Hobbes's intellectual debt to Roman law emerged, first of all, in the specific 'rights of sovereignty' that he identified. In *Elements of Law*, for example, he stated:

> The rights of sovereignty [include] ... the absolute use of the sword in peace and war, the making and abrogating of laws, supreme judicature and decision in all debates judicial and deliberative, the nomination of all magistrates and ministers.[81]

Again in *De Cive*, he remarked:

> The marks of sovereign power are: to make and repeal laws; to make decisions of war and peace; to hear and decide all disputes either in their own persons or through judges whom they appoint, and to choose all magistrates, ministers and counselors.[82]

In these early discussions of the rights of sovereignty, the specific rights, or prerogatives, that Hobbes identified were found in the Roman codebooks, as well as in Civilian commentaries.[83]

Hobbes carried this property-right analysis of sovereignty even further, by suggesting that the 'right' [*jus*] of sovereignty must be clearly distinguished from the mere 'exercise' [*exercitium*] or 'administration'

makes one very important difference by substituting *conferat* with *concessit*. This ambiguity is the source of the medieval legal debate on the jural status of the *lex regia*, whether it was a complete and irrevocable alienation [*translatio*] of sovereignty or a limited revocable delegation [*concessio*], as Azo opined.

80 *Leviathan* 196; Latin *Leviathan* 135. Cf. *De Cive* VII, para. 15: *Populus ... potest ei summum imperium tradere*.

81 *Elements of Law* 114.

82 *On the Citizen* 88; *De Cive* VI, para. 18:

83 A similar list of such sovereign rights are found in Bodin's early work, *Methodus* VI.

[*administratio*] of sovereignty, which could be performed on behalf of the sovereign by any lesser minister or officer appointed by the sovereign, as its agent. It was, as Richard Tuck observes, 'an important but often neglected distinction in Hobbes'.[84]

In the *De Corpore Politico* section of *Elements of Law*, for example, Hobbes drew the distinction in connection with his criticism of the classical theory of the mixed constitution: 'Though the sovereignty be not mixed, but be always either simple democracy, or simple aristocracy, or pure monarchy; nevertheless in the *administration* thereof, all those sorts of government may have place subordinate', such as the dictator of Republican Rome 'who had for a time the *exercise* of the whole sovereignty', even though he had no right to it.[85]

Hobbes made the point much more explicitly in *De Cive*, where he wrote not only of the 'exercise of sovereign power' [*usum summi imperii*],[86] but also of its separation from the right of sovereignty:

> We must distinguish between the *right* [*jus*] and the *exercise* [*exercitium*] of sovereign power [*summi imperii*]; for they can be separated [*separari*]; for instance, he who has the right [*is qui habet jus*] may be unwilling or unable to play a personal role in conducting trials or deliberating issues. For there are occasions when kings cannot manage their affairs because of their age, or when even though they can, they judge it more correct to content themselves with choosing ministers and counselors, and to exercise their power through them.

To explain this distinction in the concept of sovereignty, Hobbes drew a comparison between civil government (government of a civil sovereign) and divine government (government of God).

> When *right* and *exercise* are separated [*separantur jus et exercitium*], the government of the commonwealth [*regimen civitatis*] is like the ordinary government of the world [*simile est regimini mundi ordinario*], in which God the first mover of all things, produces natural effects through the order of secondary causes. But when he who has the right to reign [*jus regni*] wishes to participate himself in all judgments, consultations and public actions, it is a way of running things [*administratio*] comparable

[84] Richard Tuck, 'Hobbes and Democracy' in Annabel Brett, James Tully, Holly Hamilton-Bleakley (eds.), *Rethinking the Foundations of Modern Political Thought* (Cambridge University Press, 2006), 186.

[85] *Elements of Law* 116 [Ch. 20, para. 17], with emphasis added. This analysis of the Roman dictator – that he had mere exercise, but not right, of sovereignty for a limited term – is not original with Hobbes. Bodin makes the same point in *République*.

[86] *On the Citizen* 95; *De Cive* VII, para. 6.

to God's attending directly to every thing himself, contrary to the order of nature.[87]

After having drawn this primary distinction between the right and exercise of sovereignty, Hobbes proceeded further to delineate the 'duties of those [magistrates and officers] who exercise sovereign power whether in their own right or by someone else's [*qui summum imperium, sive proprio, sive alieno jure administrant*]'.[88] Taken together, Hobbes permitted a variety of constitutional combinations, including a scheme of popular sovereignty, where the right of sovereignty remained with the people, but was exercised or administered by executive magistrates.[89]

The critical point to stress is that these typically Hobbesian distinctions between the 'right' of sovereignty and the mere 'exercise' of sovereignty was hardly original with Hobbes, but actually were Civilian doctrines, originating in the vast juristic commentaries of Continental Civilians of the early modern period. Indeed, the first to emphasize this distinction between 'right' and 'exercise' or 'administration' of sovereignty was not Hobbes, but Andrea Alciato, the sixteenth-century Chair of Civil Law in the University of Bourges, the intellectual mecca of European legal humanism. On the distinction between 'right' and 'exercise', Alciato's starting point concerned a narrowly academic matter in Roman private law that would have far-reaching consequences for political theory. Rejecting the medieval doctrine of divided *dominium*, which allowed property to be held by multiple *domini* at once, Alciato reasserted in his humanist *Commentarii in Digesta* the classical Roman principle in the law of property – *in solidum* – that there can only be one *dominus* in a given object of property at any one time.[90] His purpose in doing so was to underscore one of the key distinctions in the Roman law of property

[87] *On the Citizen* 142–43 [Ch. 13, para. 1], emphasis appears in the original text; *De Cive* 213–214. The term, *jus regni*, and its juxtaposition against *administratio* appears in Continental juristic writing, such as in Johannes Althusius's *Politica Methodice Digesta* and Henning Arnisaeus's *De Jure Majestatis*.

[88] *De Cive* 214 [XIII, §1]. Hobbes's use of the terms 'by own right' [*proprio*] and 'by someone else's' [*alieno jure*] is without doubt drawn from the Civilian commentaries on the rubric, *De officio eius, cui iurisdictio mandata est* [Dig. 1.21], which similarly distinguished between jurisdictional powers held *suo jure* or *alieno beneficio*.

[89] Kinch Hoekstra, 'A Lion in the House: Hobbes and Democracy' in Brett *et al.*, *Rethinking the Foundations of Modern Political Thought*, 200–201. Hoekstra warns, however, that delegation of sovereignty may translate effectively into the full abdication or alienation of sovereignty, unless the sovereign has a residual effective power to recover the 'outsourced' sovereignty.

[90] Andrea Alciato, *Commentarii in Digesta* in *Opera Omnia* (Basel, 1982) 1:col. 143 [*Commentarii in Digesta*, §88]. Cf. Dig. 13.6.5; Dig. 43.14.1.pr.

which he felt the medieval Glossators and Bartolist Commentators had distorted and obscured – that is, the distinction between the legal right of ownership in some object of property and the mere use, exercise or administration of that property. As Alciato pointed out, one could enjoy and make use of a property legally belonging to someone else, as in the case of a usufruct or *emphyteusis* (long-term lease). But simply using or exercising a property did not *ipso facto* make one the *dominus* of that property, as the classical jurists took pains to stress in the *Corpus Iuris Civilis*.[91]

This background property analysis was critical for Alciato because it helped resolve one of the most celebrated debates in medieval law between the Bolognese lawyers, Azo and Lothair. According to legend, the Emperor Henry VI asked Azo and Lothair whether or not the *merum imperium* (the high imperial powers referenced in the *Digest*)[92] belonged exclusively to the Emperor. While Lothair reserved *merum imperium* for the Emperor, Azo allowed that anybody who 'exercised' or 'used' the rights of *imperium*, such as city magistrates who exercised capital jurisdiction [*jus gladii*], could claim their own share of ownership in *merum imperium*.[93] While Lothair won the Emperor's favour, Azo's dicta ultimately prevailed as the standard view throughout the Middle Ages.[94]

Going against centuries of accumulated legal tradition, however, Alciato was the first to contest Azo's dicta and suggest instead that Lothair had the better solution. Adopting Lothair's position, Alciato thought his property analysis could help explain why Azo was incorrect and why magistrates and officers could never be regarded as 'owning' their public powers, as Lothair's position entailed. For Alciato, magistrates and officers simply 'exercised' – but did not 'own' – the public *imperium* in carrying out the duties attached to their office. They, therefore, occupied the inferior jural position of a usufruct, a tenant or a borrower, but never that of a *dominus*, precisely because magistrates exercised powers which they did not own. Even the highest officers of state, such as the Roman *Praetor*, whose powers were traditionally described as being 'their own' [*imperio suo*] in the *Digest*, were entitled only to the use or exercise, but not to the ownership,

[91] However, undisturbed use and possession could 'ripen' into *dominium* by prescription or *usucapio*.

[92] Dig. 2.1.3.

[93] Azo, *Summa Azonis, Locuples Iuris Civilis Thesaurus* (Venice, 1566) 179, col. 1 [Azo, *Summa* on Cod. 3.13, §17].

[94] Myron Piper Gilmore, *Argument from Roman Law in Political Thought, 1200–1600* (Cambridge, MA: Harvard University Press, 1941).

of their official powers.[95] Thus, for Alciato, whenever the *Digest* described a magistrate 'holding' a power, what the jurists really meant to express was the mere 'exercise' [*exercitatio*] of that power, not the 'right' to that power itself [*ius ipsum*].

But if magistrates and officers were, like usufructs, merely entitled to the use or exercise of the public powers of state, the question still remained who held or retained the full ownership rights in the *merum imperium* [*meri imperii ius ipsum*]. Who was, as Alciato put it, this *proprietatis dominus*? For Alciato, there could only be one answer to that question, and that was the ruling prince, in whom full property right to *imperium* 'remains' [*remaneat*] fully intact.[96] Not only was this answer consistent with Lothair's doctrine, it was, more importantly, supported by the *Digest* which cited the crucial analysis of Papinian that, while the exercise of sovereign rights, such as capital jurisdiction [*jus gladii*], could be assigned to, and exercised by, the lesser magistrate, the full legal right over such jurisdiction always belonged to the prince.[97]

Alciato's teaching shaped an entire generation of humanist Civilians educated at Bourges in the sixteenth century, such as Eguinaire Baron, François La Douaren [Duarenus] and François Connan. In their influential published commentaries on the Roman law, humanists reinforced Alciato's separation of 'right' and 'exercise'. For example, Duarenus stressed the need to divorce conceptually the mere 'exercise' of jurisdiction [*exercere jurisdictionem*] from the essence of jural property right [*nuda proprietas*] over such delegable powers which belonged exclusively to the ruling prince.[98] Nor was this Civilian doctrine restricted to French royalist thought. By the beginning of the seventeenth century, the distinction between 'right' and 'exercise' of sovereignty had already made its way into German juristic thought, as in the thought of the Calvinist Syndic of Emden, Johannes Althusius, who, in his defence of popular sovereignty, also separated the 'rights of sovereignty' [*jura majestatis*] belonging to the people, from the mere use or exercise of the people's sovereign rights by a king, as 'guardian or trustee who is constituted over the affairs of his ward or minor [*negotia sui pupilli minorisve*]'.[99]

95 Alciato, *Opera Omnia* 4:col. 38 [*Paradoxa* 2.6, §3]; Dig. 1.21.3

96 Alciato, *Opera Omnia* 1:col. 144 [*Commentarii in Digesta*, §90].

97 Dig. 1.21.1.

98 Duarenus, *Opera Omnia* (Lucca, 1765) 1:38, col. 2 [Duarenus on Dig. 2.1, Cap. 1]; Duarenus, *Opera Omnia* 4:19, col. 2 [*Disputationum Anniversiorum* 1.17].

99 Johannes Althusius, *Politica Methodice Digesta*, edited by Carl Friedrich (Cambridge, MA: Harvard University Press, 1932), 406 [39, §18]; *Politica* 152 [18, §93].

But above all, the humanist distinction between 'right' and 'exercise' shaped the treatment of sovereignty in two political theorists who were trained in Roman law and whose writings exerted a proximate influence on Hobbes's own understanding of the right and exercise of sovereignty – Jean Bodin and Hugo Grotius. In the *République*, Bodin famously distinguished between the sovereign right belonging to the state [*république*], and the mere government of the state through the exercise or administration of that sovereign right on behalf of the sovereign authority. In Book III, Bodin explained further that sovereignty could be exercised indirectly, by concessive delegation, through officers of state. But unlike the sovereign authority, which retains the full right of property, Bodin argued that officers must treat their offices as *res commodata* because, as he writes, 'An office is a thing borrowed [*chose empruntee*; *commodatum*]'.[100] It was, thus, not within the right of the officer, merely exercising sovereignty by way of borrowing or loan, to treat his office as if it were his own property.

Grotius also followed the humanist doctrine in his analysis of sovereignty, or *imperium*, in the *De Jure Belli ac Pacis*. Grotius observed that there were varying degrees of strength by which one might hold *imperium*, what he categorized in general as 'the manner of holding a thing' [*modus rei habendi*]. *Imperium*, Grotius explained, could be held 'by full right of property' [*pleno jure proprietatis*], just as an owner [*dominus*] asserting full absolute right in his property [*dominium in rebus*] also held it by full right [*pleno jure*].[101] But just as *imperium* might be held by full right, so might *imperium* also be held by a lesser right, such as 'usufructuary right' [*jure usufructuario*], as when a civil-law usufruct exercised limited rights of use in a property belonging to another *dominus*.[102] For Grotius, then, *imperium* could variously be held by 'full right of property' or 'by a usufructuary right'. This distinction was essential for Grotius to distinguish between true patrimonial kings – those who treated the state just as private property – and 'usufructuary princes' who were, like usufructs

100 *Commonweale* 282. *République* 310: *l'office est comme une chose empruntee, que le proprietaire ne peut demander que le temps prefix ne soit expiré. De Republica* 420 [*sic* 410]: *Precarium autem semper repetere licet; commodatum non item, sed tempore definito* [marginal note cites Dig. 2.1, *de iurisdictione*]. It should be noted that *commodatum* is a type of contract in the Roman law of obligations, called contracts *re*. It is a loan of some specific thing granted for use. An essential feature of *commodatum* is its gratuitous nature; the granting party cannot receive payment or benefit for use – otherwise, it would not be a *commodatum*, but a different kind of contract, hiring-letting [*locatio-conductio*]. Dig. 13.6.

101 Grotius, *De Jure Belli ac Pacis* 1.3.11.

102 Grotius, *De Jure Belli ac Pacis* 1.3.11.1

in civil law, limited in the ways they could exercise and administer the rights belonging to another party. Remarkably, this was precisely the same analysis that appeared in *De Cive*, where Hobbes discussed the case of a 'time-limited *Monarch*', where 'sovereign power (like *Ownership* [*ut Dominium*]) remained with the *people*; only its *use* or *exercise* [*usus autem, sive exercitium*] was enjoyed by the time-limited *Monarch*, as a *usufructuary* [*ut usufructuario*]'.[103]

Thus, when Hobbes says that there is a distinction between the 'right' and the 'exercise' of sovereignty, this was actually a very specific Civilian doctrine he inherited and was reconstructing. As it turns out, Hobbes can be seen to be a participant in this long line of juristic thought framed by Roman law.

Conclusion

Understanding how Hobbes used legal texts in his writings is important because it forces us to reconsider the sources from which he drew inspiration in his thinking. In this chapter, we have seen how Hobbes used elements of Roman private law such as ownership, guardianship and suretyship to craft more precisely the different forms of authorization and representation central to his understanding of the state. We have also seen how Hobbes made use of the Civilian distinction between the right and the use of *imperium* to situate his own notion of sovereignty. Like other theorists of law and the state, such as Bodin and Grotius, Hobbes understood Roman law as a model to give content to principles that would define the contours of political modernity.

These illustrations show just how much, despite his disavowal of Roman civil law, Hobbes was nevertheless dependent upon it. Hobbes is often regarded as the first political philosopher who eschewed rhetoric or argument from history and instead insisted on grounding his civil science on deductive reasoning and the consistent use of words. But as so much recent scholarship on Hobbes has made clear, Hobbes was himself dependent on the classical learning that framed his early intellectual development. By tracing his uses of Roman law, we can see even more clearly how far this intellectual debt reached.

[103] *On the Citizen* 98–99; *De Cive* 135–136 [VII para. 16].

INDEX

For EU product safety concerns, contact us at Calle de José Abascal, 56–1°, 28003 Madrid, Spain or eugpsr@cambridge.org.

www.ingramcontent.com/pod-product-compliance
Lightning Source LLC
LaVergne TN
LVHW101501200926
848483LV00001B/185
* 9 7 8 1 1 0 7 0 2 2 7 5 1 *